core J2EE™ PATTERNS

Best Practices and Design Strategies

DEEPAK ALUR
JOHN CRUPI
DAN MALKS

Prentice Hall PTR, Upper Saddle River, NJ 07458
www.phptr.com

Sun Microsystems Press
A Prentice Hall Title

The publisher offers discounts on this book when ordered in bulk quantities.
For more information, contact Corporate Sales Department, Prentice Hall PTR ,
One Lake Street, Upper Saddle River, NJ 07458. Phone: 800-382-3419; FAX: 201- 236-7141.
E-mail: corpsales@prenhall.com.

Production Supervision: *Mary Sudul*
Composition: *FASTpages*
Acquisitions Editor: *Gregory G. Doench*
Editorial Assistant: *Brandt Kenna*
Cover Design Director: *Jerry Votta*
Cover Designer: *Anthony Gemmellaro*
Art Director: *Gail Cocker-Bogusz*
Manufacturing Manager: *Alexis R. Heydt*
Marketing Manager: *Debby vanDijk*

Sun Microsystems Press:
Marketing manager: *Michael Llwyd Alread*
Publisher: *Rachel Borden*

10   9   8   7   6   5

ISBN 0-13-064884-1

Sun Microsystems Press
A Prentice Hall Title

"The authors of *Core J2EE Patterns* have harvested a really useful set of patterns. They show you how to apply these patterns and how to refactor your system to take advantage of them. It's just like having a team of experts sitting at your side."

—Grady Booch, Chief Scientist, Rational Software Corporation,
excerpted from Foreword

"This book is an excellent collection of patterns. [It] captures vital experience for J2EE development. Don't build an enterprise bean without it. [Additionally,] refactoring is increasingly the approach of choice for making changes to an existing system. The authors are the first group to extend my work on refactoring into a new direction—into the world of J2EE design. Not just am I grateful that someone has built on my earlier work, I'm glad they've used their experience to outline how to do these transformations."

–Martin Fowler, Chief Scientist, ThoughtWorks
excerpted from Foreword

"*Core J2EE Patterns* is the gospel that should accompany every J2EE application server. The book delivers a definitive, battle-tested pattern language, along with refactoring strategies, for designing, implementing, and maintaining healthy real-world J2EE applications. Built upon the in-the-trenches expertise of its veteran architect authors, this volume unites the platform's many technologies and API's in a way that application architects can use, and provides insightful answers to the why's, when's, and how's of the J2EE platform."

—Sean Neville, JRun Enterprise Architect, Macromedia

"The authors do a great job describing useful patterns for application architectures. The section on refactoring is worth the price of the entire book!"

—Craig McClanahan, Struts Lead Architect

Contents

CHAPTER 2
J2EE Platform Overview   16

CHAPTER 5
J2EE Refactorings   72

CHAPTER 7

CHAPTER 8

CHAPTER 9

EPILOGUE

Foreword

In the world of software, a pattern is a tangible manifestation of an organization's tribal memory. A pattern provides a common solution to a common problem and so, within the culture of one specific organization or within one domain, naming and then specifying a pattern represents the codification of a common solution, drawn from proven, prior experience. Having a good language of patterns at your disposal is like having an extended team of experts sitting at your side during development: by applying one of their patterns, you in effect take the benefit of their hard-won knowledge. As such, the best patterns are not so much invented as they are discovered and then harvested from existing, successful systems. Thus, at its most mature state, a pattern is full of things that work, absent of things that don't work, and revealing of the wisdom and rationale of its designers.

Deep, really useful, patterns are typically ancient: you see one and will often remark, "Hey, I've done that before." However, the very naming of the pattern gives you a vocabulary that you didn't have previously and so helps you apply that pattern in ways you otherwise might have not have realized. Ultimately, the effect of such a pattern will be to make your system simpler.

Patterns not only help you build simpler systems that work, but they also help you build beautiful programs. In a culture of time starvation, writing beautiful software is often impossible. That's sad, for as professionals, we strive to build things of quality. By applying a good set of patterns, it is possible to bring a degree of elegance in to your systems that might otherwise have been lacking.

The authors of *Core J2EE Patterns* have harvested a really useful set of patterns. Don't get me wrong: J2EE is certainly an important platform, enabling teams to build some very powerful systems. However, reality is, there is still a wide semantic gap between the abstractions and services that J2EE provides and the final application that a team must build. Patterns such as specified in this book represent solutions that appear again and again in filling that gap. By applying these patterns, you thus carry out the primary means of reducing software risk: you write less software. Rather than discovering these solutions on your own, apply these patterns, which have already proven their utility in existing systems.

More than just naming a set of patterns, the authors make them approachable by specifying their semantics using the UML. Additionally, they show you how to apply these patterns and how to refactor your system to take advantage of them. Again, it's just like having a team of experts sitting at your side.

Grady Booch
Chief Scientist
Rational Software Corporation

Foreword

ThoughtWorks started to work with J2EE in late 1998. At that time we found a lot of cool (if somewhat immature) technology, but with little guidance on how to use it well. We coped, partly because we had a lot of experience in other OO server environments. But we've seen many clients who've struggled, not because of problems in the technology—but due to not knowing how to use it well.

For many years I've been a big fan of patterns as a way to capture design expertise—to catalog practical solutions to recurring problems. Over the last couple of years various pioneers have been working with J2EE and uncovering the patterns that make ·for an effective J2EE solution. This book is an excellent collection of those patterns, capturing many of the techniques that we had to discover by trial and error.

That's why this book is important. Knowing the APIs backwards is one thing; knowing how to design good software is something else. This book is the first book I've seen that's really concentrated on capturing this design knowledge, and I'm relieved to see they've done a damned fine job of doing it. If you're working with J2EE you need to be aware of these patterns.

Furthermore, this book recognizes that design doesn't end when you start writing code. People make decisions that don't turn out that way. In this situation you need to fix your design and you need to fix it in a disciplined way. Refactoring is increasingly the approach of choice for making changes to an existing system. The authors are the first group to extend my work on refactoring into a new direction—into the world of J2EE design. Not just am I grateful that someone has built on my earlier work, I'm glad they've used their experience to outline how to do these transformations.

In the end, it's that experience that counts. Capturing design experience in books is one of the hardest things to do, yet is so necessary for our profession to grow. This book captures vital experience for J2EE development. Don't build an enterprise bean without it.

Martin Fowler
Chief Scientist
ThoughtWorks

Preface

This book is about patterns for the Java 2 platform, Enterprise Edition (J2EE). These J2EE patterns provide solutions for problems typically encountered by designers of software applications for the J2EE platform. All the patterns documented in the catalog have been discovered in the field, where they have been used to create successful J2EE applications for our customers.

This book describes proven solutions for the J2EE platform with a particular emphasis on such key J2EE technologies as: Java Server Pages (JSP), Servlets, Enterprise JavaBeans (EJB) components, Java Message Service (JMS), JDBC, and Java Naming and Directory Interface (JNDI). We offer solutions for recurring problems for the J2EE platform through the J2EE Pattern Catalog and J2EE refactorings. You can apply these ideas when developing new systems or when improving the design of existing systems. The patterns in this book will help you quickly gain the proficiency and skills to build robust, efficient enterprise applications.

Today, as in the past, many of us naively assume that *learning a technology* is synonymous with *learning to design* with the technology. Certainly learning the technology is an important part to being successful in designing with the technology. Many existing Java books are excellent at explaining technology details, such as API specifics and so forth, but at the same time they give no insight on applying the technology. Learning to design comes from experience and from sharing knowledge on best practices and bad practices.

The experiences we have conveyed in this book are derived from the work we have done in the field. We are part of Sun Microsystems, Inc.'s Sun Java Center (SJC) consulting organization. In our work, we often encounter situations where, because technology is moving so quickly, designers and developers are still struggling to understand the technology, let alone how to design with the technology.

It is not good enough to tell designers and developers to write good code, nor is it sufficient to suggest using Servlets and JSP for developing the presentation tier and EJB components[1] for developing the business tier.

So, given this scenario, where does an aspiring J2EE architect learn not only what to do, but what not to do? What are the best practices? What are the bad practices? How do you go from problem to design to implementation?

Sun Java Center and the J2EE Pattern Catalog

Since its inception, SJC architects have been working with clients all over the world to successfully design, architect, build, and deploy various types of systems based on Java and J2EE. The SJC is a rapidly growing consulting organization constantly adding new hires to its ranks of experienced architects.

Recognizing the need to capture and share proven designs and architectures, we started to document our work on the J2EE platform in the form of patterns in 1999. Although we looked in the existing literature, we could not find a catalog of patterns that dealt specifically with the J2EE platform. We found many books dealing with one or more of the J2EE technologies, and these books do an excellent job of explaining the technology and unraveling the nuances of the specifications. Some books offered extra help by providing some design considerations.

---

1. If you are new to the J2EE platform, we discuss the platform and these technologies in Chapter 2, "J2EE Platform Overview".

Since we first publicly presented our ideas on J2EE patterns at the JavaOne Conference in June 2000, we have received an overwhelming response from architects and developers. While some individuals expressed great interest in learning more about the patterns, others confirmed that they had applied the patterns, but had never named or documented them. This interest in patterns for the J2EE platform further motivated us to continue our work.

Thus, we put together the J2EE Pattern Catalog., which was initially made available to the entire J2EE community in beta form via the Java Developer Connection in March, 2001. Based largely on community feedback, the beta documentation evolved into the release you see in this book.

We hope these patterns, best practices, strategies, bad practices, and refactorings for the J2EE platform, provide the same benefits to you as they do for us.

What This Book is About?

This book is about:

- *Using patterns for the J2EE Platform.*
  Based on our collective J2EE platform experience, we have assembled the pattern catalog in this book. The J2EE Pattern Catalog describes various best practices related to architecting and designing applications for the J2EE platform. This book focuses on the following four J2EE technologies: Servlets, JSP, EJB components, and JMS.
- *Using best practices to design applications that use JSP, Servlet, EJB components, and JMS technologies.*
  It is not sufficient to merely learn the technology and the APIs. It is equally important to learn to design with the technology. We have documented what we have experienced to be the best practices for these technologies.
- *Preventing re-inventing-the-wheel when it comes to design and architecture for the J2EE platform.*
  Patterns promote design reuse. Reusing known solutions

reduces the cycle time for designing and developing applications, including J2EE applications.

- *Identifying bad practices in existing designs and refactoring these designs to move to a better solution using the J2EE patterns.*
  Knowing what works well is good. Knowing what does not work is equally important. We have documented some of the bad practices we have experienced when designing applications for the J2EE platform.

What This Book Is Not?

This book is not about:

- *How to program with Java or J2EE technologies*
  This book is not about programming. While this book is heavily based on the J2EE technologies, we do not describe the specific APIs. If you wish to learn about programming using Java or using any of the J2EE technologies, there are a number of excellent books and online resources from which to learn. The online tutorials on the official Java home page at `http://java.sun.com` are highly recommended if you wish to learn about individual technologies. The official specifications for J2EE technologies are also available from the Java home page.
- *What process and methodology to use*
  We do not suggest any type of process or methodology to use since the material presented in this book is not related to either. Hence, this book does not teach you about a process or methodology to follow in your projects. If you would like to learn more about processes and methodologies, there are a good number of books that deal with various object-oriented methodologies and new books on lightweight processes, such as Extreme Programming.
- *How to use Unified Modeling Language (UML)*
  This book is not going to teach you about UML. We use

UML extensively (specifically class and sequence diagrams) to document the patterns and describe the static and dynamic interactions. If you want to learn more about UML, please refer to the UML User Guide [Booch] and the UML Reference Manual [Rumbaugh] by Grady Booch, Ivar Jacobson and James Rumbaugh.

Who Should Read this Book?

This book is for all J2EE enthusiasts, programmers, architects, developers, and technical managers. In short, anyone who is remotely interested in designing, architecting and developing applications for the J2EE platform.

We have attempted to distinguish this book as a training guide for J2EE architects and designers. We all recognize the importance of good designs and well-architected projects, and that we need good architects to get there.

The use of well-documented patterns, best practices, and bad practices to share and transfer knowledge and experience can prove invaluable for teams with varied experience levels, and we hope that this book answers some of these needs.

How This Book is Organized

This book is organized into three parts.

Part 1—"Patterns and J2EE", consists of Chapter 1 and Chapter 2.

Chapter 1: "Introduction" on page 4 is a brief discussion on various topics, including patterns, J2EE platform, defining a pattern, and pattern categorization. It ends by introducing the J2EE Pattern Catalog.

Chapter 2 : "J2EE Platform Overview" on page 16 provides a high level overview of the J2EE platform for those readers unfamiliar with J2EE, or who wish to refresh their knowledge of the J2EE platform.

Part 2—"Design Considerations, Bad Practices, and Refactorings" deals with design considerations for JSP, Servlets, and enterprise beans. This part also includes bad practices and refactorings for the J2EE platform. This part is comprised of Chapter 3, 4, and 5.

Chapter 3 "Presentation Tier Design Considerations and Bad Practices" on page 36 and Chapter 4 "Business Tier Design Considerations and Bad Practices" on page 56 discuss the design considerations and bad practices for the presentation tier and business/integration tiers respectively. The design considerations are issues that a J2EE developer/designer/architect needs to consider while working with the J2EE platform. The topics presented in these chapters point the reader to other sources (such as official specifications and well written books on these topics) for more detailed information on these issues.

Chapter 5: "J2EE Refactorings" on page 74 includes some of the refactorings we have experienced in our work in the field that has enabled us to move our design from a less optimal solution to a better solution. The refactorings provide another way to think about the material in the rest of the book, providing what we believe to be valuable companion material to the pattern catalog. This chapter shows how we have been influenced by Martin Fowler and his book "Refactoring" [Fowler]. For those readers who are familiar with the Refactoring book, the format of this chapter will be very familiar. However, the content of this chapter is entirely in the context of J2EE technologies, whereas Martin Fowler addresses refactoring at a different level.

Part 3—"J2EE Pattern Catalog" presents the J2EE pattern catalog. The catalog contains the fifteen patterns that form the core of this book. This part is comprised of Chapter 6, 7, 8, and 9.

Chapter 6: "J2EE Patterns Overview" on page 126 provides an overview of the J2EE pattern catalog. This chapter begins with a high level discussion of the pattern ideas and explains the way the patterns are categorized into tiers. It also explains the J2EE pattern template, which is used to present all patterns in this book. The chapter discusses all the J2EE patterns and uses a diagram to show their inter-relationships. It also provides what we have termed a roadmap to the pattern catalog. This roadmap presents common J2EE design and architecture-related questions with references to patterns or refactorings that provide solutions to these questions. Understanding the pattern relationships and the roadmap is key to using these patterns.

Chapter 7: "Presentation Tier Patterns" on page 152 presents six patterns that pertain to using Servlets, JSP, JavaBeans, and custom tags to design web-based applications for the J2EE platform. The patterns describe numerous implementation strategies, and address common problems such as request handling, application partitioning, and generating composite displays.

Chapter 8: "Business Tier Patterns" on page 250 presents seven patterns that pertain to using EJB technology to design business components for the J2EE platform. The patterns in this chapter provide the best practices for using the EJB and JMS technologies. Where relevant, these patterns include discussion on other technologies, such as JNDI and JDBC.

Chapter 9: "Integration Tier Patterns" on page 388 presents two patterns that pertain to integrating J2EE applications with the resource tier and external systems. The patterns deal with using JDBC and JMS to enable integration between business tier and resource tier components.

Epilogue: "J2EE Patterns Applied" on page 392 discusses realizing sample use cases with the patterns. This chapter discusses and demonstrates how patterns are combined and work together. This chapter reinforces the idea that patterns exist in a community, and that each pattern supports, and is supported by, other patterns.

Companion Website and Contact Information

The official companion website where we will provide updates and other material is http://www.phptr.com/corej2eepatterns.

The J2EE Patterns interest group, j2eepatterns-interest@java.sun.com is available for public subscription and participation. To subscribe to the interest group and review the discussion archives, please visit:
http://archives.java.sun.com/archives/j2eepatterns-interest.html

Acknowledgments

We wish to thank Stu Stern, Director of Global Sun Java Center and Mark Bauhaus, VP of .COM Consulting without whose support, vision, and belief in our work this effort would never have been realized.

We wish to thank Ann Betser, without whose support, encouragement and skilled advice, we would have been lost.

We wish to express our sincere thanks to the PSA/iWorkflow reference implementation team of SJC architects: Fred Bloom, Narayan Chintalapati, Anders Eliasson, Kartik Ganeshan, Murali Kalyanakrishnan, Kamran Khan, Rita El Khoury, Rajmohan Krishnamurty, Ragu Sivaraman, Robert Skoczylas, Minnie Tanglao, and Basant Verma.

We wish to thank the Sun Java Center J2EE Patterns Working Group members: Mohammed Akif, Thorbiörn Fritzon, Beniot Garbinato, Paul Jatkowski, Karim Mazouni, Nick Wilde, and Andrew X. Yang.

We wish to thank Brendan McCarthy, SJC Chief Methodologist for keeping us in balance and for all the advice.

We wish to thank Jennifer Helms and John Kapson for introducing the patterns to customers.

We wish to express our gratitude to the following SJC architects from around the world for their support, feedback, and advice: Mark Cade, Mark Cao, Torbjörn Dahlén, Peter Gratzer, Bernard Van Haecke, Patricia de las Heras, Scott Herndon, Grant Holland, Girish Ippadi, Murali Kaundinya, Denys Kim, Stephen Kirkham, Todd Lasseigne, Sunil Mathew, Fred Muhlenberg, Vivek Pande, John Prentice, Alexis Roos, Gero Vermaas, Miguel Vidal.

We wish to thank our management Hank Harris, Dan Hushon, Jeff Johnson, Nimish Radia, Chris Steel, and Alex Wong for their support and encouragement.

We wish to thank the following Sun colleagues for their collaboration:

Bruce Delagi from Software Systems group; Mark Hapner, Vlada Matena from Java Software Engineering; Paul Butterworth and Jim Dibble from Forte Products Group; Deepak Balakrishna from iPlanet Products Group; Larry Freeman, Cori Kaylor, Rick Saletta, and Inderjeet Singh from the J2EE Blueprints Team; Heidi Dailey;

Dana Nourie, Laureen Hudson, Edward Ort, Margaret Ong, and Jenny Pratt from Java Developer Connection.

We wish to thank the following for their feedback, advice, and support:

Martin Fowler and Josh Mackenzie from ThoughtWorks, Inc.; Richard Monson-Haefel; Phil Nosonowitz and Carl Reed from Goldman Sachs; Jack Greenfield, Wojtek Kozaczynski, and Jon Lawrence from Rational Software; Alexander Aptus from TogetherSoft; Kent Mitchell from Zaplets.com; Bill Dudney; David Geary; Hans Bergsten; Members of the J2EE Patterns Interest group (j2eepatterns-interest@java.sun.com).

We wish to express our special thanks and gratitude to our lead technical editor Beth Stearns, transforming our manuscripts and making them readable, at the same time keeping us on track, and working with us all the way with a heavily demanding schedule.

We wish to thank the technical editors Daniel S. Barclay, Steven J. Halter, Spencer Roberts, and Chris Taylor for their expertise, meticulous review and feedback.

We wish to thank Greg Doench, Lisa Iarkowski, Mary Sudul, and Debby Van Dijk from Prentice Hall; Michael Alread and Rachel Borden from Sun Microsystems Press, for doing everything it took to produce this book.

We thank Bill Jirsa, John Hathaway, and Darlene Khosrowpour from Sun Educational Services for their effort creating the SunEd J2EE Patterns course (SL-500), John Sharp and Andy Longshaw from Content Master Ltd., as well as all the course reviewers for SL-500.

We wish to thank the patterns and the Java communities on whose work we have built.

The authors wish to thank their families for their support.

Deepak Alur wishes to thank:
Kavya, Shivaba and Samiksha—for your support, understanding, and inspiration; My Parents and Ajay.

John Crupi wishes to thank:
Ellen and Rachel—for your support , understanding and love.
Casey and Smokey—two great dogs will be forever missed.

Dan Malks wishes to thank:

Beth, Sarah, and Jonathan—for your support and for bringing special meaning to everything in my life.

core
J2EE™ PATTERNS
Best Practices and Design Strategies

Part 1

PATTERNS AND J2EE

Part I includes the following two chapters:

- *Chapter 1—Introduction*
- *Chapter 2—J2EE Platform Overview*

Chapter 1 presents a high-level discussion on patterns and the J2EE. The chapter presents numerous pattern definitions, information on pattern categorization, and some benefits of using patterns. This chapter sets the context for our J2EE Patterns work and provides the rationale and motivation behind the J2EE Pattern Catalog.

Chapter 2 provides a high level overview of the J2EE, its background, and the platform's value proposition. The chapter also discusses the relation between the J2EE Platform and the J2EE Pattern Catalog.

INTRODUCTION

Topics in This Chapter

- What Is J2EE?
- What Are Patterns?
- J2EE Pattern Catalog
- Patterns, Frameworks, and Reuse

Chapter 1

The last few years have been extraordinary with respect to the changing landscape of enterprise software development. At the center of this change is the Java 2 Platform, Enterprise Edition (J2EE), which provides a unified platform for developing distributed, server-centric applications. The widespread adoption of the strategic, enabling technologies of the J2EE have provided the development community with open standards on which to build service-based architectures for the enterprise.

At the same time, *learning* J2EE technologies is too often confused with learning to *design* with J2EE technologies. Many existing Java books do an excellent job of explaining specific aspects of the technology, but are not always clear on how to apply it.

A J2EE architect needs to understand more than the relevant APIs, including

- What are the best practices?
- What are the bad practices?
- What are the common recurring problems and proven solutions to these problems?
- How is code refactored from a less optimal scenario, or bad practice, to a better one typically described by a pattern?

That is what this book is all about. Good designs are discovered from experience. When these designs are communicated as patterns using a standard pattern template, they become a powerful mechanism for communication exchange and reuse, and can be leveraged to improve the way we design and build software.

What Is J2EE?

J2EE is a platform for developing distributed enterprise software applications. Since the inception of the Java language, it has undergone tremendous adoption and growth. More and more technologies have become part of the Java platform, and new APIs and standards have been developed to address various needs. Eventually, Sun and a group of industry leaders, under the auspices of the open Java Community Process (JCP), unified all these enterprise-related standards and APIs into the J2EE Platform.

The J2EE Platform offers numerous advantages to the enterprise:

- J2EE establishes standards for areas of enterprise computing needs such as database connectivity, enterprise business components, message-oriented middleware (MOM), Web-related components, communication protocols, and interoperability.
- J2EE promotes best-of-breed implementations based on open standards, protecting technological investment.
- J2EE provides a standard platform for building software components that are portable across vendor implementations, avoiding vendor lock-in.
- J2EE decreases time-to-market since much of the infrastructure and plumbing is provided by the vendors' products that are implemented according to the standard J2EE specification. IT organizations can now get out of the middleware business and concentrate on building applications for their business.
- J2EE increases programmer productivity, since Java programmers can relatively easily learn J2EE technologies based on the Java language. All enterprise software development can be accomplished under the J2EE platform, using Java as the programming language.
- J2EE promotes interoperability within existing heterogenous environments.

We discuss the J2EE Platform in greater detail in Chapter 2, so refer to that chapter for more information. Now we will take a brief look at patterns, their history, and the types of patterns in the J2EE Pattern Catalog that you will find in Part 3 of this book.

What Are Patterns?

Historical References

In the 1970s, Christopher Alexander [Alex, Alex2] wrote a number of books documenting patterns in civil engineering and architecture. The software community subsequently adopted the idea of patterns based on his work, though there was burgeoning interest in the software community in these ideas already.

Patterns in software were popularized by the book *Design Patterns: Elements of Reusable Object-Oriented Software* by Erich Gamma, Richard Helm, Ralph Johnson, and John Vlissides (also known as the Gang of Four, or GoF). Of course, while the Gang of Four work resulted in patterns becoming a common discussion topic in software development teams around the world, the important point to remember is that the patterns they describe were not invented by these authors. Instead, having recognized recurring designs in numerous projects, the authors identified and documented this collection.

Many software patterns books have been published since the GoF book, covering patterns for various domains and purposes. We provide references to a selected list of these titles and encourage you to investigate the other types of patterns described in these books.

Defining a Pattern

Patterns are about communicating problems and solutions. Simply put, patterns enable us to document a known recurring problem and its solution in a particular context, and to communicate this knowledge to others. One of the key elements in the previous statement is the word *recurring,* since the goal of the pattern is to foster conceptual reuse over time.

We explore this in more detail in Chapter 6, in the section "What Is a Pattern?" on page 126.

Here we examine some well-known definitions of patterns, beginning with one from Christopher Alexander in *A Pattern Language* [Alex2]:

> Each pattern is a three-part rule, which expresses a relation between a certain context, a problem, and a solution.
> —*Christopher Alexander*

Alexander expands his definition further, and noted patterns figure Richard Gabriel [Gabriel] discusses this definition in more detail [Hillside]. Gabriel offers his own version of Alexander's definition as applied to software:

> Each pattern is a three-part rule, which expresses a relation between a certain context, a certain system of forces which occurs repeatedly in that context, and a certain software configuration which allows these forces to resolve themselves. [See A Timeless Way of Hacking.]
> —*Richard Gabriel*

This is a fairly rigorous definition, but there are also much looser ones. For example, Martin Fowler offers the following definition in *Analysis Patterns* [Fowler2]:

> A pattern is an idea that has been useful in one practical context and will probably be useful in others.
> —*Martin Fowler*

As you can see, there are many definitions for a pattern, but all these definitions have a common theme relating to the recurrence of a problem/solution pair in a particular context.

Some of the common characteristics of patterns are

- Patterns are observed through experience.
- Patterns are typically written in a structured format (see "Pattern Template" on page 138).
- Patterns prevent reinventing the wheel.
- Patterns exist at different levels of abstraction.
- Patterns undergo continuous improvement.
- Patterns are reusable artifacts.
- Patterns communicate designs and best practices.
- Patterns can be used together to solve a larger problem.

Many great minds have spent a significant amount of time attempting to define and refine the notion of a software pattern. Suffice it to say, we do not presume to be great minds, nor do we wish to spend time expanding these discussions. Instead, we attempt to be true to aspects of these various definitions, focusing on the most simple and recurring theme in each.

Categorizing Patterns

Patterns, then, represent expert solutions to recurring problems in a context and thus have been captured at many levels of abstraction and in numerous domains. Numerous categories have been suggested for classifying software patterns, with some of the most common being

- design patterns
- architectural patterns
- analysis patterns
- creational patterns
- structural patterns
- behavioral patterns

Even within this brief list of categories, we see numerous levels of abstraction and orthogonal classification schemes. Thus, while many taxonomies have been suggested, there is no one right way to document these ideas.

We refer to the patterns in the catalog simply as "J2EE patterns". Each pattern hovers somewhere between a design pattern and an architectural pattern, while the strategies document portions of each pattern at a lower level of abstraction. The only scheme we have introduced is to classify each pattern within one of the following three logical architectural tiers:

- presentation tier
- business tier
- integration tier

At some point in the evolution of the pattern catalog, perhaps it will grow to a size that will warrant its being classified using a more sophisticated scheme. Currently, however, we prefer to keep things simple and not to introduce any new terms unnecessarily.

J2EE Pattern Catalog

Continuous Evolution

The J2EE patterns described in this book are based on our collective experience of working on the J2EE platform with Sun Java Center clients around the world. The Sun Java Center, a part of Sun Professional Services, is a consulting organization focused on building Java technology-based solutions for customers. We have been creating solutions for the J2EE platform since the platform's inception, focusing on achieving Quality of Service goals such as scalability, availability, and performance.

During the early days, as we designed, developed, and implemented various systems on the J2EE platform, we started documenting our experiences in an informal way as design considerations, ideas, and notes. As the knowledge base grew, we recognized a need for a slightly more formal documentation to capture and communicate this knowledge. We transitioned to documenting these ideas as patterns, since patterns are ideally suited to capturing and communicating knowledge related to recurring problems and solutions.

The first order of business was to sort out the level of abstraction with which the patterns were to be documented. Some problems and solutions overlapped others in that the core of the problem was the same, but the solution was implemented in a different manner. To address this overlap, we had to tackle the issue of the level of abstraction and the granularity with which we defined each pattern. As you will see in the J2EE pattern catalog, we eventually settled on a level of abstraction that hovers somewhere between design pattern and architectural pattern. The details related to the solutions that deal with implementation at a lower level of abstraction are addressed in the "Strategies" sections in our pattern template (see "Pattern Template" on page 138). This allows us to describe each pattern at a higher level of abstraction and at the same time discuss the implementation details.

Each pattern has been named and renamed many times. Additionally, each pattern has been rewritten many times, based on community feedback. Needless to say, these patterns, like all patterns, are subject to continuous improvement and will certainly evolve as the technology and specifications change.

The J2EE pattern catalog currently includes 15 patterns and is presented in three chapters: Chapter 7, "Presentation Tier Patterns,"

Chapter 8, "Business Tier Patterns," and Chapter 9, "Integration Tier Patterns." Each pattern is documented in our pattern template.
Table 1-1 lists the patterns included in the catalog.

Table 1-1 Patterns in the J2EE Pattern Catalog

Tier	*Pattern Name*
Presentation Tier	"Intercepting Filter" on page 152 "Front Controller" on page 172 "View Helper" on page 186 "Composite View" on page 203 "Service to Worker" on page 216 "Dispatcher View" on page 231
Business Tier	"Business Delegate" on page 248 "Value Object" on page 261 "Session Facade" on page 291 "Composite Entity" on page 310 "Value Object Assembler" on page 339 "Value List Handler" on page 353 "Service Locator" on page 367
Integration Tier	"Data Access Object" on page 390 "Service Activator" on page 408

How to Use the J2EE Pattern Catalog

One of the challenges when using any set of patterns is understanding how to best use the patterns in combination. As Christopher Alexander says in his book, *A Pattern Language* [Alex2]:

> In short, no pattern is an isolated entity. Each pattern can exist in the world, only to the extent that is supported by other patterns: the larger patterns in which it is embedded, and the patterns of the same size that surround it, and the smaller patterns which are embedded in it. —*Christopher Alexander*

The patterns in the J2EE pattern catalog are no exception to this rule. The pattern relationships diagram, explained in Chapter 6, "J2EE Patterns Overview," describes how each pattern is supported by other patterns in the catalog. Chapter 6 also provides a roadmap to the J2EE pattern catalog, presented in tabular form, with common J2EE design and architecture-related questions paired with pattern or refactoring references, providing solutions to each question. To gain the maximum benefit from using these patterns, it is recommended that the pattern relationships and the pattern roadmap be well understood.

As you study each pattern in detail, you will see the patterns and strategies that are embedded within it, in which it is contained, and which it supports. Sometimes the pattern builds on other patterns from the J2EE pattern catalog or from other patterns described in well-known literature such as *Design Patterns: Elements of Reusable Object-Oriented Software* [GoF] or *Patterns of Software Architecture* [POSA1, POSA2].

In an attempt to aid you in further understanding the patterns, their interrelationships, pattern selection, and pattern usage, we have provided supporting chapters in Part 2 of the book.

In Part 2 of the book, we present bad practices and refactorings for the J2EE platform. For each bad practice that has been listed in these chapters, we provide links to refactorings or patterns that offer solutions to alleviate the problems created by that bad practice. In Chapter 5, "J2EE Refactorings," we present refactorings that describe the steps involved in moving from a less optimal solution to a preferred one. The mechanics section of each refactoring provides references to patterns and design considerations that influence the direction of the refactoring.

Finally, in Epilogue, "J2EE Patterns Applied," we demonstrate an example of an application based on the J2EE patterns. We present some use cases to show how these patterns interact and work together to help realize a use case.

Benefits of Using Patterns

You can use the J2EE patterns in this book to improve your system design, and you can apply them at any point in a project life cycle. The patterns in the catalog are documented at a relatively high level of abstraction and will provide great benefit when applied early in a project. Alternatively, if you apply a pattern during the implementation phase, you may have to rework existing code. In this case, the refactorings in Chapter 5 may prove quite useful.

Patterns are often quite simple to use, though not always easy to understand. However, patterns can be difficult and time consuming to document, since this effort requires an examination of the essence of what constitutes a good practice. Recognizing good practices is typically a long-term effort. It involves distilling a large volume of knowledge down to its basics and putting it into words. We have tried to ensure that our documentation is clear and that it relates well to real world issues. At the same time, we recognize that this effort will continue to evolve and to be refined and improved over time.

What are the benefits of using patterns? We describe in the following sections some of the benefits of using and applying patterns in a project. In brief, patterns

- Leverage a proven solution.
- Provide a common vocabulary.
- Constrain solution space.

Leverage a Proven Solution

A pattern is documented based on the fact that the solution it offers has been used over and over again to solve similar problems at different times in different projects. Thus, patterns provide a powerful mechanism for reuse, helping developers and architects to avoid reinventing the wheel.

Common Vocabulary

Patterns provide software designers with a common vocabulary. As designers, we use patterns not only to help us leverage and duplicate successful designs, but also to help us convey a common vocabulary and format to developers.

A designer who does not rely on patterns needs to expend more effort to communicate his design to other designers or developers. Software designers use the pattern vocabulary to communicate effectively. This is similar to the real world, where we use a common vocabulary to communicate and exchange ideas. Just as in the real world, developers can build their vocabulary by learning and understanding patterns, increasing their design vocabulary as new patterns are documented.

Once you start to use these patterns, you'll notice that you'll quickly begin to incorporate the pattern names into your vocabulary—and that you use the names of the patterns to replace lengthy descriptions. For example, suppose your problem solution entails use of a Value Object pattern. At first, you might describe the problem without putting a label on it. You may describe the need for your application to exchange data with enterprise beans, the need to maximize performance given the network overhead with remote invocations, and so forth. Later, once you've learned how to apply the Value

Object pattern to the problem, you may refer to a similar situation in terms of a "Value Object" solution and build from there.

To understand the impact of the pattern vocabulary, consider this exercise after you and another team member are familiar with the pattern catalog. Without using pattern names, try to explain what can be conveyed by simple sentences such as the following, in which the pattern names from the J2EE pattern catalog are italicized:

- We should use *Data Access Object*s in our servlets and session beans.
- How about using *Value Object* for transferring data to and from enterprise beans, and encapsulating all business services with *Business Delegates*?
- Let's use *Front Controller* and *Service to Worker*. We may have to use *Composite View*s for some complex pages.

Constrains Solution Space

Pattern application introduces a major design component—constraints. Using a pattern constrains or creates boundaries within a solution space to which a design and implementation can be applied. Thus, a pattern strongly suggests to a developer boundaries to which an implementation might adhere. Going outside of these boundaries breaks the adherence to the pattern and design, and may lead to the unwanted introduction of an anti-pattern.

However, patterns do not stifle creativity. Instead, they describe a structure or shape at some level of abstraction. Designers and developers still have many options open to them for implementing the patterns within these boundaries.

Patterns, Frameworks, and Reuse

We have been chasing the illustrious software reuse goal for years now and have only had moderate success. In fact, most of the commercial reuse success has been in the user interface area, not in business components, which is our focus. As business system architects, we strive to promote reuse, but have really been concentrating on reuse at the design and architecture levels. The pattern catalog has proven a powerful way to promote this level of reuse.

There are numerous relationships between each of the patterns in the catalog, and these relationships are sometimes referred to as

being part of a pattern language. We provide a diagram of these relationships in Chapter 6, Figure 6.2 on page 141. Another way to
describe these relationships is in terms of a pattern framework, or a
collection of patterns in a united scenario. This concept is key to
identifying end-to-end solutions and wiring components together at
the pattern level.

Developers must understand more than discrete patterns in isolation, and have been asking for best practices as to how to link patterns together to form larger solutions. Combining the patterns from
the catalog in this manner is what we refer to as leveraging a J2EE
pattern framework. A framework, in this context, is about linking
patterns together to form a solution to address a set of requirements.
We think that this type of usage will drive the next generation of
tools in J2EE development. Such automation of a pattern-driven
process requires

- Identifying scenarios and offering patterns that apply for each
  tier.
- Identifying pattern combinations, or motifs, to provide pattern
  frameworks.
- Selecting implementation strategies for each role.

We provide a bit more information on this evolving area of development in Epilogue.

Summary

By now you should have a good understanding of what constitutes a
pattern and what this book is all about. The next chapter provides
an introduction to the J2EE Platform and its various technologies.

J2EE PLATFORM
OVERVIEW

Topics in This Chapter

- A Brief Perspective
- J2EE Platform
- J2EE Patterns and J2EE Platform

Chapter 2

This chapter presents a high level overview of the Java™ 2 Platform, Enterprise Edition (J2EE) and its technologies. If you already understand the J2EE platform and its technologies and APIs, you may wish to skip this chapter. However, we suggest at a minimum that you read the section "J2EE Patterns and J2EE Platform" on page 30 to understand what J2EE patterns are all about.

Read on if you wish to refresh your memory on J2EE.

A Brief Perspective

From its introduction to the world in 1994 to current day, the Java™ programming language has revolutionized the software industry. Java has been used in a myriad of ways to implement various types of systems. As Java started becoming more and more ubiquitous, spreading from browsers to phones to all kinds of devices, we saw it gradually hone in on one particular area and establish its strength and value proposition: That area is the use of Java on servers. Over time, Java has become the chosen platform for programming servers.

Java provides its *Write Once Run Anywhere*™ advantage to IT organizations, application developers, and product vendors. IT organizations leverage the benefits of vendor independence and portability of their applications. The increasing availability of skilled Java programmers promoted Java's adoption in the industry. Unbelievably, the number of Java programmers has rocketed to 2.5 million developers in only five years.

The simplicity of the language and the explosive growth of its use on the Internet and the intranet urged numerous developers and IT organizations to embrace Java as the de facto programming language for their projects.

The client-server application architecture, a two-tier architecture, over time evolved to a multitier architecture. This natural progression occurred as additional tiers were introduced between the end-user clients and backend systems. Although a multitier architecture brings greater flexibility in design, it also increases the complexity for building, testing, deploying, administering, and maintaining application components. The J2EE platform is designed to support a multitier architecture, and thus it reduces this complexity.

During this time, corporate Internet usage changed. Corporations transitioned from providing a simple corporate Web site to exposing some of their not-so-critical applications to the external world. In this first phase of Internet experimentation, IT managers were still skeptical and the security police were adamantly unfriendly to the idea of using the Internet to run and expose business services.

Before long, more and more companies started to embrace the power of the Internet. For example, customer service organizations began to provide service on the Web, in addition to the traditional methods of supporting customers by phone and email. Such organizations recognized the major cost implications of providing online service. Customers could now help themselves for most problems, and call a customer service agent only for more serious issues.

Customers liked using the Web too, as it improved their productivity. Soon, customers started expecting more and more online services from companies, and companies had to step up and provide these services. If they did not, someone else would.

Since then, almost everything has gone online—banking, bill payment, travel, ticketing, auctioning, car buying services, mortgages and loans, pharmacies, and even pet food! New companies were created that had no business model (now we know) other than opening shop online. They thrived and they thrashed. Established companies had to make their online presence felt to face the challenges of these new kids on the block. This tremendous growth fueled the need for a robust, enterprise class, Web-centric application infrastructure.

Application Servers—The New Breed

As the acceptance and adoption of Java on the server side became more established, and the demand for Web-centric application infrastructure rose, we saw an emergence of a new breed of infrastructure applications—application servers. Application servers provided the basic infrastructure required for developing and deploying multitiered enterprise applications.

These application servers had numerous benefits. One important benefit was that IT organizations no longer needed to develop their proprietary infrastructure to support their applications. Instead, they could now rely on the application server vendor to provide the infrastructure. This not only reduced the cost of their applications, but also reduced the time-to-market.

Each application server had its own benefits and disadvantages. Because there were no standards for application servers, no two application servers were completely alike. Some application servers were based on Java, and these allowed you to write only Java components to run on that server, while others used different languages for development.

Convergence of Java Technologies

In the area of Web applications, there were significant developments in Java as well. The Common Gateway Interface (CGI) approach for developing Web-centric applications was resource-intensive and did not scale well. With the introduction of servlet technology, Java developers had an elegant and efficient mechanism to write Web-centric applications that generated dynamic content. However, writing servlets still took some effort and Java expertise.

Then, the Java Server Pages (JSP) technology was introduced, particularly for Web and graphic designers accustomed to Hypertext Markup Language (HTML) and JavaScript scripting. JSP technology made it easier for Web front developers to write Web-centric applications. One need not know Java and servlet programming to develop pages in JSP.

JSP technology addresses the need for a scripting language for Web application clients. Web designers skilled at HTML and JavaScript can quickly learn JSP technology and use it to write Web applications. Of course, the Web server translates JSPs into servlets, but that happens "under the wraps." Effectively, servlets and JSPs separate Web application development roles.

The standard approach for database access in Java applications is Java Database Connectivity (JDBC). The JDBC API (application programming interface) gives programmers the ability to make their Java applications independent of the database vendor. One can write a JDBC application that accesses a database using standard Structured Query Language (SQL). If the underlying database changes from one vendor's product to another, the JDBC application works without any code change, provided that the code is properly written and does not use any proprietary extensions from the first vendor. JDBC API is offered as part of the core APIs in the Java^{TM} 2 Platform, Standard Edition (J2SE^{TM}).

J2SE (formerly known as Java Development Kit or JDK) is the foundation for all Java APIs. J2SE consists of a set of core APIs that define the Java programming language interfaces and libraries. Java developers use the J2SE as the primary API for developing Java applications. As requirements expand and the Java language matures over the years, the J2SE offers additional APIs as standard extensions.

As Java established its permanent role on the server side, and the adoption of various Java APIs became widespread, Sun put together an initiative to unify standards for various Java technologies into a single platform. The initiative to develop standards for enterprise Java APIs was formed under the open Java Community Process (JCP). Enterprise Java APIs are a collection of various APIs that provide vendor-independent programming interfaces to access various types of systems and services. The enterprise Java APIs emerged as the Java^{TM} 2 Platform, Enterprise Edition (J2EE™).

The Rise of the J2EE Platform

The Enterprise Java Beans™ (EJB™) technology is one of the prominent, promising technologies in the J2EE platform. The EJB architecture provides a standard for developing reusable Java server components that run in an application server. The EJB specification and APIs provide a vendor-independent programming interface for application servers. EJB components, called *enterprise beans,* provide for persistence, business processing, transaction processing, and distributed processing capabilities for enterprise applications. In short, the EJB technology offers portability of business components.

Various application vendors, having come together with Sun under the open JCP to develop this standard, adopted and implemented the EJB specification into their application server products. Similar to JDBC application portability, EJB applications are portable from one application server vendor to another. Again, this is true if the application does not use any vendor-dependent feature of the application server. J2EE technologies are now a proven and established platform for distributed computing for the enterprise.

Java Message Service (JMS) is another standard API in the J2EE platform. It brings the same kind of standardization to messaging as JDBC brought for databases. JMS provides a standard Java API for using message-oriented middleware (MOM) for point-to-point and publish/subscribe types of enterprise messaging. As with the other technologies, JMS brings vendor independence in the MOM products for Java.

In each of these areas, Sun and other companies collaborated in coming up with an acceptable standard under the auspices of the open JCP. The JCP coordinated the activities to develop these standards. This cooperation is a foundation for the success of these APIs.

J2EE Value Proposition

The J2EE platform, built on the Java programming language and Java technologies, is the application architecture that is best suited for an enterprise-distributed environment. The J2EE platform is a standard that brings the following benefits to IT organizations, application developers, and product vendors:

- Vendors develop products that can run on any system that supports the J2EE platform. With virtually no extra effort, their products are available on a wide range of system platforms.

- Corporate IT developers benefit from the advantages of portable component technology. IT applications become vendor-independent and release the IT organizations from the clutches of vendor lock-in.

- IT developers can focus on supporting business process requirements rather than building in-house application infrastructure. The application servers handle the complex issues of multithreading, synchronization, transactions, resource allocation, and life-cycle management.

- IT organizations can take advantage of the best available products built on a standard platform. They can choose among products and select the most suitable and cost-effective development products, deployment products, and deployment platforms based on their requirements.

- Adopting the J2EE platform results in a significant productivity increase. Java developers can quickly learn the J2EE APIs.

- Companies protect their investment by adopting the J2EE platform, since it is an industry-supported standard and not a vendor-defined lock-in architecture.

- Development teams can build new applications and systems more rapidly. This decreases time-to-market and reduces the cost of development.

- A standard development platform for distributed computing ensures that robust applications are built on a proven platform.

- The J2EE platform provides a clear, logical, and physical partitioning of applications into various tiers, thus naturally addressing multitiered application requirements.

- Developers can either build their own J2EE component or procure it from the rapidly growing third-party components market. Vendors are able to offer their components individually, and customers are able to buy these software parts as needed.

J2EE Platform

The previous section described the core technology components of the J2EE platform, such as servlet, JSP, EJB, JDBC, and JMS. In this section, we take a look at the J2EE architecture model and describe other aspects of the J2EE platform that complete the platform definition.

J2EE Architecture

The J2EE architecture is a multitiered architecture. See Figure 2.1.

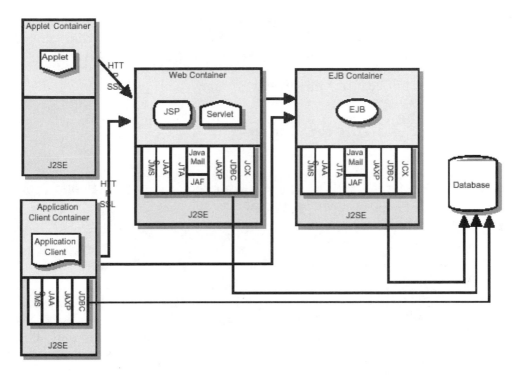

Figure 2.1 J2EE architecture

The J2EE architecture consists of the following tiers:

- ***Client tier***—The client tier interacts with the user and displays information from the system to the user. The J2EE platform supports different types of clients, including HTML clients, Java applets, and Java applications.

- ***Web tier***—The Web tier generates presentation logic and accepts user responses from the presentation clients, which are typically HTML clients, Java applets, and other Web clients. Based on the received client request, The presentation tier generates the appropriate response to a client request that it receives. In the J2EE platform, servlets and JSPs in a Web container implement this tier.

- ***Business tier***—This tier handles the core business logic of the application. The business tier provides the necessary interfaces to the underlying business service components. The business components are typically implemented as EJB components with support from an EJB container that facilitates the component life cycle and manages persistence, transactions, and resource allocation.

- **EIS tier**—This tier is responsible for the enterprise information systems, including database systems, transaction processing systems, legacy systems, and enterprise resource planning systems. The EIS tier is the point where J2EE applications integrate with non-J2EE or legacy systems.

Java 2 Standard Edition

J2SE is the underlying base platform for J2EE, hence a brief discussion on the J2SE platform is relevant to the J2EE platform. The J2SE platform includes two deliverables:

- Java 2 SDK, Standard Edition (J2SE SDK)

- Java 2 Runtime Environment, Standard Edition (JRE)

J2SE SDK, formerly the JDK, is the Java programming language's core API set. J2SE provides the Java language functionality as well as the core libraries required for Java development. The core libraries are the classes within the `java.*` packages. In addition, J2SE provides auxiliary interfaces and libraries as extensions. It makes these standard extensions available as `javax.*` packages.

J2SE includes tools and APIs for developing applications with graphical user interfaces (GUIs), database access, directory access, Common Object Request Broker Architecture (CORBA), fine-grained security, input/output functions, and many other functions. See Table 2-1 .

Table 2-1

Function	*Package Name*
Graphical user interface	`java.awt.*`, `javax.swing.*`
Database access	`java.sql.*`
Directory access	`javax.naming.*`
CORBA	`javax.rmi.CORBA.*`
Security	`java.security.*`
Input/output	`java.io.*`

Figure 2.2 shows the various components of the J2SE platform.

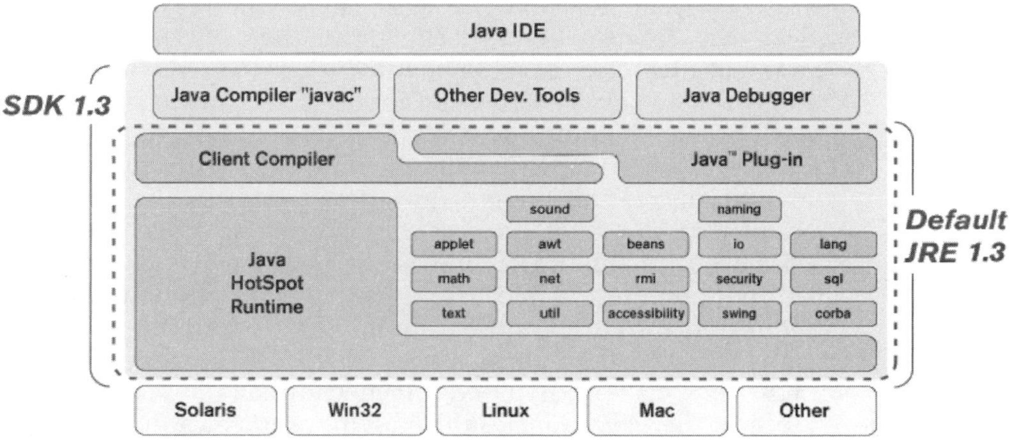

Figure 2.2 J2SE platform

J2EE Application Components and Containers

The J2EE component container supports application components in the J2EE platform. A container is a service that provides the necessary infrastructure and support for a component to exist and for the component to provide its own services to clients. A container usually provides its services to the components as a Java compatible runtime environment.

The core application components in the J2EE platform are as follows:

- *Java application components*—standalone Java programs that run inside an application container.
- *Applet components*—Java applets that run inside an applet container, and which are usually supported via a Web browser.
- *Servlets and JSPs*—Web-tier components that run in a Web container. Servlets and JSPs provide mechanisms for dynamic content preparation, processing, and formatting related to presentation.
- *EJB components*—Coarse-grained business components that are run inside an EJB container (usually bundled in an application server product). EJB components, or enterprise beans, come in two types: session beans and entity beans. Session beans are enterprise beans that are suitable for

processing or workflow. Session beans come in two flavors: stateful and stateless. A stateful session bean retains client state between method invocations. A stateless session bean does not retain client-specific state between client-invoked methods. Stateless session beans are used when no state needs to be stored between method invocations, and they may offer performance benefits over stateful session beans, which must be used when some state needs to be retained between invocations. Session bean instances pertain to a single user session and are not shared between users. Entity beans are used when a business component needs to be persisted and shared among multiple users. Entity bean persistence can be managed in two ways: bean-managed persistence (BMP) and container-managed persistence (CMP). BMP is used when the bean developer implements all mechanisms for persisting the state in the bean. CMP is used when the bean developer does not implement the persistence mechanisms in the bean. Instead, the bean developer specifies the necessary mapping between the bean attributes and the persistent storage and lets the container do the job.

The core focus of the J2EE patterns in this book is the design and architecture of applications using servlets, JSPs, and enterprise bean components.

Standard Services

The J2EE platform specifies the following standard services that every J2EE product supports. These services include APIs, which every J2EE product must also provide to application components so that the components may access the services.

- *HTTP*—Standard protocol for Web communications. Clients can access HTTP via the `java.net` package
- *HTTP over Secure Socket Layer (HTTPS)*—Same as HTTP, but the protocol is used over Secure Socket Layer for security.
- *JDBC*—A standard API to access database resources in a vendor-independent manner.
- *JavaMail*—An API that provides a platform-independent and protocol-independent framework to build mail and messaging applications in Java.
- *Java Activation Framework (JAF)*—APIs for an activation framework that is used by other packages, such as JavaMail. Developers can use JAF to determine the type of an arbitrary

piece of data, encapsulate access to it, discover the operations available on it, and instantiate the appropriate bean to perform these operations. For example, JavaMail uses JAF to determine what object to instantiate depending on the mime type of the object.

- ***Remote Method Invocation/Internet Inter-ORB Protocol (RMI/IIOP)***—Protocol that enables Remote Method Invocation (RMI) programmers to combine the benefits of using the RMI APIs and robust CORBA IIOP communications protocol to communicate with CORBA-compliant clients that have been developed using any language compliant with CORBA.

- ***Java Interface Definition Language (JavaIDL)***—A service that incorporates CORBA into the Java platform to provide interoperability using standard IDL defined by the Object Management Group. Runtime components include Java ORB (Object Request Broker) for distributed computing using IIOP communication.

- ***Java Transaction API (JTA)***—A set of APIs that allows transaction management. Applications can use the JTA APIs to start, commit, and abort transactions. JTA APIs also allow the container to communicate with the transaction manager, and allow the transaction manager to communicate with the resource manager.

- ***JMS***—An API to communicate with MOM to enable point-to-point and publish/subscribe messaging between systems. JMS offers vendor independence for using MOMs in Java applications.

- ***Java Naming and Directory Interface (JNDI)***—A unified interface to access different types of naming and directory services. JNDI is used to register and look up business components and other service-oriented objects in a J2EE environment. JNDI includes support for Lightweight Directory Access Protocol (LDAP), the CORBA Object Services (COS) Naming Service, and the Java RMI Registry.

J2EE Platform Roles

The J2EE platform uses a set of defined roles to conceptualize the tasks related to the various workflows in the development and deployment life cycle of an enterprise application. These role definitions provide a logical separation of responsibilities for team mem-

bers involved in the development, deployment, and management of a
J2EE application. See Figure 2.3.

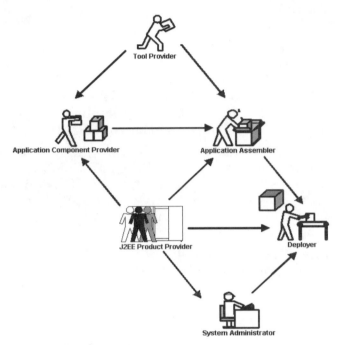

Figure 2.3 J2EE platform roles

The J2EE roles are as follows:

- **J2EE product provider**—Provides component containers,
  such as application servers and Web servers, that are built to
  conform to the J2EE specification. The product provider must
  also provide tools to deploy components into the component
  containers. These tools are typically used by the deployer. In
  addition, the product provider must provide tools to manage
  and monitor the applications in the container. The system
  administrator typically uses these latter tools. This role is fulfilled by the product vendors.
- **Application component provider**—Provides business components built using the J2EE APIs. These components include
  components for Web applications as well as for EJB applications. This role is fulfilled by programmers, developers, Web
  designers, and so forth.
- **Application assembler**—Assembles, or puts together, a set of
  components into a deployable application. The assembler
  obtains the application components from the component pro-

viders. The application assembler packages the application and provides the necessary assembly and deployment instructions to the deployer.

- *Application deployer*—Deploys the assembled application into a J2EE container. The deployer may deploy Web applications into containers—Web containers, EJB containers, and so on—using the tools provided by the J2EE product provider. The deployer is responsible for installation, configuration, and execution of the J2EE application.

- *System administrator*—Has the responsibility of monitoring the deployed J2EE applications and the J2EE containers. The system administrator uses the management and monitoring tools provided by the J2EE product provider.

- *Tool provider*—Provides tools used for development, deployment, and packaging of components.

Deployment Descriptors

An application assembler puts a J2EE application together for deployment, and at the same time provides the assembly and deployment instructions in special files called *deployment descriptors*. The J2EE specification defines deployment descriptors as the contract between the application assembler and the deployer. Deployment descriptors are XML documents that include all the necessary configuration parameters required to deploy the J2EE application or J2EE components. Such configuration parameters specify external resource requirements, security requirements, environment parameters, and other component-specific and application-specific parameters. The deployer may use a deployment tool provided by the J2EE product provider to inspect, modify, customize, and add configuration parameters in these deployment descriptors to tailor the deployment to the capabilities of the deployment environment.

Deployment descriptors offer flexibility for the development and deployment of J2EE application components by allowing changes to configurations and dependencies as needed during the different application phases: the development, deployment, and administration phases. Much of this flexibility is due to descriptors defining parameters in a declarative fashion, rather than having the parameters be embedded in the program code.

J2EE Patterns and J2EE Platform

As you can see from the overview, the J2EE platform standardizes a number of different technologies to provide a robust platform for building distributed multitier enterprise class applications. The J2EE platform is built on the J2SE platform. Since the J2SE platform forms the foundation of the J2EE platform, a Java developer can learn the J2EE technologies with relative ease.

However, there is a belief that learning a new technology by itself is sufficient to make us adept at designing systems based on that new technology. We respectfully disagree with this. We believe that in addition to learning the technology, we need other insights to build successful systems. Patterns can help facilitate the process of knowledge accumulation and knowledge transfer. Patterns help us to document and communicate proven solutions to recurring problems in different environments. Using patterns effectively, we can prevent the "re-invent the wheel" syndrome.

Our J2EE patterns are derived from our experience with the J2EE platform and technologies. The J2EE patterns described in this book address different requirements spread across all the J2EE tiers. In our tiered approach (see "The Tiered Approach" on page 128), we have modeled the J2EE multiple tiers as five tiers: client, presentation, business, integration, and resource tiers. This model allows us to logically separate responsibilities into individual tiers. In our model, for example, we separate the EIS tier into an integration tier and a resource tier. By doing so, we make it easier to separately address the requirements of integration and resources. Thus, the tiers in our model are a logical separation of concerns.

We've categorized the J2EE patterns described in this book into three of these five tiers—*presentation*, *business*, and *integration*. In our opinion, the client and resource tiers are not direct concerns of the J2EE platform. The patterns related to servlets and JSP technologies are described in Chapter 7, *"Presentation Tier Patterns."* The patterns related to enterprise beans and JNDI technologies, and those related to bridging the presentation and business tier components, are described in Chapter 8, *"Business Tier Patterns."* Finally, the patterns related to JDBC and JMS technologies, aimed at bridging the business tier with the resource tier, are described in Chapter 9, *"Integration Tier Patterns."*

Because our most intensive work has been in these core areas of the J2EE platform, we currently do not address patterns other than these aforementioned technologies. We feel that the developer community gains a huge benefit if we first document the patterns in these core areas. We also believe that this categorization allows us to be flexible, and as new patterns are observed, we will categorize and document them.

We believe that these patterns will prove useful to you as they did to us and our fellow architects. They may be reused as solutions to the problems you may encounter during your J2EE design and architecture experience. We are also aware that patterns evolve over time, and we expect that our patterns are no exception. The patterns presented here have been refined many times. They have been written and rewritten to make them better. This process of evolution will continue.

Summary

While this chapter provided an overview of the J2EE platform, it also included a flurry of terminologies and acronyms. If you are interested in learning more, the following online resources are recommended:

- The Story of the Java Platform—http://java.sun.com/nav/whatis/storyofjava.html
- Java Technology—An Early History—http://java.sun.com/features/1998/05/birthday.html
- Java Community Process—http://java.sun.com/aboutJava/communityprocess/
- J2SE Platform Documentation—http://java.sun.com/docs/index.html
- J2EE home page—http://java.sun.com/j2ee
- J2EE Blueprints—http://java.sun.com/j2ee/blueprints/index.html
- EJB home page—http://java.sun.com/products/ejb
- Servlets home page—http://www.java.sun.com/products/servlet
- JSP home page—http://www.java.sun.com/products/jsp
- JDBC home page—http://www.java.sun.com/products/jdbc
- JMS home page—http://www.java.sun.com/products/jms
- JNDI home page—http://java.sun.com/products/jndi
- Connector home page—http://java.sun.com/j2ee/connector

DESIGN CONSIDERATIONS, BAD PRACTICES, AND REFACTORINGS

Part 2 includes the following three chapters:

- *Chapter 3—Presentation Tier Design Considerations and Bad Practices*
- *Chapter 4—Business Tier Design Considerations and Bad Practices*
- *Chapter 5—J2EE Refactorings*

Chapter 3 and 4, as their names suggest, discuss various design considerations and bad practices.

When applying the patterns from the catalog, developers will need to consider numerous adjunct design issues, such as the ones discussed in these chapters. These include issues affecting numerous aspects of the system, including security, data integrity, manageability, and scalability.

Many of these design issues could be captured in pattern form, as well, although they primarily focus on issues at a lower level of abstraction than those described in the J2EE Pattern Catalog. Instead of documenting each as a pattern, we have chosen to document them more informally, simply describing each as a design issue to be considered when implementing systems based on the pattern catalog. While a complete discussion of each issue is outside the scope of this book, we wanted to mention these concerns, and encourage the reader to investigate these issues.

Chapter 3 and 4 also highlight less than optimal ways to solve certain problems—solutions which we term bad practices. Each bad practice provides a brief problem summary accompanied by a list of solution references. The solution references are a list of pointers to other sections of the book with related material, suggesting preferred ways to solve these problems. Typically, these references are to a pattern in the catalog, to a refactoring, or to a combination of the two.

Chapter 5 presents refactorings for the J2EE Platform. The presentation format of this chapter is based on that in Martin Fowler's book Refactoring [Fowler], an excellent guide for those wishing to learn more about software design. Each refactoring identifies a simple problem and solution statement, offers motivations for improving the problem, and suggests mechanics for doing so.

PRESENTATION TIER DESIGN CONSIDERATIONS AND BAD PRACTICES

Topics in This Chapter

- Presentation Tier Design Considerations
- Presentation Tier Bad Practices

Chapter 3

Presentation Tier Design Considerations

When developers apply the presentation patterns that appear in the catalog in this book, there will be adjunct design issues to consider. These issues relate to designing with patterns at a variety of levels, and they may affect numerous aspects of a system, including security, data integrity, manageability, and scalability. We discuss these issues in this chapter.

Although many of these design issues could be captured in pattern form, we chose not to do so because they focus on issues at a lower level of abstraction than the presentation patterns in the catalog. Rather than documenting each issue as a pattern, we have chosen to document them more informally: We simply describe each issue as one that you should consider when implementing systems based on the pattern catalog.

Session Management

The term *user session* describes a conversation that spans multiple requests between a client and a server. We rely on the concept of user session in the discussion in the following sections.

Session State on Client

Saving session state on the client involves serializing and embedding the session state within the view markup HTML page that is returned to the client.

There are benefits to persisting session state on the client:

- It is relatively easy to implement.
- It works well when saving minimal amounts of state.

Additionally, this strategy virtually eliminates the problem of replicating state across servers in those situations that implement load balancing across physical machines.

There are two common strategies for saving session state on the client—HTML hidden fields and HTTP cookies—and we describe these strategies below. A third strategy entails embedding the session state directly into the URIs referenced in each page (for example, `<form action=someServlet?var1=x&var2=y method=GET>`). Although this third strategy is less common, it shares many of the limitations of the following two methods.

HTML Hidden Fields

Although it is relatively easy to implement this strategy, there are numerous drawbacks to using HTML hidden fields to save session state on the client. These drawbacks are especially apparent when saving large amounts of state. Saving large amounts of state negatively affects performance. Since all view markup now embeds or contains the state, it must traverse the network with each request and response.

Additionally, when you utilize hidden fields to save session state, the persisted state is limited to string values, so any object references must be "stringified". It is also exposed in clear text in the generated HTML source, unless specifically encrypted.

HTTP Cookies

Similar to the hidden fields strategy, it is relatively easy to implement the HTTP cookies strategy. This strategy unfortunately shares many of the same drawbacks as well. In particular, saving large amounts of state causes performance to suffer, because all the session state must traverse the network for each request and response.

We also run into size and type limitations when saving session state on the client. There are limitations on the size of cookie headers, and this limits the amount of data that can be persisted. Moreover, as with hidden fields, when you use cookies to save session state, the persisted state is limited to stringified values.

Security Concerns of Client-Side Session State

When you save session state on the client, security issues are introduced that you must consider. If you do not want your data exposed to the client, then you need to employ some method of encryption to secure the data.

Although saving session state on the client is relatively easy to implement initially, it has numerous drawbacks that take time and thought to overcome. For projects that deal with large amounts of data, as is typical with enterprise systems, these drawbacks far outweigh the benefits.

Session State in the Presentation Tier

When session state is maintained on the server, it is retrieved using a session ID and typically persists until one of the following occurs:

- A predefined session timeout is exceeded.
- The session is manually invalidated.
- The state is removed from the session.

Note that after a server shutdown, some in-memory session management mechanisms may not be recoverable.

It is clearly preferable for applications with large amounts of session state to save their session state on the server. When state is saved on the server, you are not constrained by the size or type limitations of client-side session management. Additionally, you avoid raising the security issues associated with exposing session state to the client, and you do not have the performance impact of passing the session state across the network on each request.

You also benefit from the flexibility offered by this strategy. By persisting your session state on the server, you have the flexibility to trade off simplicity versus complexity and to address scalability and performance.

If you save session state on the server, you must decide how to make this state available to each server from which you run the application. This issue is one that requires you to deal with the replication of session state among clustered software instances across load-balanced hardware, and it is a multidimensional problem. However, numerous application servers now provide a variety of out-of-the-box solutions. There are solutions available that are above the application server level. One such solution is to maintain a "sticky" user experience, where you use traffic management software, such as that available from Resonate [Resonate], to route users to the same server to handle each request in their session. This is also referred to as *server affinity*.

Another alternative is to store session state in either the business tier or the resource tier. Enterprise JavaBeans components may be used to hold session state in the business tier, and a relational database may be used in the resource tier. For more information on the business-tier option, please refer to "Using Session Beans" on page 55.

Controlling Client Access

There are numerous reasons to restrict or control client access to certain application resources. In this section, we examine two of these scenarios.

One reason to restrict or control client access is to guard a view, or portions of a view, from direct access by a client. This issue may occur, for example, when only registered or logged-in users should be allowed access to a particular view, or if access to portions of a view should be restricted to users based on role.

After describing this issue, we discuss a secondary scenario relating to controlling the flow of a user through the application. The latter discussion points out concerns relating to duplicate form submissions, since multiple submissions could result in unwanted duplicate transactions.

Guarding a View

In some cases, a resource is restricted in its entirety from being accessed by certain users. There are several strategies that accomplish this goal. One is including application logic that executes when the controller or view is processed, disallowing access. A second strategy is to configure the runtime system to allow access to certain resources only via an internal invocation from another application resource. In this case, access to these resources must be routed through another presentation-tier application resource, such as a servlet controller. Access to these restricted resources is not available via a direct browser invocation.

One common way of dealing with this issue is to use a controller as a delegation point for this type of access control. Another common variation involves embedding a guard directly within a view. We cover controller-based resource protection in "Presentation Tier Refactorings" on page 73 and in the pattern catalog, so we will focus here on view-based control strategies. We describe these strategies first, before considering the alternative strategy of controlling access through configuration.

Embedding Guard Within View

There are two common variations for embedding a guard within a view's processing logic. One variation blocks access to an entire resource, while the other blocks access to portions of that resource.

Including an All-or-Nothing Guard per View

In some cases, the logic embedded within the view processing code allows or denies access on an all-or-nothing basis. In other words, this logic prevents a particular user from accessing a particular view in its entirety. Typically, this type of guard is better encapsulated within a centralized controller, so that the logic is not sprinkled throughout the code. This strategy is reasonable to use when only a small fraction of pages need a guard. Typically, this scenario occurs when a nontechnical individual needs to rotate a small number of static pages onto a site. If the client must still be logged into the site to view these pages, then add a custom tag helper to the top of each page to complete the access check, as shown in Example 3.1.

Example 3.1 Including an All-or-Nothing Guard per View

```
<%@ taglib uri="/WEB-INF/corej2eetaglibrary.tld"
  prefix="corePatterns" %>

<corePatterns:guard/>
<HTML>
.
.
.
</HTML>
```

Including a Guard for Portions of a View

In other cases, the logic embedded within the view processing code simply denies access to portions of a view. This secondary strategy can be used in combination with the previously mentioned all-or-nothing strategy. To clarify this discussion, let's use an analogy of controlling access to a room in a building. The all-or-nothing guard tells users whether they can walk into the room or not, while the secondary guard logic tells users what they are allowed to see once they are in the room. Following are some examples of why you might want to utilize this strategy.

Portions of View Not Displayed Based on User Role

A portion of the view might not be displayed based on the user's role. For example, when viewing her organizational information, a manager has access to a subview dealing with administering review materials for her employees. An employee might only see his own organizational information, and be restricted from the portions of the user interface that allow access to any review-related information, as shown in Example 3.2.

Example 3.2 Portions of View Not Displayed Based on User Role

```
<%@ taglib uri="/WEB-INF/corej2eetaglibrary.tld"
  prefix="corePatterns" %>

<HTML>
.
.
.
<corePatterns:guard role="manager">
<b>This should be seen only by managers!</b>
<corePatterns:guard/>
.
.
.
</HTML>
```

Portions of View Not Displayed Based on System State or Error Conditions

Depending on the system environment, the display layout may be modified. For example, if a user interface for administering hardware CPUs is used with a single-CPU hardware device, portions of the display that relate solely to multiple CPU devices may not be shown.

Guarding by Configuration

To restrict the client from directly accessing particular views, you can configure the presentation engine to allow access to these resources only via other internal resources, such as a servlet controller using a RequestDispatcher. Additionally, you can leverage the security mechanisms that are built into the Web container, based on the servlet specification, version 2.2 and later. Security constraints are defined in the deployment descriptor, called web.xml.

The *basic* and *form-based* authentication methods, also described in the Servlet specification, rely on this security information. Rather than repeat the specification here, we refer you to the current specification for details on these methods. (See *http://java.sun.com/products/servlet/index.html*.)

So that you understand what to expect when adding declarative security constraints to your environment, we present a brief discussion of this topic and how it relates to all-or-nothing guarding by configuration. Finally, we describe one simple and generic alternative for all-or-nothing protection of a resource.

Resource Guards via Standard Security Constraints

Applications may be configured with a security constraint, and this declarative security may be used programmatically to control access based on user roles. Resources can be made available to certain roles of users and disallowed to others. Moreover, as described in "Embedding Guard Within View" on page 39, portions of a view can be restricted based on these user roles as well. If there are certain resources that should be disallowed in their entirety for all direct browser requests, as in the all-or-nothing scenario described in the previous section, then those resources can be constrained to a security role that is not assigned to any users. Resources configured in this manner remain inaccessible to all direct browser requests, as long as the security role remains unassigned. See Example 3.3 for an excerpt of a web.xml configuration file that defines a security role to restrict direct browser access.

The role name is "sensitive" and the restricted resources are named sensitive1.jsp, sensitive2.jsp, and sensitive3.jsp. Unless a user or group is assigned the "sensitive" role, then clients will not be able to directly access these Java Server Pages (JSPs). At the same time, since internally dispatched requests are not restricted by these security constraints, a request that is handled initially by a servlet controller and then forwarded to one of these three resources will indeed receive access to these JSPs.

Finally, note that there is some inconsistency in the implementation of this aspect of the Servlet specification version 2.2 across vendor products. Servers supporting Servlet 2.3 should all be consistent on this issue.

Example 3.3 Unassigned Security Role Provides All-or-Nothing Control

```
<security-constraint>
      <web-resource-collection>
      <web-resource-name>SensitiveResources
  </web-resource-name>
      <description>A Collection of Sensitive Resources
  </description>
        <url-pattern>/trade/jsp/internalaccess/
sensitive1.jsp</url-pattern>
    <url-pattern>/trade/jsp/internalaccess/
sensitive2.jsp</url-pattern>
    <url-pattern>/trade/jsp/internalaccess/
sensitive3.jsp</url-pattern>
        <http-method>GET</http-method>
      <http-method>POST</http-method>
    </web-resource-collection>
    <auth-constraint>
      <role-name>sensitive</role-name>
    </auth-constraint>
  </security-constraint>
```

Resource Guards via Simple and Generic Configuration

There is a simple and generic way to restrict a client from directly accessing a certain resource, such as a JSP. This method requires no configuration file modifications, such as those shown in Example 3.3. This method simply involves placing the resource under the `/WEB-INF/` directory of the Web application. For example, to block direct browser access to a view called `info.jsp` in the `securityissues` Web application, we could place the JSP source file in the following subdirectory:
`/securityissues/WEB-INF/internalaccessonly/info.jsp`.

Direct public access is disallowed to the `/WEB-INF/` directory, its subdirectories, and consequently to `info.jsp`. On the other hand, a controller servlet can still forward to this resource, if desired. This is an all-or-nothing method of control, since resources configured in this manner are disallowed in their entirety to direct browser access.

For an example, please refer to "Hide Resource From a Client" on page 100.

Duplicate Form Submissions

Users working in a browser client environment may use the Back button and inadvertently resubmit the same form they had previously submitted, possibly invoking a duplicate transaction. Similarly, a user might click the Stop button on the browser before receiving a confirmation page, and subsequently resubmit the same form. In most cases, we want to trap and disallow these duplicate submissions, and using a controlling servlet provides a control point for addressing this problem.

Synchronizer (or Déjà vu) Token

This strategy addresses the problem of duplicate form submissions. A synchronizer token is set in a user's session and included with each form returned to the client. When that form is submitted, the synchronizer token in the form is compared to the synchronizer token in the session. The tokens should match the first time the form is submitted. If the tokens do not match, then the form submission may be disallowed and an error returned to the user. Token mismatch may occur when the user submits a form, then clicks the Back button in the browser and attempts to resubmit the same form.

On the other hand, if the two token values match, then we are confident that the flow of control is exactly as expected. At this point, the token value in the session is modified to a new value and the form submission is accepted.

You may also use this strategy to control direct browser access to certain pages, as described in the sections on resource guards. For example, assume a user bookmarks page A of an application, where page A should only be accessed from page B and C. When the user selects page A via the bookmark, the page is accessed out of order and the synchronizer token will be in an unsynchronized state, or it may not exist at all. Either way, the access can be disallowed if desired.

Please refer to "Introduce Synchronizer Token" in the "Presentation Tier Refactorings" section, p. 77 for an example of this strategy.

Validation

It is often desirable to perform validation both on the client and on the server. Although client validation processing is typically less sophisticated than server validation, it provides high-level checks, such as whether a form field is empty. Server-side validation is often much more comprehensive. While both types of processing are appropriate in an application, it is not recommended to include only client-side validation. One major reason not to rely solely on client-side validation is that client-side scripting languages are user-configurable and thus may be disabled at any time.

Detailed discussion of validation strategies is outside the scope of this book. At the same time, we want to mention these issues as ones to consider while designing your systems, and hope you will refer to the existing literature in order to investigate further.

Validation on Client

Input validation is performed on the client. Typically, this involves embedding scripting code, such as JavaScript, within the client view. As stated, client-side validation is a fine complement for server-side validation, but should not be used alone.

Validation on Server

Input validation is performed on the server. There are several typical strategies for doing server validation. These strategies are form-centric validation and validation based on abstract types.

Form-Centric Validation

The form-centric validation strategy forces an application to include lots of methods that validate various pieces of state for each form submitted. Typically, these methods overlap with respect to the logic they include, such that reuse and modularity suffer. Since there is a validation method that is specific to each Web form that is posted, there is no central code to handle required fields or numeric-only fields. In this case, although there may be a field on multiple different forms that is considered a required field, each is handled separately and redundantly in numerous places in the application. This strategy is relatively easy to implement and is effective, but it leads to duplication of code as an application grows.

To provide a more flexible, reusable, and maintainable solution, the model data may be considered at a different level of abstraction. This approach is considered in the following alternative strategy, "Validation Based on Abstract Types. An example of form-centric validation is shown in the listing in Example 3.4.

Example 3.4 Form-Centric Validation

```
/**If the first name or last name fields were left
   blank, then an error will be returned to client.
   With this strategy, these checks for the existence
   of a required field are duplicated. If this valida-
   tion logic were abstracted into a separate compo-
   nent, it could be reused across forms (see
   Validation Based on Abstract Types strategy)**/
public Vector validate()
{
Vector errorCollection = new Vector();
    if ((firstname == null) ||
    (firstname.trim().length() < 1))
      errorCollection.addElement("firstname required");
    if ((lastname == null) || (lastname.trim().length()
   < 1))
      errorCollection.addElement("lastname required");
return errorCollection;
}
```

Validation Based on Abstract Types

This strategy could be utilized on either the client or server, but is preferred on the server in a browser-based or thin-client environment.

The typing and constraints information is abstracted out of the model state and into a generic framework. This separates the validation of the model from the application logic in which the model is being used, thus reducing their coupling.

Model validation is performed by comparing the metadata and constraints to the model state. The metadata and constraints about the model are typically accessible from some sort of simple data store, such as a properties file. A benefit of this approach is that the system becomes more generic, because it factors the state typing and constraint information out of the application logic.

An example is to have a component or subsystem that encapsulates validation logic, such as deciding whether a string is empty, whether a certain number is within a valid range, whether a string is formatted in a particular way, and so on. When various disparate application components want to validate different aspects of a model, each component does not write its own validation code. Rather, the centralized validation mechanism is used. The centralized validation mechanism will typically be configured either programmatically, through some sort of factory, or declaratively, using configuration files.

Thus, the validation mechanism is more generic, focusing on the model state and its requirements, independent of the other parts of the application. A drawback to using this strategy is the potential reduction in efficiency and performance. Also, more generic solutions, although often powerful, are sometimes less easily understood and maintained.

An example scenario follows. An XML-based configuration file describes a variety of validations, such as "required field," "all-numeric field," and so on. Additionally, handler classes can be designated for each of these validations. Finally, a mapping links HTML form values to a specific type of validation. The code for validating a particular form field simply becomes something similar to the code snippet shown in Example 3.5.

Example 3.5 Validation Based on Abstract Types

```
//firstNameString="Dan"
//formFieldName="form1.firstname"
Validator.getInstance().validate(firstNameString,
    formFieldName);
```

Helper Properties—Integrity and Consistency

JavaBean helper classes are typically used to hold intermediate state when it is passed in with a client request. JSP runtime engines provide a mechanism for automatically copying parameter values from a servlet request object into properties of these JavaBean helpers. The JSP syntax is as follows:

```
<jsp:setProperty name="helper" property="*"/>
```

This tells the JSP engine to copy all *matching* parameter values into the corresponding properties in a JavaBean called "helper," shown in Example 3.6:

Example 3.6 Helper Properties - A Simple JavaBean Helper

```
public class Helper
{
  private String first;
  private String last;

  public String getFirst()
  {
    return first;
  }

  public void setFirst(String aString)
  {
    first=aString;
  }

  public String getLast()
  {
    return last;
  }


  public void setLast(String aString)
  {
    last=aString;
  }

}
```

How is a match determined, though? If a request parameter exists with the same name and same type as the helper bean property, then it is considered a match. Practically, then, each parameter is compared to each bean property name and the type of the bean property setter method.

Although this mechanism is simple, it can produce some confusing and unwanted side effects. First of all, it is important to note what happens when a request parameter has an empty value. Many developers assume that a request parameter with an empty string value should, if matched to a bean property, cause that bean property to take on the value of an empty string, or null. The spec-compliant behavior is actually to make no changes to the matching bean property in this case, though. Furthermore, since JavaBean helper instances are typically reused across requests, such confusion can lead to data values being inconsistent and incorrect. Figure 3.1 shows the sort of problem that this might cause.

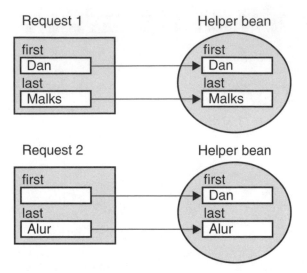

Figure 3.1 Helper properties

Request 1 includes values for the parameter named "first" and the one named "last," and each of the corresponding bean properties is set. Request 2 includes a value only for the "last" parameter, causing only that one property to be set in the bean. The value for the "first" parameter is unchanged. It is not reset to an empty string, or null, simply because there is no value in the request parameter. As you can see in Figure 3.1, this may lead to inconsistencies if the bean values are not reset manually between requests.

Another related issue to consider when designing your application is the behavior of HTML form interfaces when controls of the form are not selected. For example, if a form has multiple checkboxes, it is not unreasonable to expect that *un*checking every checkbox would result in clearing out these values on the server. In the case of the request object created based on this interface, however, there would simply not be a parameter included in this request object for any of the checkbox values. Thus, no parameter values relating to these checkboxes are sent to the server (see *http://www.w3.org* for full HTML specification).

Since there is no parameter passed to the server, the matching bean property will remain unchanged when using the <jsp:setProperty> action, as described. So, in this case, unless the developer manually modifies these values, there is the potential for inconsistent and incorrect data values to exist in the application. As stated, a simple design solution to this problem is to reset all state in the JavaBean between requests.

Presentation Tier Bad Practices

Bad practices are less than optimal solutions that conflict with many of the patterns' recommendations. When we documented the patterns and best practices, we naturally discarded those practices that were less than optimal.

In this part of the book, we highlight what we consider to be bad practices in the presentation tier.

In each section, we briefly describe the bad practice and provide numerous references to design issues, refactorings, and patterns that provide further information and preferable alternatives. We do not provide an in-depth discussion of each bad practice, but rather present a brief synopsis as a starting point for further investigation.

The "Problem Summary" section provides a quick description of a less than optimal situation, while the "Solution Reference" section includes references to:

- *Patterns* that provide information on context and trade-offs;
- *Design considerations* that provide related details;
- *Refactorings* that describe the journey from the less than optimal situation (bad practice) to a more optimal one, a best practice, or pattern.

Consider this part of the book as a roadmap, using the references to locate further detail and description in other parts of the book.

Control Code in Multiple Views

Problem Summary

Custom tag helpers may be included at the top of a JSP View to perform access control and other types of checks. If a large number of views include similar helper references, maintaining this code becomes difficult, since changes must be made in multiple places.

Solution Reference

Consolidate control code, introducing a controller and associated Command helpers.

Refactoring • See "Introduce a Controller" on page 74.

Refactoring • See "Localize Disparate Logic" on page 83.

Pattern   • See "Front Controller – "Command and Controller Strategy"
               on page 179.
When there is a need to include similar control code in multiple
places, such as when only a portion of a JSP View is to be restricted
from a particular user, delegate the work to a reusable helper class.

Pattern   • See "View Helper" on page 186

Design   • See "Guarding a View" on page 38.

Exposing Presentation-Tier Data Structures to Business Tier

Problem Summary

Presentation-tier data structures, such as HttpServletRequest,
should be confined to the presentation tier. Sharing these details
with the business tier, or any other tier, increases coupling between
these tiers, dramatically reducing the reusability of the available
services. If the method signature in the business service accepts a
parameter of type HttpServletRequest, then any other clients to this
service (even those outside of the Web space) must wrap their
request state in an HttpServletRequest object. Additionally, in this
case the business-tier services need to understand how to interact
with these presentation tier-specific data structures, increasing the
complexity of the business-tier code and increasing the coupling
between the tiers.

Solution Reference

Instead of sharing data structures specific to the presentation tier
with the business tier, copy the relevant state into more generic data
structures and share those. Alternatively, extract and share the relevant state from the presentation tier-specific data structure as individual parameters.

Refactoring • See "Hide Presentation Tier-Specific Details From the Busi-
                 ness Tier" on page 91.

Exposing Presentation-Tier Data Structures to Domain Objects

Problem Summary

Sharing request handling data structures, such as HttpServletRequest, with domain objects needlessly increases the coupling between these two distinct aspects of the application. Domain objects should be reusable components, and if their implementation relies on protocol or tier-specific details, their potential for reuse is reduced. Furthermore, maintaining and debugging tightly coupled applications is more difficult.

Solution Reference

Instead of passing an HttpServletRequest object as a parameter, copy the state from the request object into a more generic data structure and share this object with the domain object. Alternatively, extract the relevant state from the HttpServletRequest object and provide each piece of state as an individual parameter to the domain object.

Refactoring
- See "Hide Presentation Tier-Specific Details From the Business Tier" on page 91.

Allowing Duplicate Form Submissions

Problem Summary

One of the limitations of the browser-client environment is the lack of control an application has over client navigation. A user might submit an order form that results in a transaction that debits a credit card account and initiates shipment of a product to a residence. If after receiving the confirmation page, the user clicks the Back button, then the same form could be resubmitted.

Solution Reference

To address these issues, monitor and control the request flow.

Refactoring
- See "Introduce Synchronizer Token" on page 77.

Refactoring
- See "Controlling Client Access" on page 38.

Design
- See "Synchronizer (or Déjà vu) Token" on page 43.

Exposing Sensitive Resources to Direct Client Access

Problem Summary

Security is one of the most important issues in enterprise environments. If there is no need for a client to have direct access to certain information, then this information must be protected. If specific configuration files, property files, JSPs, and class files are not secured appropriately, then clients may inadvertently or maliciously retrieve sensitive information.

Solution Reference

Protect sensitive resources, disallowing direct client access

Refactoring   • See "Hide Resource From a Client" on page 100.

Refactoring   • See "Controlling Client Access" on page 38.

Assuming <jsp:setProperty> Will Reset Bean Properties

Problem Summary

While the expected behavior of the `<jsp:setProperty>` standard tag is to copy request parameter values into JavaBean helper properties of the same name, its behavior when dealing with parameters that have empty values is often confusing. For example, a parameter with an empty value is ignored, although many developers incorrectly assume that the matching JavaBean property will be assigned a null or empty string value.

Solution Reference

Take into account the less than intuitive nature of how properties are set when using the `<jsp:setProperty>` tag, and initialize bean properties before use.

Design   • See "Helper Properties—Integrity and Consistency" on page 46.

Creating Fat Controllers

Problem Summary

Control code that is duplicated in multiple JSP views should, in many cases, be refactored into a controller. If too much code is added to a controller, though, it becomes too heavyweight and cumbersome to maintain, test, and debug. For example, unit testing a servlet controller, particularly a "fat controller," is more complicated than unit testing individual helper classes that are independent of the HTTP protocol.

Solution Reference

A controller is typically the initial contact point for handling a request, but it should also be a delegation point, working in coordination with other control classes. Command objects are used to encapsulate control code to which the controller delegates. It is much easier to unit test these JavaBean command objects, independent of the servlet engine, than it is to test less modular code.

Refactoring	• See "Introduce a Controller" on page 74.
Pattern	• See "Front Controller–"Command and Controller Strategy" on page 179.
Refactoring	• See "Localize Disparate Logic" on page 83.
Pattern	• See "View Helper" on page 186.

BUSINESS TIER DESIGN CONSIDERATIONS AND BAD PRACTICES

Topics in This Chapter

- Business Tier Design Considerations
- Business and Integration Tiers Bad Practices

Chapter 4

Business Tier Design Considerations

When developers apply the business tier and integration tier patterns that appear in the catalog in this book, there may be adjunct design issues about which they may be concerned. These issues relate to designing with patterns at a variety of levels, and they may affect numerous aspects of a system. We discuss these issues in this chapter.

The discussions in this chapter simply describe each issue as a design issue that you should consider when implementing systems based on the J2EE pattern catalog.

Using Session Beans

Session beans are distributed business components with the following characteristics, per the EJB specification:

- A session bean is dedicated to a single client or user.
- A session bean lives only for the duration of the client's session.
- A session bean does not survive container crashes.
- A session bean is not a persistent object.

- A session bean can time out.
- A session bean can be transaction-aware.
- A session bean can be used to model stateful or stateless conversations between the client and the business tier components.

Note

In this section, we use the term "workflow" in the context of EJB to represent the logic associated with the enterprise beans communication. For example, workflow encompasses how session bean A calls session bean B, then entity bean C.

Session Bean—Stateless Versus Stateful

Session beans come in two flavors—stateless and stateful. A stateless session bean does not hold any conversational state. Hence, once a client's method invocation on a stateless session beans is completed, the container is free to reuse that session bean instance for another client. This allows the container to maintain a pool of session beans and to reuse session beans among multiple clients. The container pools stateless session beans so that it can reuse them more efficiently by sharing them with multiple clients. The container returns a stateless session bean to the pool after the client completes its invocation. The container may allocate a different instance from the pool to subsequent client invocations.

A stateful session bean holds conversational state. A stateful session bean may be pooled, but since the session bean is holding state on behalf of a client, the bean cannot simultaneously be shared with and handle requests from another client.

The container does not pool stateful session beans in the same manner as it pools stateless session beans because stateful session beans hold client session state. Stateful session beans are allocated to a client and remain allocated to the client as long as the client session is active. Thus, stateful session beans need more resource overhead than stateless session beans, for the added advantage of maintaining conversational state.

Many designers believe that using stateless session beans is a more viable session bean design strategy for scalable systems. This belief stems from building distributed object systems with older technologies, because without an inherent infrastructure to manage component life cycle, such systems rapidly lost scalability characteristics as resource demands increased. Scalability loss was due to the lack of component life cycle, causing the service to continue to consume resources as the number of clients and objects increased.

An EJB container manages the life cycle of enterprise beans and is responsible for monitoring system resources to best manage enterprise bean instances. The container manages a pool of enterprise beans and brings enterprise beans in and out of memory (called *activation* and *passivation*, respectively) to optimize invocation and resource consumption.

Scalability problems are typically due to the misapplication of stateful and stateless session beans. The choice of using stateful or stateless session beans must depend upon the business process being implemented. A business process that needs only one method call to complete the service is a non-conversational business process. Such processes are suitably implemented using a stateless session bean. A business process that needs multiple method calls to complete the service is a conversational business process. It is suitably implemented using a stateful session bean.

However, some designers choose stateless session beans, hoping to increase scalability, and they may wrongly decide to model all business processes as stateless session beans. When using stateless session beans for conversational business processes, every method invocation requires the state to be passed by the client to the bean, reconstructed at the business tier, or retrieved from a persistent store. These techniques could result in reduced scalability due to the associated overheads in network traffic, reconstruction time, or access time respectively.

Session Beans as Business-Tier Facades

In our patterns in the J2EE Pattern Catalog and best practices, one application of session beans is to use them as facades to the business tier. Session bean facades, or simply session facades, can be viewed as a coarse-grained controller layer for the business tier. Clients of the session beans are typically Business Delegates.

- See "Session Facade" on page 291.
- See "Business Delegate" on page 248.
- See also "Mapping Each Use Case to a Session Bean" on page 64.

Storing State on the Business Tier

Some design considerations for storing state on the Web server are discussed in "Session State in the Presentation Tier" on page 37.

Here we continue that discussion to explore when it is appropriate to store state in a stateful session bean instead of in an HttpSession. One of the considerations is to determine what types of clients access the business services in your system. If the architecture is solely a Web-based application, where all the clients come through a Web server either via a servlet or a JSP, then conversational state may be maintained in an HttpSession in the Web tier. This scenario is shown in Figure 4.1.

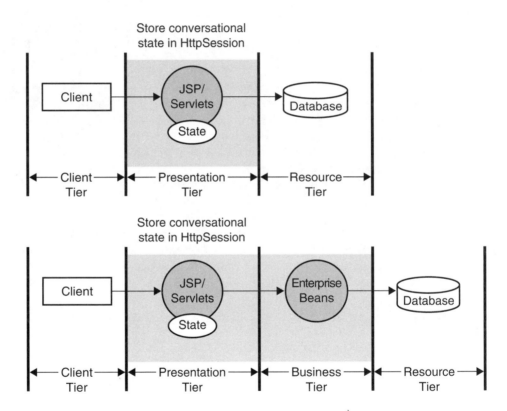

Figure 4.1 Storing state in HttpSession

On the other hand, if your application supports various types of clients, including Web clients, Java applications, other applications, and even other enterprise beans, then conversational state may be maintained in the EJB layer using stateful session beans. This is shown in Figure 4.2.

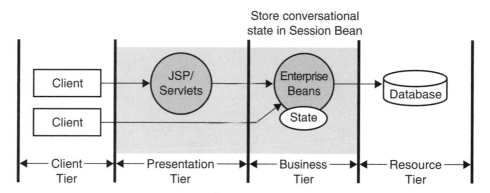

Figure 4.2 Storing state in session beans

We have presented some basic discussion on the subject of state management here and in the previous chapter (see "Session State on Client" on page 36). A full-scale discussion is outside the scope of this book, since the problem is multi-dimensional and depends very much on the deployment environment, including:

- Hardware
- Traffic management
- Clustering of Web container
- Clustering of EJB container
- Server affinity
- Session replication
- Session persistence

We touch on this issue because it is one that should be considered during development and deployment.

Using Entity Beans

Using entity beans appropriately is a question of design heuristics, experience, need, and technology. Entity beans are best suited as coarse-grained business components. Entity beans are distributed objects and have the following characteristics, per the EJB specification:

- Entity beans provide an object view of persistent data.
- Entity beans are transactional.
- Entity beans are multiuser.
- Entity beans are long-lived.

- Entity beans survive container crashes. Such crashes are typically transparent to the clients.

Summarizing this definition, the appropriate use of an entity bean is as a distributed, shared, transactional, and persistent object. In addition, EJB containers provide other infrastructure necessary to support such system qualities as scalability, security, performance, clustering, and so forth. All together, this makes for a very reliable and robust platform to implement and deploy applications with distributed business components.

Entity Bean Primary Keys

Entity beans are uniquely identified by their primary keys. A primary key can be a simple key, made up of a single attribute, or it can be a composite key, made up of a group of attributes from the entity bean. For entity beans with a single-field primary key, where the primary key is a primitive type, it is possible to implement the entity bean without defining an explicit primary key class. The deployer can specify the primary key field in the deployment descriptor for the entity bean. However, when the primary key is a composite key, a separate class for the primary key must be specified. This class must be a simple Java class that implements the serializable interface with the attributes that define the composite key for the entity bean. The attribute names and types in the primary key class must match those in the entity bean, and also must be declared public in both the bean implementation class and primary key class.

As a suggested best practice, the primary key class must implement the optional java.lang.Object methods, such as `equals` and `hashCode`.

- Override the `equals()` method to properly evaluate the equality of two primary keys by comparing values for each part of the composite key.
- Override the `Object.hashCode()` method to return a unique number representing the hash code for the primary key instance. Ensure that the hash code is indeed unique when you use your primary key attribute values to compute the hash code.

Business Logic in Entity Beans

A common question in entity bean design is what kind of business logic it should contain. Some designers feel that entity beans should contain only persistence logic and simple methods to get and set data contain only persistence logic and simple methods to get and set data values. They feel that entity beans should not contain business logic, which is often misunderstood to mean that only code related to getting and setting data must be included in the entity bean.

Business logic generally includes any logic associated with providing some service. For this discussion, consider business logic to include all logic related to processing, workflow, business rules, data, and so forth. The following is a list of sample questions to explore the possible results of adding business logic into an entity:

- Will the business logic introduce entity-entity relationships?

- Will the entity bean become responsible for managing workflow of user interaction?

- Will the entity bean take on the responsibilities that should belong in some other business component?

- Will the entity bean include code related to data access logic, such as Java Database Connectivity (JDBC) code when implemented using bean-managed persistence?

A "yes" answer to any of these questions helps identify whether introducing business logic into the entity bean can have an adverse impact. It is desirable to investigate the design to avoid inter-entity-bean dependencies as much as possible, since such dependences create overheads that may impede overall application performance.

In general, the entity bean should contain business logic that is self-contained to manage its data and its dependent objects' data. Thus, it may be necessary to identify, extract, and move business logic that introduces entity-bean-to-entity-bean interaction from the entity bean into a session bean by applying the Session Facade pattern. The Composite Entity pattern and some of the refactorings discuss the issues related to entity bean design.

If any workflow associated with multiple entity beans is identified, then such workflow can be suitably implemented in a session bean instead of in an entity bean. Such workflow can be consolidated into a session facade.

- See "Merge Session Beans" on page 108.

- See "Reduce Inter-Entity Bean Communication" on page 110.

- See "Move Business Logic to Session" on page 112.

- See "Session Facade" on page 291.

- See "Composite Entity" on page 310.

For bean-managed persistence in entity beans, data access code is best implemented outside entity beans.

- See "Separate Data Access Code" on page 113.
- See "Data Access Object" on page 390.

Caching Enterprise Bean Remote References and Handles

When clients use an enterprise bean, they may need to cache some reference to an enterprise bean for future use. You will encounter this when using business delegates (see "Business Delegate" on page 248), where a delegate connects to a session bean and invokes the necessary business methods on the bean on behalf of the client. When the client uses the business delegate for the first time, the delegate needs to perform a lookup using the EJB Home object to obtain a remote reference to the session bean. For subsequent requests, the business delegate can avoid lookups by caching a remote reference or its handle as necessary. The EJB Home handle can also be cached to avoid an additional Java Naming and Directory Interface (JNDI) lookup for the enterprise bean home. For more details on using an EJB Handle or the EJB Home Handle, please refer to the current EJB specification.

Business and Integration Tiers Bad Practices

Mapping Object Model Directly to Entity Bean Model

Problem Summary

One of the common practices in designing an EJB application is to map the object model directly into entity beans; that is, each class in the object model is transformed into an entity bean. This results in a large number of fine-grained entity beans.

The container and network overhead increases as the number of enterprise beans increases. Such mapping also transforms object relationships into entity-bean-to-entity-bean relationships. This is best avoided, since entity-bean-to-entity-bean relationships introduce severe performance implications.

Solution Reference

Identify the parent-dependent object relationships in the object model and design them as coarse-grained entity beans. This results in fewer entity beans, where each entity bean composes a group of related objects from the object model.

Refactoring   •   See "Eliminate Inter-Entity Bean Communication" on page 110.

Pattern   •   See "Composite Entity" on page 310.

Consolidate related workflow operations into session beans to provide a uniform coarse-grained service access layer.

Refactoring   •   See "Merge Session Beans" on page 108.

Pattern   •   See "Session Facade" on page 291.

Mapping Relational Model Directly to Entity Bean Model

Problem Summary

When designing an EJB model, it is bad practice to model each row in a table as an entity bean. While entity beans are best designed as coarse-grained objects, this mapping results in a large number of fine-grained entity beans, and it affects scalability.

Such mapping also implements inter-table (i.e., primary key/foreign key) relationships as entity-bean-to-entity-bean relationships.

Solution Reference

Design your enterprise bean application using an object-oriented approach instead of relying on the preexisting relational database design to produce the EJB model.

Bad Practice   • See solution reference for "Mapping Object Model Directly to Entity Bean Model" on page 63.

Avoid inter-entity relationships by designing coarse-grained business objects by identifying parent-dependent objects.

Refactoring   • See "Eliminate Inter-Entity Bean Communication" on page 110.

Refactoring   • See "Move Business Logic to Session" on page 112.

Pattern   • See "Composite Entity" on page 310.

Mapping Each Use Case to a Session Bean

Problem Summary

Some designers implement each use case with its own unique session bean. This creates fine-grained controllers responsible for servicing only one type of interaction. The drawback of this approach is that it may result in a large number of session beans and significantly increase the complexity of the application.

Solution Reference

Apply the Session Facade pattern to aggregate a group of the related interactions into a single session bean. This results in fewer session beans for the application, and leverages the advantages of applying the Session Facade pattern.

Refactoring   • See "Merge Session Beans" on page 108.

Pattern   • See "Session Facade" on page 291.

Exposing All Enterprise Bean Attributes via Getter/Setter Methods

Problem Summary

Exposing each enterprise bean attribute using getter/setter methods is a bad practice. This forces the client to invoke numerous fine-grained remote invocations and creates the potential to introduce a significant amount of network chattiness across the tiers. Each method call is potentially remote and carries with it a certain network overhead that impacts performance and scalability.

Solution Reference

Use a value object to transfer aggregate data to and from the client instead of exposing the getters and setters for each attribute.

Pattern
- See "Value Object" on page 261.

Embedding Service Lookup in Clients

Problem Summary

Clients and presentation tier objects frequently need to look up the enterprise beans. In an EJB environment, the container uses JNDI to provide this service.

Putting the burden of locating services on the application client can introduce a proliferation of lookup code in the application code. Any change to the lookup code propagates to all clients that look up the services. Also, embedding lookup code in clients exposes them to the complexity of the underlying implementation and introduces dependency on the lookup code.

Solution Reference

Encapsulate implementation details of the lookup mechanisms using a Service Locator.

Pattern
- See "Service Locator" on page 367.

Encapsulate the implementation details of business-tier components, such as session and entity beans, using Business Delegates. This simplifies client code since they no longer deal with enterprise beans and services. Business Delegates may in turn use the Service Locator.

Refactoring   • See "Introduce Business Delegate" on page 106.

Pattern   • See "Business Delegate" on page 248.

Using Entity Bean as Read-Only Object

Problem Summary

Any entity bean method is subject to transaction semantics based on its transaction isolation levels specified in the deployment descriptor. Using an entity bean as a read-only object simply wastes expensive resources and results in unnecessary update transactions to the persistent store. This is due to the invocation of the `ejb-Store()` methods by the container during the entity bean's life cycle. Since the container has no way of knowing if the data was changed during a method invocation, it must assume that it has and invoke the `ejbStore()` operation. Thus, the container makes no distinction between read-only and read-write entity beans. However, some containers may provide read-only entity beans, but these are vendor proprietary implementations.

Solution Reference

Encapsulate all access to the data source using Data Access Object pattern. This provides a centralized layer of data access code and also simplifies entity bean code.

Pattern   • See "Data Access Object" on page 390.

Implement access to read-only functionality using a session bean, typically as a Session Facade that uses a DAO.

Pattern   • See "Session Facade" on page 291.

For obtaining a list of value objects, Value List Handler pattern may be implemented.

Pattern   • See "Value List Handler" on page 353.

For obtaining a complex data model from the business tier, the Value Object Assembler pattern may be implemented.

Pattern   • See "Value Object Assembler" on page 339.

Using Entity Beans as Fine-Grained Objects

Problem Summary

Entity beans are meant to represent coarse-grained transactional persistent business components. Using an entity bean to represent fine-grained objects increases the overall network communication and container overhead. This impacts application performance and scalability.

A fine-grained object is best thought of as an object that has little meaning without its association to another object (typically a coarse-grained parent object). For example, an item object can be thought of as a fined-grained object because it has little value until it is associated with an order object. In this example, the order object is the coarse-grained object and the item object is the fine-grained (dependent) object.

Solution Reference

When designing enterprise beans based on a preexisting RDBMS schema,

Bad Practice
- See "Mapping Relational Model Directly to Entity Bean Model" on page 63.

When designing enterprise beans using an object model,

Bad Practice
- See "Mapping Object Model Directly to Entity Bean Model" on page 63.

Design coarse-grained entity beans and session beans. Apply the following patterns and refactorings that promote coarse-grained enterprise beans design.

Pattern
- See "Composite Entity" on page 310.

Pattern
- See "Session Facade" on page 291.

Refactoring
- See "Eliminate Inter-Entity Bean Communication" on page 110.

Refactoring
- See "Move Business Logic to Session" on page 112.

Refactoring
- See "Business Logic in Entity Beans" on page 60.

Refactoring
- See "Merge Session Beans" on page 108.

Storing Entire Entity Bean-Dependent Object Graph

Problem Summary

When a complex tree structure of dependent objects is used in an entity bean, performance can degrade rapidly when loading and storing an entire tree of dependent objects. When the container invokes the entity bean's `ejbLoad()` method, either for the initial load or for reloads to synchronize with the persistent store, loading the entire tree of dependent objects can prove wasteful. Similarly, when the container invokes the entity bean's `ejbStore()` method at any time, storing the entire tree of objects can be quite expensive and unnecessary.

Solution Reference

Identify the dependent objects that have changed since the previous store operation and store only those objects to the persistent store.

Pattern
- See "Composite Entity" on page 310 and "Store Optimization (Dirty Marker) Strategy" on page 318.

Implement a strategy to load only data that is most accessed and required. Load the remaining dependent objects on demand.

Pattern
- See "Composite Entity" on page 310 and "Lazy Loading Strategy" on page 317.

By applying these strategies, it is possible to prevent loading and storing an entire tree of dependent objects.

Exposing EJB-related Exceptions to Non-EJB Clients

Problem Summary

Enterprise beans can throw business application exceptions to clients. When an application throws an application exception, the container simply throws the exception to the client. This allows the client to gracefully handle the exception and possibly take another action. It is reasonable to expect the application developer to understand and handle such application-level exceptions.

However, despite employing such good programming practices as designing and using application exceptions, the clients may still receive EJB-related exceptions, such as a java.rmi.RemoteException.

This can happen if the enterprise bean or the container encounters a system failure related to the enterprise bean.

The burden is on the application developer, who may not even be aware of or knowledgeable about EJB exceptions and semantics, to understand the implementation details of the non-application exceptions that may be thrown by business tier components. In addition, non-application exceptions may not provide relevant information to help the user rectify the problem.

Solution Reference

Decouple the clients from the business tier and hide the business-tier implementation details from clients, using business delegates. Business delegates intercept all service exceptions and may throw an application exception. Business delegates are plain Java objects that are local to the client. Typically, business delegates are developed by the EJB developers and provided to the client developers.

Refactoring
Pattern

- See "Introduce Business Delegate" on page 106.
- See "Business Delegate" on page 248.

Using Entity Bean Finder Methods to Return a Large Results Set

Problem Summary

Frequently, applications require the ability to search and obtain a list of values. Using an EJB finder method to look up a large collection of entity beans will return a collection of remote references. Consequently, the client has to invoke a method on each remote reference to get the data. This is a remote call and can become very expensive, especially impacting performance, when the caller invokes remote calls on each entity bean reference in the collection.

Solution Reference

Implement queries using session beans and DAOs to obtain a list of value objects instead of remote references. Use a DAO to perform searches instead of EJB finder methods.

Pattern
Pattern

- See "Value List Handler" on page 353.
- See "Data Access Object" on page 390.

Client Aggregates Data from Business Components

Problem Summary

The application clients (in the client or presentation tier) typically need the data model for the application from the business tier. Since the model is implemented by business components—such as entity beans, session beans, and arbitrary objects in the business tier—the client must locate, interact with, and extract the necessary data from various business components to construct the data model.

These client actions introduce network overhead due to multiple invocations from the client into the business tier. In addition, the client becomes tightly coupled with the application model. In applications where there are various types of clients, this coupling problem multiplies: A change to the model requires changes to all clients that contain code to interact with those model elements comprised of business components.

Solution Reference

Decouple the client from model construction. Implement a business-tier component that is responsible for the construction of the required application model.

Pattern   • See "Value Object Assembler" on page 339.

Using Enterprise Beans for Long-Lived Transactions

Problem Summary

Enterprise beans (pre-EJB 2.0) are suitable for synchronous processing. Furthermore, enterprise beans do well if each method implemented in a bean produces an outcome within a predictable and acceptable time period.

If an enterprise bean method takes a significant amount of time to process a client request, or if it blocks while processing, this also blocks the container resources, such as memory and threads, used by the bean. This can severely impact performance and deplete system resources.

An enterprise bean transaction that takes a long time to complete potentially locks out resources from other enterprise bean instances that need those resources, resulting in performance bottlenecks.

Solution Reference

Implement asynchronous processing service using a message-oriented middleware (MOM) with a Java Message Service (JMS) API to facilitate long-lived transactions.

Pattern
- See "Service Activator" on page 408.

Stateless Session Bean Reconstructs Conversational State for Each Invocation

Problem Summary

Some designers choose stateless session beans to increase scalability. They may inadvertently decide to model all business processes as stateless session beans even though the session beans require conversational state. But, since the session bean is stateless, it must rebuild conversational state in every method invocation. The state may have to be rebuilt by retrieving data from a database. This completely defeats the purpose of using stateless session beans to improve performance and scalability and can severely degrade performance.

Solution Reference

Analyze the interaction model before choosing the stateless session bean mode. The choice of stateful or stateless session bean depends on the need for maintaining conversational state across method invocations in stateful session bean versus the cost of rebuilding the state during each invocation in stateless session bean.

Pattern
- See "Session Facade" on page 291, "Stateless Session Facade Strategy" on page 296, and "Stateful Session Facade Strategy" on page 297.

Design
- See "Session Bean—Stateless Versus Stateful" on page 56 and "Storing State on the Business Tier" on page 57.

J2EE
REFACTORINGS

Topics in This Chapter

- Presentation Tier Refactorings
- Business and Integration Tier Refactorings
- General Refactorings

Chapter 5

This chapter discusses refactoring for the presentation, business, and integration tiers.

Presentation Tier Refactorings

The refactorings in this section apply to the presentation tier.

Introduce a Controller

Control logic is scattered throughout the application, typically dupli-cated in multiple Java Server Page (JSP) views.

Extract control logic into one or more controller classes that serve as the initial contact point for handling a client request.

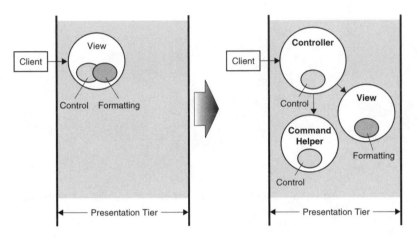

Figure 5.1 Introduce a controller

Motivation

Control code that is duplicated in multiple JSPs also needs to be maintained in each JSP. Extracting this code into one or more cen-tralized controller class improves the modularity, reusability, and maintainability of the application.

Mechanics

❑ Use the Front Controller pattern as a guide for applying Extract Class [Fowler] to create a controller class, moving duplicate control logic from individual JSPs into this control-ler.

⇨ *See "Front Controller" on page 172.*

⇨ *Remember that the controller is a delegation point for con-trolling the request handling. Partition the code with an eye toward modularity and reuse. Do not necessarily embed all*

*the control code directly within a single controller, but
rather consider creating helper components to which it may
delegate. See "Creating Fat Controllers" on page 53.*

❏ Control code may also be encapsulated in command objects
that work in coordination with the controller, utilizing the
Command pattern [GoF].

⇒ See "Front Controller" on page 172, "Command and Controller Strategy."

Example

Assume we have the structure shown in Example 5.1 in many of our
JSPs.

Example 5.1 Introduce a Controller – JSP Structure

```
<HTML>
<BODY>
  <control:grant_access/>
 .
 .
 .

</BODY>
  </HTML>
```

The three vertical dots represent the body of each JSP, which is
not being shown in this example. While this body portion differs for
each JSP, the helper at the top of the page, implemented as a custom
tag, is the same. This helper is responsible for controlling access to
this page. It is an "all-or-nothing" type of control, meaning that a client is either granted access to the whole page or is denied access
entirely.

If we change the design and introduce a controller, as described in
the mechanics, then each of our JSPs will no longer include the
<control:grant_access/> tag, as seen in Example 5.1 .

Instead, we have a centralized controller that manages this behavior, handling the access control check that we removed from each
JSP. Example 5.2 is a snippet of code from the controller, which is
implemented as a servlet.

Example 5.2 Introduce a Controller - Controller Structure

```
if (grantAccess())
{
    dispatchToNextView();
}
else
{
    dispatchToAccessDeniedView();
}
```

Of course, there are some cases where helpers are suitable for control code. For example, if only a small fraction of our JSPs need this type of access control, then it is not unreasonable to include a custom tag helper in each of these few pages to accomplish this goal. Another reason we might use custom tags in individual JSPs is to control access to specific subviews of a composite view (see "Composite View" on page 203).

If we are already using a controller, then we still might want to add this behavior in this centralized place, since the number of pages we want to protect might grow over time. To handle the case of an existing controller, we simply extract control code from our views and add it to the existing controller. In effect, we are moving methods (using Move Method [Fowler]) instead of extracting a new class.

Introduce Synchronizer Token

Clients make duplicate resource requests that should be monitored and controlled, or clients access certain views out of order by returning to previously bookmarked pages.

Use a shared token to monitor and control the request flow and client access to certain resources.

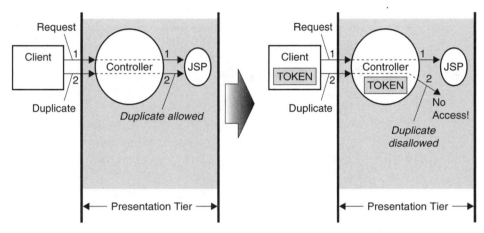

Figure 5.2 Introduce synchronizer token

Motivation

There are a number of scenarios in which control of an incoming request is desired. One of the most common reasons is the desire to control duplicate request submissions from a client. Such duplicate submissions may occur when the user clicks the Back or Stop browser buttons and resubmits a form.

While this issue is mainly one of controlling the order or flow of the requests, there is also the issue of controlling access based on permissions. For introducing permission-based control, see "Hide Resource From a Client" on page 100.

Mechanics

❑ Create one or more helper classes responsible for generating and comparing one-time-use, unique tokens.

⇒ *Alternatively, this logic may be added to already existing control components.*

⇒ *The component managing this activity (typically a controller, but possibly a JSP) delegates to these helpers, managing the temporary storage of a fresh token for each client submission.*

⇒ *A copy of the token is stored per user on the server and on the client browser. The token is typically stored on the client browser as a hidden field and on the server in a user session.*

When Is a Token Generated and Stored? When Is a Token Checked?

A synchronizer token is compared for a match before processing an arriving request. A new token value is generated and stored after processing this request, but before the response is prepared and sent to the client.

For more information, see "Introduce Synchronizer Token" on page 77 and Figure 5.3.

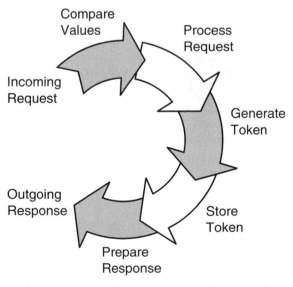

Figure 5.3 Synchronizer token life cycle

❏ Add logic to check whether the token arriving with the client request matches the token in the user session.

⇒ *The token arriving from the client in the current request should be the same token that the server sent to the client with its last response. Thus a match of these two values confirms that this is not a duplicate submission, while a mismatch suggests this possibility.*

⇒ *As stated, a mismatch might also occur for other reasons, such as a user navigating directly to a bookmarked page, but a duplicate request submission is the most common reason. (See Presentation Tier Design Considerations - Controlling Client Access" on page 38 for more information.)*

❏ A controller typically manages token generation and comparison. Consider introducing a controller, if one does not already exist.

⇒ *See "Introduce a Controller" on page 74.*

⇒ *Without a controller to centralize management of token generation and comparison, this behavior must be referenced from each JSP.*

⇒ *Typically, the JSP delegates to a helper component, implemented as either a JavaBean or custom tag (see "View Helper" on page 186), which encapsulates the responsibilities token management.*

The source code excerpts in Introduce Synchronizer Token are reprinted with permission under the Apache Software License, Version 1.1. See page 425 to view the terms of this license.

Example

The Struts presentation framework applies several of the J2EE patterns and refactorings. It introduces this exact type of request flow control, and we use excerpts from this open source framework in our example.

Instead of creating a separate utility class to encapsulate the token generation and matching logic, Struts simply adds this functionality to a preexisting class that is part of its control mechanism. The class is called *Action*, and it is a common superclass for all actions. Actions are Command objects that extend the controller functionality. This is an application of the Front Controller pattern, Command and Controller strategy.

As shown in Example 5.3, the `saveToken()` method, which is part of the Action class, generates and stores token values.

Example 5.3 Generate and Store Token

```
/**
 * Save a new transaction token in the
 * user's current session, creating
 * a new session if necessary.
 *
 * @param request The servlet request we are processing
 */
protected void saveToken(HttpServletRequest request) {

HttpSession session = request.getSession();
String token = generateToken(request);
if (token != null)
   session.setAttribute(TRANSACTION_TOKEN_KEY, token);
}
```

This method generates a unique token, calculated using the session ID and the current time, and stores this value into the user session.

At some point (usually immediately) prior to generating the HTML display for the client responsible for submitting a request that we do not want to duplicate (this display typically includes a form to be posted back to the server), a one-time token value is set, as previously described, by making the following method invocation:

```
saveToken(request);
```

Additionally, the JSP responsible for generating this HTML display also includes logic that delegates to a helper class to generate a hidden field that includes this token value. Thus, the page sent to the client, which typically includes a form that will be submitted back to the server, includes a hidden field of the following form:

```
<input type="hidden"
   name="org.apache.struts.taglib.html.TOKEN"
   value="8d2c392e93a39d299ec45a22">
```

The value attribute of this hidden field is the value of the token that was generated by the `saveToken()` method.

When the client submits the page that includes this hidden field, the controller delegates to a Command object (again, a subclass of the Action class) that compares the token value in the user session with the value in the request object parameter that came from the hidden field in the page. The Command object uses the method shown in Example 5.4, also excerpted from its superclass (the Action class again), to compare the values.

Example 5.4 Check For a Valid Token

```
/**
 * Return <code>true</code> if there is a transaction
 * token stored in the user's current session, and
 * the value submitted as a request request parameter
 * with this action matches it.
 *
 * Returns <code>false</code>
 * under any of the following circumstances:
 * <ul>
 * <li>No session associated with this request</li>
 * <li>No transaction token saved in the session</li>
 * <li>No transaction token included as a request
 * parameter</li>
 * <li>The included transaction token value does not
 *     match the transaction token in the user's
 *     session</li>
 * </ul>
 *
 * @param request The servlet request we are processing
 */

protected boolean isTokenValid(HttpServletRequest
   request) {

    // Retrieve the saved transaction token from our
    // session
    HttpSession session = request.getSession(false);
    if (session == null)
        return (false);
    String saved = (String)
        session.getAttribute(TRANSACTION_TOKEN_KEY);
    if (saved == null)
        return (false);
    // Retrieve the transaction token included in this
    // request
```

Example 5.4 Check For a Valid Token

```
String token = (String)
    request.getParameter(Constants.TOKEN_KEY);
if (token == null)
    return (false);

// Do the values match?
return (saved.equals(token));

}
```

If there is a match, then we are certain that this request submission is not a duplicate. If the tokens do not match, then we are able to take appropriate action to deal with this potentially duplicate form submission.

Localize Disparate Logic

Business logic and presentation formatting are
intermingled within a JSP view.

*Extract business logic into one or more helper classes that can be used
by the JSP or by a controller.*

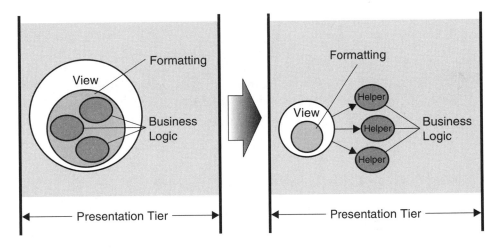

Figure 5.4 Localize Disparate Logic: Factor Back

Figure 5.4 shows logic being extracted from a view and into helpers.

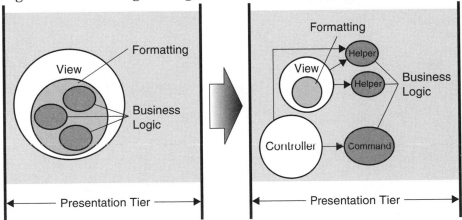

Figure 5.5 Localize Disparate Logic: Factor Forward

Figure 5.5 shows logic being extracted from a view and into a controller, a command object, and helpers.

Motivation

To create cleaner abstractions, increase cohesion and reduce coupling, which improves modularity and reusability. Well-partitioned, modular applications also provide better separation of developer roles, since Web developers own formatting code, while software developers own business logic.

Mechanics

❑ Use the View Helper pattern as a guide for applying Extract Class [Fowler] to create new helper classes, moving business logic from the JSP into these helpers.

❑ Delegate to these helper classes from the JSP.

⇒ *See "View Helper" on page 186.*

⇒ *The initial contact point for handling the client request could be the view, as shown in the Factor Back diagram in Figure 5.4. See "Dispatcher View" on page 231.*

❑ Consider introducing a controller, if one does not already exist.

⇒ *See "Introduce a Controller" on page 74.*

⇒ *As shown in the Factor Forward diagram in Figure 5.5, the controller may use a command helper.*

⇒ *The initial contact point for handling the client request could be the controller, as shown in the Factor Forward diagram. See "Service to Worker" on page 216.*

Example

We start with the sample code listed in Example 5.5. It is a JSP that includes lots of scriptlet code, intermingling business logic with the view.

Example 5.5 JSP with Scriptlet Code

```
<html>
<head><title>Employee List</title></head>
<body>
<%-- Display All employees belonging to a department
   and earning at most the given salary --%>

<%

    // Get the department for which the employees are
    // to be listed
    String deptidStr = request.getParameter(
        Constants.REQ_DEPTID);

    // Get the max salary constraint
    String salaryStr = request.getParameter(
        Constants.REQ_SALARY);

    // validate parameters

    // if salary or department not specified, go to
    // error page
    if ( (deptidStr == null) || (salaryStr == null ) )
    {
       request.setAttribute(Constants.ATTR_MESSAGE,
        "Insufficient query parameters specified" +
        "(Department and Salary)");
       request.getRequestDispatcher("/error.jsp").
         forward(request, response);
    }

    // convert to numerics
    int deptid = 0;
    float salary = 0;
    try
    {
        deptid = Integer.parseInt(deptidStr);
        salary = Float.parseFloat(salaryStr);
    }
    catch(NumberFormatException e)
    {
       request.setAttribute(Constants.ATTR_MESSAGE,
          "Invalid Search Values" +
          "(department id and salary )");
       request.getRequestDispatcher("/error.jsp").
          forward(request, response);
```

Example 5.5 JSP with Scriptlet Code

```
      }

      // check if they within legal limits
      if ( salary < 0  )
      {
        request.setAttribute(Constants.ATTR_MESSAGE,
          "Invalid Search Values" +
          "(department id and salary )");
        request.getRequestDispatcher("/error.jsp").
          forward(request, response);
      }

  %>

  <h3><center> List of employees in department #
    <%=deptid%> earning at most <%= salary %>. </h3>

  <%
      Iterator employees = new EmployeeDelegate().
                                  getEmployees(deptid);
  %>

  <table border="1" >
      <tr>
          <th> First Name </th>
          <th> Last Name </th>
          <th> Designation </th>
          <th> Employee Id </th>
          <th> Tax Deductibles </th>
          <th> Performance Remarks </th>
          <th> Yearly Salary</th>
      </tr>
  <%
      while ( employees.hasNext() )
      {
          EmployeeVO employee = (EmployeeVO)
                                  employees.next();

          // display only if search criteria is met
          if ( employee.getYearlySalary() <= salary )
          {
  %>
          <tr>
            <td> <%=employee.getFirstName()%></td>
```

Example 5.5 JSP with Scriptlet Code

```
            <td> <%=employee.getLastName()%></td>
            <td> <%=employee.getDesignation()%></td>
            <td> <%=employee.getId()%></td>
            <td> <%=employee.getNoOfDeductibles()%></td>
            <td> <%=employee.getPerformanceRemarks()%>
                </td>
            <td> <%=employee.getYearlySalary()%></td>
        </tr>
  <%
            }
      }
%>
</table>

<%@ include file="/jsp/trace.jsp" %>
<P> <B>Business logic and presentation formatting are
   intermingled within this JSP view. </B>

</body>
</html>
```

This JSP generates an HTML table that lists employees at a certain salary level. The JSP encapsulates formatting and business logic, as shown in Figure 5.6.

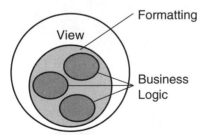

Figure 5.6 View with intermingled business logic and formatting code

As Example 5.6 shows, we apply the View Helper pattern, changing the design and extracting scriptlet code from the JSP view.

Example 5.6 JSP with Scriptlet Code Extracted

```
<%@ taglib uri="/WEB-INF/corepatternstaglibrary.tld"
    prefix="corepatterns" %>
<html>
<head><title>Employee List</title></head>
<body>

<corepatterns:employeeAdapter />

<h3><center>List of employees in
  <corepatterns:department attribute="id"/>
  department - Using Custom Tag Helper Strategy </h3>

<table border="1" >
    <tr>
        <th> First Name </th>
        <th> Last Name </th>
        <th> Designation </th>
        <th> Employee Id </th>
        <th> Tax Deductibles </th>
        <th> Performance Remarks </th>
        <th> Yearly Salary</th>
    </tr>
    <corepatterns:employeelist id="employeelist_key">
    <tr>
      <td><corepatterns:employee
           attribute="FirstName"/></td>
      <td><corepatterns:employee
           attribute="LastName"/></td>
      <td><corepatterns:employee
           attribute="Designation"/> </td>
        <td><corepatterns:employee
           attribute="Id"/></td>
        <td><corepatterns:employee
           attribute="NoOfDeductibles"/></td>
        <td><corepatterns:employee
           attribute="PerformanceRemarks"/></td>
        <td><corepatterns:employee
           attribute="YearlySalary"/></td>
        <td>
     </tr>
    </corepatterns:employeelist>
</table>

</body>
</html>
```

Additionally, we have written two custom tag helpers to encapsulate our business and presentation formatting processing logic by adapting the data model into the rows and columns of our HTML table.

The two helpers are the `<corepatterns:employeelist>` tag and the `<corepatterns:employee>` tag.

Figure 5.7 shows that we have moved from the design represented by the left side of the arrow to the one represented on the right side.

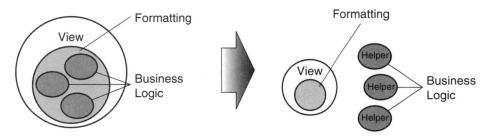

Figure 5.7 Extracting business logic into helper classes

Business logic has been extracted into helper classes instead of being embedded directly within the JSP. These helpers handle a variety of tasks, including content retrieval, access control, and adapting model state for display. In the second case, the helper actually encapsulates some of the presentation processing logic, such as formatting a result set into an HTML table. See also "Remove Conversions from View" on page 96. This helps us meet our goal of extracting as much programming logic from the view as possible, thus using the JSP to ask the helper for the completed table, instead of including scriptlet code in the JSP to generate the table.

Helper components may be implemented as JavaBeans or custom tags (see "View Helper" on page 186). JavaBean helpers are well suited to encapsulating content retrieval logic and storing the results, while custom tag helpers are well suited to the aforementioned task of converting the model for display, such as creating a table from a result set. There is quite a bit of overlap, though, so other factors, such as developer experience and manageability issues, may affect the decision about how to implement a helper.

Applying the second bullet of the mechanics, we simply delegate the work to the helpers, as shown in Figure 5.8.

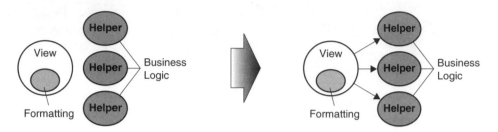

Figure 5.8 Delegate work to helpers

The JSP view uses the helper classes to perform the view process-ing and generation. Typically, a controller is used in front of the JSP as the initial contact point for client requests (see "Front Controller" on page 172 and "Introduce a Controller" on page 74). The controller dispatches to the view, but prior to doing so, the controller may also delegate work to the helper components (see "Service to Worker" on page 216). Having introduced a controller, we have made the transi-tion shown in Figure 5.9.

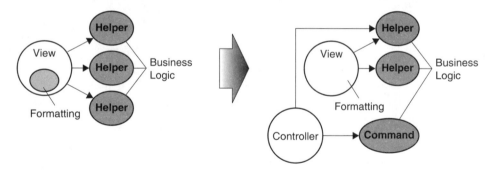

Figure 5.9 Introducing a controller

Hide Presentation Tier-Specific Details From the Business Tier

Request handling and/or protocol-related data structures are exposed from the presentation tier to the business tier.

Remove all references to request handling and protocol-related presentation tier data structures from the business tier. Pass values between tiers using more generic data structures.

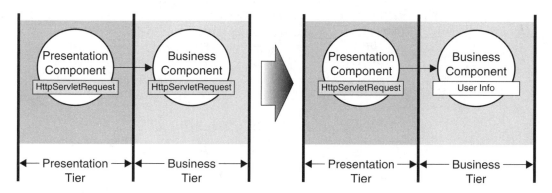

Figure 5.10 Hide presentation tier-specific details from the business tier

Motivation

Implementation details specific to one tier should not be introduced in another tier. The service API exposed by the business tier to the presentation tier will likely be used by other clients as well. If the service API accepts parameters with types, such as HttpServletRequest, then every client to the service is forced to package its data in a servlet request data structure. This drastically reduces the service's reusability.

Mechanics

❑ Replace all references to presentation-tier data structures in the business tier with references to more generic data structures and types.

⇒ *These are typically business-tier methods accepting parameters with types such as HttpServletRequest that might be replaced with parameters of more generic types, such as String, int, or UserInfo.*

❑ Modify client code in the presentation tier that invokes these methods.

⇒ *Pieces of the presentation tier data structure may be passed to the business tier methods as individual arguments. For example, if the HttpServletRequest has parameters x, y, and z, a method in the business tier, instead of accepting the HttpServletRequest as a parameter, might accept these three arguments individually as Strings. One drawback of passing fine-grained, individual arguments is that this strategy more tightly couples the details of the presentation tier with the business service API. Thus, if the state required by the service changes, then the service API must change.*

⇒ *A slightly more flexible alternative is to copy the relevant state from the presentation tier data structure into a more generic data structure, such as a value object, which is passed into the business tier. In this case the service API continues to accept this object, even if its implementation details change.*

❑ Alternatively, implement a strategy of overlaying interface types, if a presentation-tier framework, such as the popular Struts project [Struts], is used.

⇒ *When handling a request, frameworks typically create numerous data structures. For example, typically a framework will transparently complete the step of copying the relevant state from the HttpServletRequest data structure to a more generic data structure, massaging request parameters into a framework-specific data type. While this data type may fulfill the same basic role as a value object, it is a framework-specific data type. Thus, passing this data structure into the business tier introduces coupling between the request-handling framework and the business services. In this case, one could still take the approach just described and copy the framework-specific data structure into a generic structure before passing it to the business tier. Instead, a more efficient solution is to simply create a generic type of interface that mirrors the methods of the framework-specific type. If this interface type is overlaid onto the framework-specific object, then this object can be shared with the business tier without any coupling to the specific framework.*

⇒ *For example, if the framework instantiates a subclass of a.framework.StateBean called my.stuff.MyStateBean, it will be of type StateBean:*

```
//Note:Instance creation is typically done via a factory
//Note:Parameters not shown for simplicity
a.framework.StateBean bean = new my.stuff.MyState-
  Bean(…);
```

⇒ *If the business tier accepted this bean as a parameter, the type would be StateBean:*

```
public void aRemoteBizTierMethod(a.framework.StateBean
                                 bean)
```

⇒ *Instead of passing the bean of type StateBean into the business tier, introduce a new Interface called my.stuff.MyStateVO, implemented by my.stuff.MyStateBean:*

```
public class MyStateBean extends a.framework.StateBean
  implements MyStateVO
```

⇒ *Now the business tier can include the following method signature:*

```
public void aRemoteBizTierMethod(my.stuff.MyStateVO
                                 bean)
```

⇒ *There is no need to copy parameters into a more generic value object, and the framework type is no longer exposed across tiers.*

❏ Finally, on a separate note, remember that you can further reduce the coupling among the logically unrelated parts of the application by applying this refactoring to presentation-tier domain objects, as well.

⇒ *Visually, we are describing something similar to Figure 5.11.*

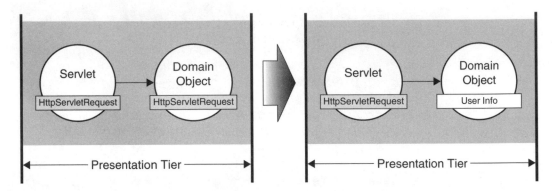

Figure 5.11 Hiding presentation tier-specific details from domain objects

⇨ *The same motivation and mechanics apply to this situation, since we don't want to reduce the reusability of our basic domain objects, such as Customer objects.*

⇨ *This localizes all references to protocol-related data structures in and around the request handling components, such as the controller. An example of decoupling the HttpServletRequest from a domain object is shown in Example 5.7 and Example 5.8 in the "Example" section.*

Example

The Customer class in Example 5.7 accepts an HttpServletRequest instance as a parameter, which greatly reduces the generic nature of this domain object. If a non-web client wanted to use this Customer class, it would somehow need to first generate an HttpServletRequest object, which is inappropriate.

Example 5.7 Tight Coupling between a Domain Object and HttpServletRequest object

```
/** The following excerpt shows a domain object that
   is too tightly coupled with HttpServletRequest **/
public class Customer
{
  public Customer ( HttpServletRequest request )
  {
      firstName = request.getParameter("firstname");
      lastName = request.getParameter("lastname ");
  }
}
```

Instead of exposing the HttpServletRequest object to a general Customer object, simply decouple the two, as shown in Example 5.8 :

Example 5.8 Reduced Coupling between a Domain Object and HttpServletRequest object

```
// Domain Object not coupled with HttpServletRequest
public class Customer
{
  public Customer ( String first, String last )
  {
    firstName - first;
    lastName = last;
  }
}
```

Remove Conversions from View

Portions of the model are converted for display within
a view component.

*Extract all conversion code from view and encapsulate it in one or
more helper classes.*

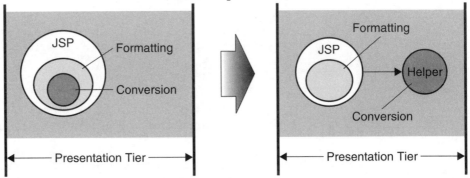

Figure 5.12 Remove conversions from view

Motivation

Directly embedding logic that converts the model for display in the
JSP view reduces the application's modularity and reusability. Since
such conversions might occur in multiple JSPs, the code would need
to be duplicated, creating a copy-and-paste type of reuse that is a
maintenance headache.

Mechanics

❑ Apply Extract Class [Fowler] to move the converting and
adapting logic from individual JSPs into helper classes.

⇒ *An example is adapting a database result set into an HTML
table via some application code.*

❑ Invoke these helpers from the JSPs to process the conversions
and adaptations as desired.

⇒ *The conversion is performed by the helper class to which the
JSP delegates.*

Example

In this example, we examine logic that converts a collection of items, such as a result set, into an HTML table. While this is indeed formatting logic in one sense, it is also conversion code, generating a table of results from an intermediate model. The implementation of this dynamic conversion is reusable if it is encapsulated in a custom tag instead of being embedded directly within a JSP.

Example 5.9 is an example of a JSP that includes this type of conversion logic embedded directly in its source.

Example 5.9 Conversion Logic Embedded Within View

```
<html>
<head><title>Employee List</title></head>
<body>

<h3><head><center> List of employees</h3>

<%
    String firstName =
       (String)request.getParameter("firstName");
    String lastName   =
       (String)request.getParameter("lastName");
    if ( firstName == null )
      // if none specific, fetch all
      firstName = "";
    if ( lastName == null )
      lastName = "";

    EmployeeDelegate empDelegate = new
          EmployeeDelegate();
    Iterator employees =
       empDelegate.getEmployees(
         EmployeeDelegate.ALL_DEPARTMENTS);
%>

<table border="1" >
    <tr>
        <th> First Name </th>
        <th> Last Name </th>
        <th> Designation </th>
    </tr>
<%
    while ( employees.hasNext() )
    {
```

Example 5.9 Conversion Logic Embedded Within View

```
          EmployeeVO employee = (EmployeeVO)
                                employees.next();

          if ( employee.getFirstName().
              startsWith(firstName) &&
              employee.getLastName().
              startsWith(lastName) ) {
%>
 <tr>
  <td><%=employee.getFirstName().toUpperCase() %></td>
  <td> <%=employee.getLastName().toUpperCase() %></td>
  <td> <%=employee.getDesignation()%></td>
 </tr>
<%
        }
    }
%>
</table>
```

The first step is to extract this logic into helper classes. Custom tag helpers make the most sense in this case, since we want to remove as much scriptlet code from the JSP as possible (see See "Note on Helpers:" on page 197.). The JSP is then modified to delegate to these helpers to complete the processing. Example 5.10 shows how the JSP might look after these steps.

Example 5.10 Logic Extracted into Helper Classes

```
<html>
<head><title>Employee List - Refactored </title>
</head>
<body>

<h3> <center>List of employees</h3>

<corepatterns:employeeAdapter />

<table border="1" >
    <tr>
        <th> First Name </th>
        <th> Last Name </th>
        <th> Designation </th>
    </tr>
```

Example 5.10 Logic Extracted into Helper Classes

```
<corepatterns:employeelist id="employeelist"
    match="FirstName, LastName">
<tr>

    <td><corepatterns:employee attribute= "FirstName"
  case="Upper" /> </td>
    <td><corepatterns:employee attribute= "LastName"
  case="Upper" /></td>
    <td><corepatterns:employee attribute=
  "Designation" /> </td>
    <td>
  </tr>
</corepatterns:employeelist>
</table>
```

Now let us examine another type of conversion. In some cases, portions of the model are converted to HTML via XSL transformations. This can also be accomplished using custom tag helpers. Once again, this allows us to extract the logic from the JSP itself, providing us with more modular and reusable components. Here is an example of a JSP that uses custom tag helpers to perform its conversions, instead of performing such conversions inline:

```
<%@taglib uri="http://jakarta.apache.org/taglibs/xsl-1.0"
  prefix="xsl" %>
<xsl:apply nameXml="model" propertyXml="xml"
  xsl="/stylesheet/transform.xsl"/>
```

The Jakarta taglibs [JakartaTaglibs] XSL apply tag is used to generate the entire output of this page. It could be used to simply generate component pieces of the page in the same manner. The tag invocation relies on the fact that a bean exists in a page scope called "model," with a property named "xml." In other words, there is an instance of a bean in a page scope that has a method with the following signature:

```
public String getXml()
```

It is worth noting that these types of conversions can be performed entirely independent of JSP. Depending on numerous factors, such as the storage format of the content and existence of various legacy technologies, one might choose this route.

Hide Resource From a Client

Certain resources, such as JSP Views, are directly accessible to clients, though access should be restricted.

Hide certain resources via container configuration or by using a control component.

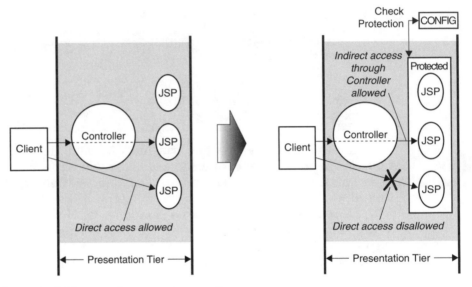

Figure 5.13 Restricted via container configuration

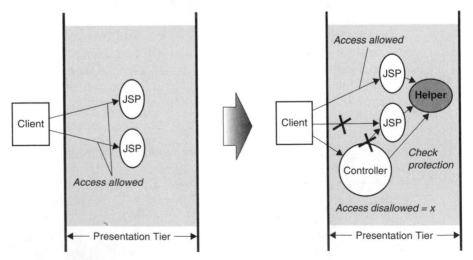

Figure 5.14 Restricted by using a control component

Motivation

Control of an incoming request is often desired. This refactoring describes permission-based control and protection.

If the order or flow of the client requests must be controlled, then apply Introduce Synchronizer Token (see "Introduce Synchronizer Token" on page 77).

Mechanics

❑ Restrict access to certain resources (such as Web resources, servlets, among others) via configuration, by moving these resources into a subdirectory of the `/WEB-INF/` subdirectory of the Web application.

⇒ *For example, to block direct browser access to a view called* `info.jsp`, *in the* `securityissues` *Web application, we could place the JSP source file in the following subdirectory:* `/securityissues/WEB-INF/internalaccessonly/` `info.jsp`.

❑ Restrict access using a control component.

⇒ *Introduce a controller (see "Introduce a Controller" on page 74) may be applied and the controller can manage access to protected resources.*

⇒ *Additionally, each resource to be protected can manage its own access control, meaning it would delegate to a helper class to perform this processing.*

❑ Create one or more helper classes.

⇒ *Depending on the implementation, either the controller or each JSP itself delegates to these helper classes to check whether the resource should be served.*

Example

Restricted by Container Configuration

We can make a JSP called `info.jsp` inaccessible to our client, except via a controller, by moving the JSP under the `/WEB-INF/` directory.

If we have a Web application called `corepatterns`, then we might start with the following configuration under our server root directory:

```
/corepatterns/secure_page.jsp
```

By default, this allows direct client access to this resource, as shown in the following URL:

```
http://localhost:8080/corepatterns/secure_page.jsp
```

To restrict direct access, we can simply move the JSP file to a subdirectory of the `/WEB-INF/` directory, giving us the following under our server root:

```
/corepatterns/WEB-INF/privateaccess/secure_page.jsp
```

The `/WEB-INF/` directory hierarchy is accessible only indirectly via internal requests, such as those coming through a controller and a RequestDispatcher. Thus, a browser client can only access this file now using a URL similar to the following:

```
http://localhost:8080/corepatterns/controller?view=/
   corepatterns/WEB-INF/privateaccess/secure_page.jsp
```

Note: The above URL is for example purposes only and is *not* a recommended way to pass path information to the server. The view query parameter should not expose the server's directory structure. It does so in this example only to clarify the example's intent.

If this request is handled by a servlet controller, then it can forward the request to `secure_page.jsp`, using the RequestDispatcher.

On the other hand, if an attempt is made to access the resource directly, as follows,

```
http://localhost:8080/corepatterns/WEB-INF/
   privateaccess/secure_page.jsp
```

the server responds that the requested resource is not available, as shown in Figure 5.15.

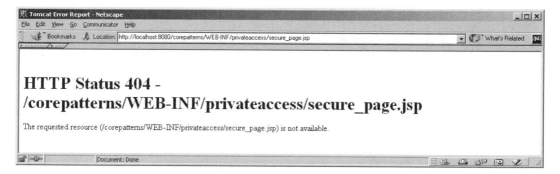

Figure 5.15 Screen shot: Restricting direct browser access via simple file configuration

Restricted by Using a Control Component

Another option for restricting access is to delegate to a control component, as shown in Figure 5.14 and Example 5.11.

Example 5.11 Controlling Access Using a Control Component

```
<%@ taglib uri="/WEB-INF/corepatternstaglibrary.tld"
  prefix="corepatterns" %>
<corepatterns:guard/>
<html>
<head><title>Hide Resource from Client</title></head>
<body>

<h2>This view is shown to the client only if the
control component allows access. The view delegates
the control check to the guard tag at the top of the
page.</h2>
</body>
</html>
```

Business and Integration Tier Refactorings

Wrap Entities With Session

Entity beans from the business tier are exposed to
clients in another tier.

Use a Session Facade to encapsulate the entity beans.

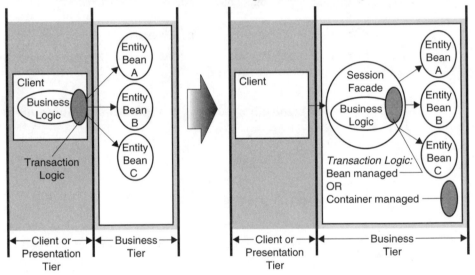

Figure 5.16 Wrap Entities With Session

Motivation

Entity beans are coarse-grained distributed persistent objects. Exposing the entity bean to clients in a different tier results in network overhead and performance degradation. Each client invocation on the entity bean is a remote network method call, which is expensive.

Entity beans mandate container-managed transaction. Exposing the entity bean to the clients may put the burden on the client developer to understand, design, and demarcate transactions when dealing with multiple entity beans. The client developer has to obtain a user transaction from the transaction manager and code the interaction with entity beans to occur within the context of that transaction. Since the client implements the transaction management, it is not possible to use the benefits of container-managed transaction demarcation.

Mechanics

❏ Move the business logic to interact with the entity beans out of the application client.

⇒ *Use Extract Class [Fowler] to extract the logic from the client.*

❏ Use a session bean as a facade to the entity beans.

⇒ *This session bean can contain the entity bean interaction logic and associated workflow logic.*

⇒ *See "Session Facade" on page 291 for details.*

❏ Implement session beans to provide a consolidated uniform access layer to the entity beans by applying the Session facade pattern.

⇒ *The number of interactions between the client and the entity beans is now moved into the Session facade in the business tier.*

⇒ *Thus, the number of remote method invocations from the client is reduced.*

❏ Implement transaction logic in session beans if using bean-managed transactions. For container-managed transactions, specify the transaction attributes for the session bean in the deployment descriptor.

⇒ *Since the session bean interacts with the entity beans, the client is no longer responsible for demarcating transactions.*

⇒ *Thus, all transaction demarcation is now delegated to either the session bean or the container, depending on whether the designer has chosen user-managed or container-managed transactions.*

Introduce Business Delegate

Session beans in the business tier are exposed to clients
in other tiers.

*Use a business delegate to decouple the tiers and to hide the
implementation details.*

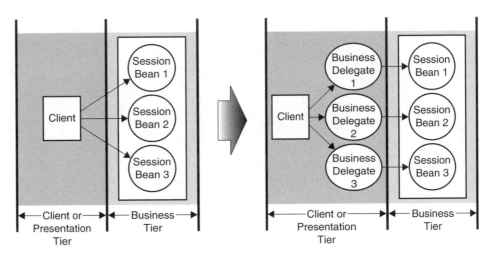

Figure 5.17 Introduce Business Delegate

Motivation

Session beans are used to implement facades for entity beans, as discussed in "Wrap Entities With Session" on page 104. Session beans provide coarse-grained interfaces to business services. But, exposing the session bean directly to the application client creates a tight coupling between the application client code and the session bean.

Exposing the session bean to the application client increases the prevalence of session bean calls throughout the client code. Thus, any change to the session bean interface impacts every point in the application client code where the session bean is called, and thus creates highly brittle code. The clients also are exposed to service level exceptions encountered when dealing with enterprise beans. This effect is further exaggerated if you consider applications with different types of clients, where each such client uses the session bean interface to obtain some service.

Mechanics

❑ For each session bean that is directly exposed to clients across the tier, introduce a business delegate.

⇒ *Business delegates are plain Java classes that encapsulate the business tier details and intercept service level exceptions on behalf of the client.*

⇒ *See "Business Delegate" on page 248.*

❑ Implement each Business Delegate to deal with its session bean, typically as a facade. A business delegate is designed with a one-to-one relationship with its session facade.

⇒ *Business delegates reduce the coupling between the client tier and the business services (session beans) by hiding the implementation details.*

⇒ *The clients deal with the business delegates by invoking methods on them locally.*

❑ Encapsulate code related to lookup services and caching in business delegates.

⇒ *Business delegates can use a service locator to look up business services.*

⇒ *See See "Service Locator" on page 367.*

Merge Session Beans

There is a one-to-one mapping between session beans and entity beans.

Map coarse-grained business services to session beans. Eliminate or combine session beans that act solely as entity bean proxies into session beans that represent coarse-grained business services.

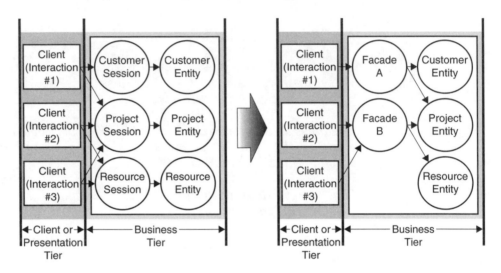

Figure 5.18 Merge Session Beans

Motivation

A one-to-one mapping of a session bean to an entity bean does not yield any benefits. Such mapping only introduces a layer of session beans acting as proxies. Typically this happens when developers create session beans to front entity beans, rather than to represent coarse-grained services.

Some designers interpret "Wrap Entities With Session" to mean that every entity bean should be protected by its own session bean. This is not a correct interpretation, since it results in design of session beans as proxies rather than as facades. The drawbacks of exposing the entity beans to clients is discussed in "Wrap Entities With Session" on page 104.

In Figure 5.18, different clients are servicing different interactions. Each interaction involves one or more entity beans. With a one-to-one mapping of a session bean to an entity bean, the client has to interact with each session bean fronting an entity bean. Since the session bean is essentially a proxy to the entity, this scenario is similar to exposing the entity bean directly to the client.

Mechanics

❑ Implement session beans as facades to entity beans. Thus, each session bean provides a coarse-grained business service interface to the clients.

❑ Consolidate fine-grained session beans or a set of session beans that are proxies to entity beans into a single session bean.

⇒ *Session beans represent coarse-grained business service.*

⇒ *Entity beans represent coarse-grained, transactional persistent data.*

⇒ *See "Session Facade" on page 291.*

❑ Consolidate a set of related interactions that involve one or more entity beans into a single session facade instead of implementing each interaction using a unique session bean.

⇒ *This results in a fewer number of session beans that provide a uniform coarse-grained business service access to entity beans.*

⇒ *The number of Session facades is related to the grouping of interactions and not to the number of entity beans.*

Reduce Inter-Entity Bean Communication

Inter-entity bean relationships introduce overhead in the model.

Reduce the inter-entity bean relationships by using coarse-grained entity bean (Composite Entity) with dependent objects.

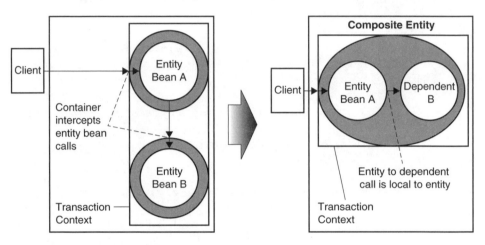

Figure 5.19 Reduce Inter-Entity Bean Communication

Motivation

Entity beans have significantly more overhead than plain Java objects. Calls to entity bean methods are remote and incur network overhead. Also, entity beans must interact with an external data source.

Even if two entity beans are in the same container, remote method invocation semantics apply (the container is involved in the communication) when one entity bean calls the other bean. Some container implementations may optimize such calls, because they recognize that the call comes from an object within the same container, but this is vendor-specific and cannot be relied upon.

Another issue is the inability for the entity bean to demarcate a transaction. When using entity beans, you are only allowed to have container-managed transactions. This means that, depending on the transaction attribute of the entity bean method, the container may start a new transaction, participate in the current transaction, or do neither. When a client invokes a method on an entity bean, the transaction includes the chain of dependent entity beans and binds them into the transaction's context. This reduces the performance throughput of the entity beans as a whole, because any transaction may lock multiple entity beans and possibly introduce deadlock situations.

Mechanics

❏ Design and implement entity beans as coarse-grained objects with root and dependent objects.

⇒ *Transform an entity-bean-to-entity-bean relationship into an entity-bean-to-dependent-object relationship.*

⇒ *Dependent objects are not entity beans. Rather, they are objects contained within an entity bean. A relationship between an entity bean and its dependent objects is a local relationship with no network overhead.*

⇒ *Optimize load and store operations for Composite Entity using the Lazy Loading Strategy and Store Optimization (Dirty Marker) Strategy respectively.*

⇒ *See "Composite Entity" on page 310.*

❏ Extract and move business logic related to working with other entities from the entity bean into a session bean.

⇒ *Use Extract Method [Fowler] and / or Move Method [Fowler] to move such business logic into a session bean, applying the Session facade pattern.*

⇒ *See "Session Facade" on page 291.*

Move Business Logic to Session

Inter-entity bean relationships introduce overhead in the model.

Encapsulate the workflow related to inter-entity bean relationships in a session bean (Session Facade).

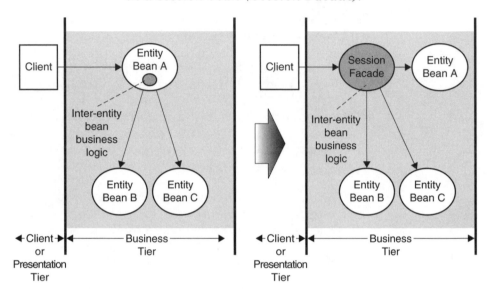

Figure 5.20 Move Business Logic to Session

Motivation

In "Reduce Inter-Entity Bean Communication" on page 110, we discussed the problems associated with direct inter-entity-bean dependencies. The problem is that an entity may contain business logic that deals with other entity beans. This creates a direct or indirect dependency on another entity bean. The same problems discussed in Reduce Inter-Entity Bean Communication apply to this scenario too.

Mechanics

❏ Extract and move business logic related to working with other entities from the entity bean into a session bean.

⇒ *Use Extract Method [Fowler] and / or Move Method [Fowler] to move such business logic into a session bean applying the Session facade pattern.*

⇒ *See "Session Facade" on page 291.*

⇒ *See "Wrap Entities With Session" on page 104.*

General Refactorings

Separate Data Access Code

Data access code is embedded directly within a class that has other unrelated responsibilities.

Extract the data access code into a new class and move the new class logically and / or physically closer to the Data Source.

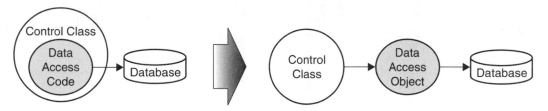

Figure 5.21 Separate Data Access Code

Motivation

Create cleaner abstractions, increase cohesion, and reduce coupling, thus improving modularity and reusability.

Mechanics

❑ Identify and extract the data access logic from the controller object.

⇛ *Use Extract Class [Fowler] to create a new class and move data access code from the original class into the new Data Access Object (DAO) class.*

⇛ *Consider including the DAO as part of the name of the new class in order to flag its role as a Data Access Object.*

⇛ *See "Data Access Object" on page 390.*

❑ Use the new DAO from the controller to access data.

❑ For related information on application partitioning, see "Refactor Architecture by Tiers" on page 116.

Example

Consider an example where a servlet has embedded data access code to access some user information. Applying the first two bullets, assume we change the design, as shown in Figure 5.22.

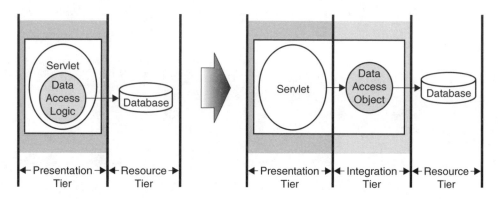

Figure 5.22 Separate Data Access Code – Servlet example

We now have two classes: one for the servlet, which acts as a controller, and the other a new object called "UserDAO," which acts as a data access object to access user information. The UserDAO encapsulates all Java Database Connectivity (JDBC) code and decouples the servlet from the implementation details. The servlet code is much simpler as a result.

Consider another example where the persistence logic is embedded in an enterprise bean using bean-managed persistence. Combining the persistence code with the enterprise bean code creates brittle, tightly coupled code. When the persistence code is part of the enterprise bean, any change to the persistence store requires changing the bean's persistence code. Such coupling has a negative impact on enterprise bean code maintenance. This is another example of how this refactoring can help.

Applying this refactoring, we change the design as shown in Figure 5.23.

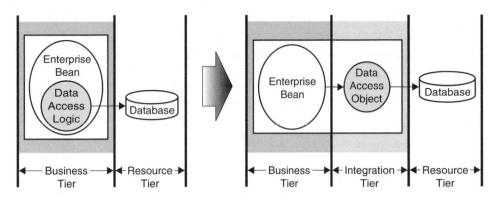

Figure 5.23 Separate Data Access Code – Enterprise bean example

Refactor Architecture by Tiers

Increasing architectural sophistication requires changing the localization of data access logic and processing logic.

Move Data Access code logically and / or physically closer to the actual Data Source. Move processing logic out of the client and presentation tiers into the business tier.

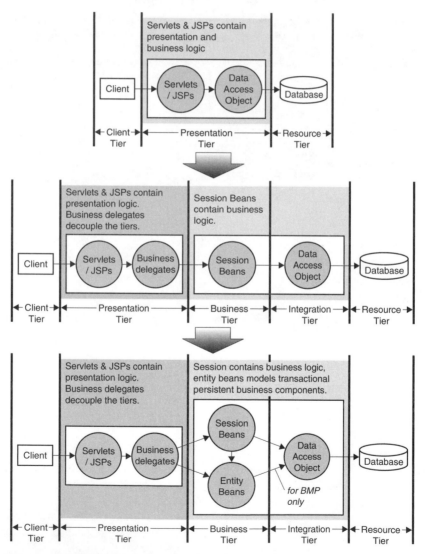

Figure 5.24 Refactor Architecture by Tiers

Motivation

"Separate Data Access Code" on page 113 demonstrates refactoring data access logic, while this refactoring discusses other types of business logic in an application.

The J2EE platform offers clear separation of concerns into the roles of servlets, JSPs, and EJB components to provide maximum benefits in terms of scalability, flexibility, transactions, security, and so forth.

As business requirements become more sophisticated, the design needs to better address issues related to persistence, transactions, security, and scalability of business services. At some point in this increasing complexity, session beans and entity beans are introduced to provide centralized business processing for all clients and to leverage the benefits of the EJB container.

Some designers use heavyweight components like enterprise beans without ensuring that the application requirements warrant their use. Some sophisticated application requirements that influence this decision are transactions, security, scalability, and distributed processing.

Mechanics

❑ Separate data access code from control and entity objects into data access objects.

⇒ *See "Separate Data Access Code" on page 113.*

❑ Separate presentation and business processing. Introduce session beans for business processing. Retain presentation processing in servlets and JSPs.

⇒ *Apply this step when application requirements become more sophisticated, and as business logic consolidation is required at the business tier to offer the same business service to all clients (i.e., not only to presentation clients).*

⇒ *Introducing session beans as business service processing components enables this functionality. Session beans access the persistent storage via the data access objects.*

⇒ *Container-managed or bean-managed transaction demarcation can be utilized as appropriate for the session beans.*

⇒ *See "Session Facade" on page 291.*

❑ Introduce entity beans to model-shared, transactional, coarse-grained persistent business objects. If requirements do not warrant using entity beans, then skip this step.

> ⇒ *Apply this step when the persistent business components become increasingly complex and you wish to leverage the entity bean benefits, including container-managed transactions and container-managed persistence (CMP).*

> ⇒ *Entity beans offer container-managed transaction for transaction demarcation. This allows declarative programming for transaction demarcation without hardcoding the transaction logic into the enterprise beans.*

> ⇒ *See "Value Object" on page 261 and "Composite Entity" on page 310.*

❑ Decouple presentation-tier and business-tier components, using business delegates.

> ⇒ *Business Delegate decouples the presentation-tier components from business-tier components and hides the complexity of lookup and other implementation details.*

> ⇒ *See "Business Delegate" on page 248.*

Use A Connection Pool

Database connections are not shared. Instead, clients manage their own connections for making database invocations.

Use a Connection Pool to pre-initialize multiple Connections, improving scalability and performance.

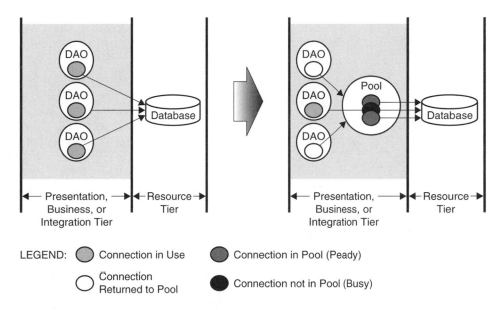

LEGEND: ⬤ Connection in Use   ⬤ Connection in Pool (Peady)

◯ Connection Returned to Pool   ⬤ Connection not in Pool (Busy)

Figure 5.25 Use A Connection Pool

Motivation

Opening a connection to a database is a fairly expensive operation that takes time and resources to perform. Both performance and scalability are affected. Since database connections are limited, if each client manages its own connection, the total number of connections will likely be exhausted far sooner than desired.

This issue arises in the presentation tier on projects that use a phased approach to introducing EJB technology. In this case, components in the presentation tier initially interact directly with a database, and the data access code is later moved into the business tier and encapsulated in an EJB layer. See "Separate Data Access Code" on page 113 and "Refactor Architecture by Tiers" on page 116.

Mechanics

❑ Create an interface for connection management, including methods for retrieving and returning a connection.

❑ Apply Extract Class [Fowler] and/or Move Method [Fowler], moving the existing connection retrieval code into a class that implements the connection management interface.

⇒ *At the points from which the connection code was extracted, substitute invocations to an instance of this new class; that is,*
`connectionMgr.getConnection()` *and*
`connectionMgr.returnConnection(conn)`.

⇒ *Note that the JDBC specification, version 2, includes a standard mechanism for introducing connection pooling. This mechanism, if available, is the recommended way to introduce connection pooling. In the JDBC specification version 2, the management interface is named* `javax.sql.DataSource` *and it provides a factory for pooled Connection objects.*

⇒ *At this point, only the structure and interface has been standardized, but the functionality is the same.*

⇒ *Still no pooling is implemented, unless the JDBC 2.0 Data-Source factory is utilized, which is recommended.*

❑ Modify the implementation of the connection retrieval methods within the connection manager implementation to pre-initialize some Connection instances and share them among users, thus introducing pooling.

⇒ *There are numerous publicly available implementations from which to choose.*

⇒ *Clients of these connection manager instances are typically DAOs. See "Separate Data Access Code" on page 113.*

⇒ *Data access code typically migrates logically closer to the database as a project evolves. See "Refactor Architecture by Tiers" on page 116.*

Part 3

J2EE PATTERN CATALOG

Part 3 includes the following four chapters:

- *Chapter 6—J2EE Patterns Overview*
- *Chapter 7—Presentation Tier Patterns*
- *Chapter 8—Business Tier Patterns*
- *Chapter 9—Integration Tier Patterns*
- *Epilogue—J2EE Patterns Applied*

Chapter 6 provides an overview of the J2EE Pattern Catalog with a discussion on our tiered approach. The chapter provides a guide to the pattern catalog and describes the terminology and UML Stereotypes used to describe each pattern. The template used to document each pattern is also defined and discussed. One of the important aspects of the chapter is the discussion of the relationships among various patterns in the catalog - both with each other, as well as with patterns in other literature such as Design Patterns [GoF], Patterns of Software Architecture, Volume 1 [POSA1] and Volume 2 [POSA2]. Another useful artifact in this chapter is the J2EE Patterns roadmap, which presents a table of common requirements mapped to various patterns and refactorings.

Chapter 7, 8 and 9 describe the patterns in the J2EE Pattern Catalog.

Chapter 7 provides six patterns for the presentation tier dealing with Servlets and Java Server Pages (JSP) technologies.

Chapter 8 provides seven business-tier patterns related to the use of Enterprise JavaBeans (EJB), Java Database Connectivity (JDBC), Java Naming and Directory Interface (JNDI) technologies.

Chapter 9 provides 2 patterns related to the use of Java Database Connectivity (JDBC) and Java Messaging Service (JMS) technologies.

Epilogue presents a brief discussion on pattern selection and usage with sample use cases. It also discusses and demonstrates how multiple patterns work together to create a solution.

J2EE PATTERNS
OVERVIEW

Topics in This Chapter

- The Tiered Approach
- J2EE Patterns
- J2EE Pattern Relationships
- Relationship to Known Patterns
- Patterns Roadmap

Chapter 6

The J2EE patterns are a collection of J2EE-based solutions to common problems. They reflect the collective expertise and experience of Java architects at the Sun Java Center, gained from successfully executing numerous J2EE engagements. The Sun Java Center is Sun's consulting organization, focused on architecting Java technology-based solutions for customers. The Sun Java Center has been architecting solutions for the J2EE platform since its early days, focusing on achieving Quality of Service (QoS) qualities such as scalability, availability, performance, securability, reliability, and flexibility.

These J2EE patterns describe typical problems encountered by enterprise application developers and provide solutions for these problems. We have formulated these solutions based on our ongoing work with numerous J2EE customers and on exchanges with other Java architects experiencing similar problems. The patterns capture the essence of these solutions, and they represent the solution refinement that takes place over the course of time and from collective experience. To put it another way, they extract the core issues of each problem, offering solutions that represent an applicable distillation of theory and practice.

Our work has focused on the J2EE area, especially regarding such J2EE components as Enterprise Java Beans (EJB), Java Server Pages (JSP), and servlets. During our work with J2EE customers implementing the various components, we have come to recognize the common problems and difficult areas that may impede a good implementation. We've also developed effective best practices and approaches for using the J2EE components in combination.

The patterns presented here extract these "best practice" approaches and present them to you in a way that enables you to apply the patterns to your own particular application and to accommodate your own needs. The patterns clearly and simply express proven techniques. They make it easier for you to reuse successful designs and architectures. Simply put, you can use the patterns to design your J2EE system successfully and quickly.

What Is a Pattern?

In Chapter 1, we discussed how different experts define a pattern. We also discussed some of the peripheral issues around patterns including the benefits of using patterns. Here, we revisit this discussion in the context of the J2EE Pattern Catalog.

As discussed in Chapter 1, some experts define a pattern as a recurring *solution* to a *problem* in a *context*. These terms—context, problem, and solution—deserve a bit of explanation. First, what is a context? A context is the environment, surroundings, situation, or interrelated conditions within which something exists. Second, what is a problem? A problem is an unsettled question, something that needs to be investigated and solved. Typically, the problem is constrained by the context in which it occurs. Finally, the solution refers to the answer to the problem in a context that helps resolve the issues.

So, if we have a solution to a problem in a context, is it a pattern? Not necessarily. The characteristic of recurrence also needs to be associated with the definition of a pattern. That is, a pattern is only useful if it can be applied repeatedly. Is that all? Perhaps not. As you can see, while the concept of a pattern is fairly simple, actually defining the term is more complex.

We point you to the references so that you can dig more deeply into the pattern history and learn about patterns in other areas. In our catalog, a pattern is described according to its main characteristics: *context, problem,* and *solution,* along with other important aspects, such as *forces* and *consequences.* The section describing the pattern template (see "Pattern Template" on page 138) explains these characteristics in more detail.

Identifying a Pattern

We have handled many J2EE projects at the Sun Java Center, and over time we have noticed that similar problems recur across these projects. We have also seen similar solutions emerge for these problems. While the implementation strategies varied, the overall solutions were quite similar. Let us discuss, in brief, our pattern identification process.

When we see a problem and solution recur, we try to identify and document its characteristics using the pattern template. At first, we consider these initial documents to be candidate patterns. However, we do not add candidate patterns to the pattern catalog until we are able to observe and document their usage multiple times on different projects. We also undertake the process of pattern mining by looking for patterns in implemented solutions.

As part of the pattern validation process, we use the *Rule of Three,* as it is known in the pattern community. This rule is a guide for transitioning a candidate pattern into the pattern catalog. According to this rule, a solution remains a candidate pattern until it has been verified in at least three different systems. Certainly, there is much room for interpretation with rules such as this, but they help provide a context for pattern identification.

Often, similar solutions may represent a single pattern. When deciding how to form the pattern, it is important to consider how to best communicate the solution. Sometimes, a separate name improves communication among developers. If so, then consider documenting two similar solutions as two different patterns. On the other hand, it might be better to communicate the solution by distilling the similar ideas into a pattern/strategy combination.

Patterns Versus Strategies

When we started documenting the J2EE patterns, we made the decision to document them at a relatively high level of abstraction. At the same time, each pattern includes various strategies that provide lower level implementation details. Through the strategies, each pattern documents a solution at multiple levels of abstraction. We could have documented some of these strategies as patterns in their own right; however, we feel that our current template structure most clearly communicates the relationship of the strategies to the higher level pattern structure in which they are included.

While we continue to have lively debates about converting these strategies to patterns, we have deferred these decisions for now, believing the current documentation to be clear. We have noted some of the issues with respect to the relationship of the strategies to the patterns:

- The patterns exist at a higher level of abstraction than the strategies.
- The patterns include the most recommended or most common implementations as strategies.
- Strategies provide an extensibility point for each pattern. Developers discover and invent new ways to implement the patterns, producing new strategies for well-known patterns.
- Strategies promote better communication by providing names for lower level aspects of a particular solution.

The Tiered Approach

Since this catalog describes patterns that help you build applications that run on the J2EE platform, and since a J2EE platform (and application) is a multitiered system, we view the system in terms of *tiers*. A tier is a logical partition of the separation of concerns in the system. Each tier is assigned its unique responsibility in the system. We view each tier as logically separated from one another. Each tier is loosely coupled with the adjacent tier. We represent the whole system as a stack of tiers. See Figure 6.1.

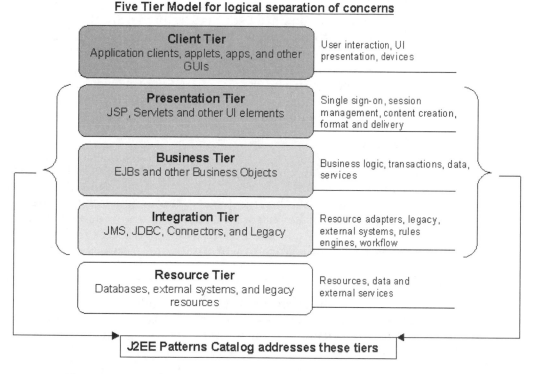

Figure 6.1 Tiered approach

Client Tier

This tier represents all device or system clients accessing the system or the application. A client can be a Web browser, a Java or other application, a Java applet, a WAP phone, a network application, or some device introduced in the future. It could even be a batch process.

Presentation Tier

This tier encapsulates all presentation logic required to service the clients that access the system. The presentation tier intercepts the client requests, provides single sign-on, conducts session management, controls access to business services, constructs the responses, and delivers the responses to the client. Servlets and JSPs reside in this tier. Note that servlets and JSPs are not themselves UI elements, but they produce UI elements.

Business Tier

This tier provides the business services required by the application clients. The tier contains the business data and business logic. Typically, most business processing for the application is centralized into this tier. It is possible that, due to legacy systems, some business processing may occur in the resource tier. Enterprise bean components are the usual and preferred solution for implementing the business objects in the business tier.

Integration Tier

This tier is responsible for communicating with external resources and systems such as data stores and legacy applications. The business tier is coupled with the integration tier whenever the business objects require data or services that reside in the resource tier. The components in this tier can use JDBC, J2EE connector technology, or some proprietary middleware to work with the resource tier.

Resource Tier

This is the tier that contains the business data and external resources such as mainframes and legacy systems, business-to-business (B2B) integration systems, and services such as credit card authorization.

J2EE Patterns

We used the tiered approach to divide the J2EE patterns according to functionality, and our pattern catalog follows this approach. The presentation tier patterns contain the patterns related to servlets and JSP technology. The business tier patterns contain the patterns related to the EJB technology. The integration tier patterns contain the patterns related to JMS and JDBC. See Figure 6.2 on page 141.

Presentation Tier Patterns

Table 6-1 lists the presentation tier patterns, along with a brief description of each pattern.

Table 6-1 Presentation Tier Patterns

Pattern Name	Synopsis
Intercepting Filter	Facilitates preprocessing and post-processing of a request.
Front Controller	Provides a centralized controller for managing the handling of a request.
View Helper	Encapsulates logic that is not related to presentation formatting into Helper components.
Composite View	Creates an aggregate View from atomic subcomponents.
Service To Worker	Combines a Dispatcher component with the FrontController and View Helper Patterns.
Dispatcher View	Combines a Dispatcher component with the FrontController and View Helper Patterns, deferring many activities to View processing.

Business Tier Patterns

Table 6-2 lists the business tier patterns, along with a brief synopsis of each pattern.

Table 6-2 Business Tier Patterns

Pattern Name	Synopsis
Business Delegate	Decouples presentation and service tiers, and provides a facade and proxy interface to the services.
Value Object	Facilitates data exchange between tiers by reducing network chattiness.
Session Facade	Hides business object complexity; centralizes workflow handling.
Composite Entity	Represents a best practice for designing coarse-grained entity beans by grouping parent-dependent objects into a single entity bean.
Value Object Assembler	Assembles a composite value object from multiple data sources.

Table 6-2 Business Tier Patterns (continued)

Pattern Name	Synopsis
Value List Handler	Manages query execution, results caching, and results processing.
Service Locator	Encapsulates complexity of business service lookup and creation; locates business service factories.

Integration Tier Patterns

Table 6-3 lists the integration tier patterns and provides a brief description of each pattern.

Table 6-3 Integration Tier Patterns

Pattern Name	Synopsis
Data Access Object	Abstracts data sources; provides transparent access to data.
Service Activator	Facilitates asynchronous processing for EJB components.

Guide to the Catalog

To help you effectively understand and use the J2EE patterns in the catalog, we suggest that you familiarize yourself with this section before reading the individual patterns. Here we introduce the pattern terminology and explain our use of the Unified Modeling Language (UML), stereotypes, and the pattern template. In short, we explain how to use these patterns. We also provide a high-level roadmap to the patterns in the catalog.

Terminology

Players in the enterprise computing area, and particularly establishments using Java-based systems, have incorporated a number of terms and acronyms into their language. While many readers are familiar with these terms, sometimes their use varies from one setting to another. To avoid misunderstandings and to keep things consistent, we define in Table 6-4 how we use these terms and acronyms.

Table 6-4 Terminology

Term	*Description/Definition*	*Used in*
BMP	Bean-managed persistence: a strategy for entity beans where the bean developer implements the persistence logic for entity beans.	Business tier patterns
Business Object	An object that implements business logic and/or business data. Business data and business logic are implemented in coarse-grained objects called business objects. In J2EE, business objects are implemented as session or entity beans. In some cases, a business object could be an arbitrary Java object that provides some service.	Business tier patterns
CMP	Container-managed persistence: a strategy for entity beans where the container services transparently manage the persistence of entity beans.	Business tier patterns
Composite	A complex object that holds other objects. Also related to the Composite pattern described in the GoF book. (See GoF below.)	Composite View, Composite Entity
Controller	Interacts with a client, controlling and managing the handling of each request.	Presentation and business tier patterns

Table 6-4 Terminology (continued)

Term	Description/Definition	Used in
Data Access Object	An object that encapsulates and abstracts access to data from a persistent store or an external system. Currently, Data Access Objects are closely related to bean-managed persistence.	Business and integration tier patterns
Delegate	A stand-in, or surrogate, object for another component; an intermediate layer. A Delegate has qualities of a proxy and facade.	Business Delegate and many other patterns
Dependent Object	An object that does not exist by itself and whose lifecycle is managed by another object.	Composite Entity pattern
Dispatcher	Some of the responsibilities of a Controller include managing the choice of and dispatching to an appropriate View. This behavior may be partitioned into a separate component, referred to as a Dispatcher.	Dispatcher View, Service To Worker
Enterprise Bean	Refers to an Enterprise JavaBean component; can be a session or entity bean instance. When this term is used, it means that the bean instance can be either an entity or a session bean.	Many places in this literature
Entity Bean	Refers to an entity bean. May also refer collectively to the entity bean's home interface, remote object, bean implementation, and primary key objects.	Many places in this literature

Table 6-4 Terminology (continued)

Term	Description/Definition	Used in
Facade	A pattern for hiding underlying complexities; described in the GoF book.	Session Façade pattern
Factory (Abstract Factory or Factory Method)	Patterns described in the GoF book for creating objects or families of objects.	Business tier patterns: Data Access Object, Value Object
Iterator	A pattern to provide accessors to underlying collection facilities; described in the GoF book.	Value List Handler
GoF	Gang of Four—refers to the authors of the popular design patterns book, *Design Patterns: Elements of Reusable Object-Oriented Software,* by Erich Gamma, Richard Helm, Ralph Johnson, and John Vlissides. [GoF]	Many places in this literature
Helper	Responsible for helping the Controller and/or View. For example, the Controller and View may delegate the following to a Helper: content retrieval, validation, storing the model or adapting it for use by the display.	Presentation tier patterns, Business Delegate
Independent Object	An object that can exist by itself and may manage the lifecycles of its dependent objects.	Composite Entity pattern
Locator	An object that aids in locating service and business objects.	Service Locator pattern

Table 6-4 Terminology (continued)

Term	Description/Definition	Used in
Model	A physical or logical representation of the system or its subsystem.	Presentation and business tier patterns
Persistent Store	Represents persistent storage systems such as RDBMSs, ODBMSs, file systems, and so forth.	Business and integration tier patterns
Proxy	A pattern to provide a placeholder for another object to control access to it; described in the GoF book.	Many places in this literature
Scriptlet	Application logic embedded directly within a JSP.	Presentation tier patterns
Session Bean	Refers to a stateless or stateful session bean. May also refer collectively to the session bean's home, remote object, and bean implementation.	Business tier patterns
Singleton	A pattern that provides a single instance of an object, as described in the GoF book.	Many places in this literature
Template	Template text refers to the literal text encapsulated within a JSP View. Additionally, a template may refer to a specific layout of components in a display.	Presentation tier patterns
Value Object	An arbitrary Java object that is used to carry data from one object/tier to another. Usually does not contain any business methods. May be designed with public attributes or provided with get methods to obtain attribute values.	Business tier patterns

Table 6-4 Terminology (continued)

Term	Description/Definition	Used in
View	The View manages the graphics and text that make up the display. It interacts with Helpers to get data values with which to populate the display. Additionally, it may delegate activities, such as content retrieval, to its Helpers.	Presentation tier patterns

Use of UML

We have used UML extensively in the pattern catalog, particularly as follows:

- *Class diagrams.* We use the class diagrams to show the structure of the pattern solution and the structure of the implementation strategies. This provides the static view of the solution.

- *Sequence (or Interaction) diagrams.* We use these diagrams to show the interactions between different participants in a solution or a strategy. This provides the dynamic view of the solution.

- *Stereotypes.* We use stereotypes to indicate different types of objects and roles in the class and interaction diagrams. The list of stereotypes and their meanings is included in Table 6-5 .

Each pattern in the pattern catalog includes a class diagram that shows the structure of the solution and a sequence diagram that shows the interactions for the pattern. In addition, patterns with multiple strategies use class and sequence diagrams to explain each strategy.

To learn more about UML, please see the Bibliography.

UML Stereotypes

While reading the patterns and their diagrams, you will encounter certain stereotypes. Stereotypes are terms coined or used by designers and architects. We created and used these stereotypes in order to present the diagrams in a concise and easy to understand manner.

Note that some of the stereotypes relate to the terminology explained in the previous section.

Table 6-5 UML Stereotypes

Stereotype	Meaning
EJB	Represents an enterprise bean component; associated with a business object. This is a role that is usually fulfilled by a session or entity bean.
SessionEJB	Represents a session bean as a whole without specifying the session bean remote interface, home interface, or the bean implementation.
EntityEJB	Represents an entity bean as a whole without specifying the entity bean remote interface, home interface, the bean implementation, or the primary key.
View	A View represents and displays information to the client.
JSP	A Java Server Page; a View is typically implemented as a JSP.
Servlet	A Java servlet; a Controller is typically implemented as a Servlet.
Singleton	A class that has a single instance in accordance with the Singleton pattern.
Custom Tag	JSP Custom Tags are used to implement Helper objects, as are JavaBeans. A Helper is responsible for such activities as gathering data required by the View and for adapting this data model for use by the View. Helpers can service requests for data from the View by simply providing access to the raw data or by formatting the data as Web content.

Pattern Template

The J2EE patterns are all structured according to a defined pattern template. The pattern template consists of sections presenting various attributes for a given pattern. You'll also notice that we've tried to give each J2EE pattern a descriptive pattern name. While it is difficult to fully encompass a single pattern in its name, the pattern names are intended to provide sufficient insight into the function of the pattern. Just as with names in real life, those assigned to patterns affect how the reader will interpret and eventually use that pattern.

We have adopted a pattern template that consists of the following sections:

- *Context:* Sets the environment under which the pattern exists.

- *Problem:* Describes the design issues faced by the developer.

- *Forces:* Lists the reasons and motivations that affect the problem and the solution. The list of forces highlights the reasons why one might choose to use the pattern and provides a justification for using the pattern.

- *Solution:* Describes the solution approach briefly and the solution elements in detail. The solution section contains two subsections:

  - *Structure:* Uses UML class diagrams to show the basic structure of the solution. The UML Sequence diagrams in this section present the dynamic mechanisms of the solution. There is a detailed explanation of the participants and collaborations.

  - *Strategies:* Describes different ways a pattern may be implemented. Please see "Patterns Versus Strategies" on page 127 to gain a better understanding of strategies. Where a strategy can be demonstated using code, we include a code snippet in this section. If the code is more elaborate and lengthier than a snippet, we include it in the "Sample Code" section of the pattern template.

- *Consequences:* Here we describe the pattern trade-offs. Generally, this section focuses on the results of using a particular pattern or its strategy, and notes the pros and cons that may result from the application of the pattern.

- *Sample Code:* This section includes example implementations and code listings for the patterns and the strategies. This section is rendered optional if code samples can be adequately included with the discussion in the "Strategies" section.

- *Related Patterns:* This section lists other relevant patterns in the J2EE Pattern Catalog or from other external resources, such as the GoF design patterns. For each related pattern, there is a brief description of its relationship to the pattern being described.

J2EE Pattern Relationships

A recent focus group of architects and designers raised a major concern: There seems to be a lack of understanding of how to apply patterns in combination to form larger solutions. We address this problem with a high-level visual of the patterns and their relationships. This diagram is called the J2EE Pattern Relationships Diagram and is shown in Figure 6.2. In Epilogue "J2EE Patterns Applied," we explore example use cases to demonstrate how many patterns come together to form a patterns framework to realize a use case.

Individual patterns offer their context, problem, and solution when addressing a particular need. However, it is important to step back and grasp the big picture to put the patterns to their best use. This grasping the big picture results in better application of the patterns in a J2EE application.

Reiterating Christopher Alexander's quote from Chapter 1, a pattern does not exist in isolation and needs the support of other patterns to bring meaning and usefulness. Virtually every pattern in the catalog has a relationship to other patterns. Understanding these relationships when designing and architecting a solution helps in the following ways:

- Enables you to consider what other new problems may be introduced when you consider applying a pattern to solve your problem. This is the domino effect: What new problems are introduced when a particular pattern is introduced into the architecture? It is critical to identify these conflicts before coding begins.

- Enables you to revisit the pattern relationships to determine alternate solutions. After possible problems are identified, revisit the pattern relationships and collect alternate solutions. Perhaps the new problems can be addressed by selecting a different pattern or by using another pattern in combination with the one you have already chosen.

Figure 6.2 shows the relationships between the patterns.

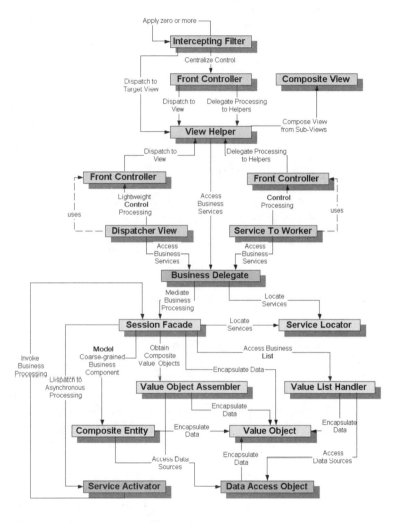

Figure 6.2 J2EE pattern relationships

Intercepting Filter intercepts incoming requests and outgoing responses and applies a filter. These filters may be added and removed in a declarative manner, allowing them to be applied unobtrusively in a variety of combinations. After this preprocessing and/or post-processing is complete, the final filter in the group vectors control to the original target object. For an incoming request, this is often a Front Controller, but may be a View.

Front Controller is a container to hold the common processing logic that occurs within the presentation tier and that may otherwise be erroneously placed in a View. A controller handles requests and manages content retrieval, security, view management, and navigation, delegating to a Dispatcher component to dispatch to a View.

View Helper encourages the separation of formatting-related code from other business logic. It suggests using Helper components to encapsulate logic relating to initiating content retrieval, validation, and adapting and formatting the model. The View component is then left to encapsulate the presentation formatting. Helper components typically delegate to the Business Services via a Business Delegate, while a View may be composed of multiple subcomponents to create its template.

Composite View suggests composing a View from numerous atomic pieces. Multiple smaller views, both static and dynamic, are pieced together to create a single template.

Business Delegate reduces coupling between tiers and provides an entry point for accessing the services that are provided by another tier. The Delegate may also provide results caching for common requests to improve performance. A Business Delegate typically uses a Service Locator to locate service objects, such as an EJB Home object and JMS Connection factory.

The *Service to Worker* and *Dispatcher View* patterns represent a common combination of other patterns from the catalog. The two patterns share a common structure, consisting of a controller working with a Dispatcher, Views, and Helpers. The *Service to Worker* and the *Dispatcher View* patterns are identical with respect to the components involved, but differ in the division of labor among those components. Unlike the *Service to Worker* pattern, the *Dispatcher View* pattern suggests deferring content retrieval and error handling to the time of View Processing. Also, the *Dispatcher View* pattern suggests the Dispatcher plays a more limited role in View Management, as the choice of View is typically already included in the request.

The *Session Façade* provides coarse-grained services to the clients by hiding the complexities of the business object interactions. The Session Façade may use the Service Locator pattern to locate services. The Session façade may also use other patterns to provide its services: *Value Object, Value Object Assembler, Value List Handler, Service Activator,* and *Data Access Object.*

The *Value Object* pattern provides the best techniques and strategies to exchange data across tiers (that is, across system boundaries). This pattern attempts to reduce the network overhead by minimizing the number of network calls to get data from the business tier.

The *Value Object Assembler* constructs a composite value object from various sources. These sources could be EJB components, Data Access Objects, or other arbitrary Java objects. This pattern is most useful when the client needs to obtain data for the application model or part of the model.

The *Value List Handler* uses the GoF iterator pattern to provide query execution and processing services. The Value List Handler may also cache the results and return subsets of the result to the clients as requested. By using this pattern, it is possible to avoid overheads associated with finding large numbers of entity beans.

The *Composite Entity* pattern groups parent-dependent objects into a coarse grained entity bean. It shows how to aggregate objects into a tree with a parent object that manages its dependent objects.

The *Service Activator* pattern enables asynchronous processing for enterprise bean components. The EJB specification version 2.0 defines a new type of enterprise bean called *message-driven bean* that provides similar functionality. However, this pattern can be leveraged by all EJB applications that have a need for asynchronous processing with enterprise bean components.

The *Data Access Object* pattern provides loose coupling between the business and resource tiers for enterprise beans that use bean-managed persistence. The Data Access Object intercepts and services all access to the resource tier, making the implementation details of the resource tiers transparent to the clients. The data in the resource tier can reside in database systems, proprietary systems, other external systems and services. By using this pattern, you can build applications that are more flexible and portable.

Relationship to Known Patterns

There is a wealth of software pattern documentation available today. The patterns in these different books are at various levels of abstraction. There are architecture patterns, design patterns, analysis patterns, and programming patterns. The most popular and influential of these books is *Design Patterns: Elements of Reusable Object-Oriented Software,* [GoF] better known as the Gang of Four, or GoF book. The patterns in the GoF book describe expert solutions for object design.

Our pattern catalog includes patterns that describe the structure of an application and others that describe design elements.

The unifying theme of the pattern catalog is its support of the J2EE platform. In some cases, the patterns in the catalog are based on or related to an existing pattern in the literature. In these cases, we communicate this relationship by referencing the existing pattern in the name of the J2EE pattern and/or including a reference and citation in the "Related Patterns" section at the end of each pattern description. For example, some patterns are based on GoF patterns but are considered in a J2EE context. In those cases, the J2EE pattern name includes the GoF pattern name as well as a reference to the GoF pattern in the related patterns section.

Patterns Roadmap

Here we present a list of common requirements that architects encounter when creating solutions with the J2EE. We present the requirement or motivation in a brief statement, followed by a list of one or more patterns addressing that requirement. While this requirements list is not exhaustive, we hope that it helps you to quickly identify the relevant patterns based on your needs.

Table 6-6 shows the functions typically handled by the presentation tier patterns and indicates which pattern provides a solution.

Table 6-6 Presentation Tier Patterns

If you are looking for this	Find it here	
Preprocessing or post-processing of your requests	"Intercepting Filter" on page 152	Pattern
Centralizing control for request handling	"Front Controller" on page 172, "Intercepting Filter" on page 152	Pattern
Adding logging, debugging, or some other behavior to be completed for each request	"Front Controller" on page 172, "Intercepting Filter" on page 152	Pattern
Creating a generic command interface for delegating processing from a controller to helper components	"Front Controller" on page 172	Pattern
Whether to implement your Controller as a servlet or JSP	"Front Controller" on page 172	Pattern

Table 6-6 Presentation Tier Patterns (continued)

If you are looking for this	*Find it here*	
Creating a View from numerous sub-Views	"Composite View" on page 203	**Pattern**
Whether to implement your View as a servlet or JSP	"View Helper" on page 186	**Pattern**
How to partition your View and Model	"View Helper" on page 186	**Pattern**
Where to encapsulate your presentation-related data formatting logic	"View Helper" on page 186	**Pattern**
Whether to implement your Helper components as JavaBeans or Custom tags	"View Helper" on page 186	**Pattern**
Combining multiple presentation patterns	"Service to Worker" on page 216, "Dispatcher View" on page 231	**Pattern**
Where to encapsulate View Management and Navigation logic, which involves choosing a View and dispatching to it	"Service to Worker" on page 216, "Dispatcher View" on page 231	**Pattern**
Where to store session state	"Session State on Client" on page 36, "Session State in the Presentation Tier" on page 37, and "Storing State on the Business Tier" on page 57	**Design**
Controlling client access to a certain View or sub-View	"Controlling Client Access" on page 38 "Hide Resource From a Client" on page 100	**Design** **Refactoring**
Controlling the flow of requests into the application	"Duplicate Form Submissions" on page 43 "Introduce Synchronizer Token" on page 77	**Design** **Refactoring**
Controlling duplicate form submissions	"Duplicate Form Submissions" on page 43 "Introduce Synchronizer Token" on page 77	**Design** **Refactoring**

Table 6-6 Presentation Tier Patterns (continued)

If you are looking for this	*Find it here*	
Design issues using JSP standard property auto-population mechanism via <jsp:setProperty>	"Helper Properties—Integrity and Consistency" on page 46	**Design**
Reducing coupling between presentation tier and business tier	"Hide Presentation Tier-Specific Details From the Business Tier" on page 91 "Introduce Business Delegate" on page 106	**Refactoring**
Partitioning Data Access Code	"Separate Data Access Code" on page 113	**Refactoring**

Table 6-7 shows the functions handled by the business tier patterns and indicates where you can find the particular pattern or patterns that may provide solutions.

Table 6-7 Business Tier Patterns

If you are looking for this	*Find it here*	
Minimize coupling between presentation and business tiers	"Business Delegate" on page 248	**Pattern**
Cache business services for clients	"Business Delegate" on page 248	**Pattern**
Hide implementation details of business service lookup/creation/access	"Business Delegate" on page 248, "Service Locator" on page 367	**Pattern**
Isolate vendor and technology dependencies for services lookup	"Service Locator" on page 367	**Pattern**
Provide uniform method for business service lookup and creation	"Service Locator" on page 367	**Pattern**
Hide the complexity and dependencies for enterprise bean and JMS component lookup	"Service Locator" on page 367	**Pattern**
Transfer data between business objects and clients across tiers	"Value Object" on page 261	**Pattern**

Table 6-7 Business Tier Patterns (continued)

If you are looking for this	Find it here	
Minimize code duplication between entity beans and Value Object classes	"Value Object" on page 261	Pattern
Provide simpler uniform interface to clients	"Business Delegate" on page 248	Pattern
Reduce remote method invocations by providing coarse-grained method access to business tier components	"Session Facade" on page 291	Pattern
Manage relationships between enterprise bean components and hide the complexity of interactions	"Session Facade" on page 291	Pattern
Protect the business tier components from direct exposure to clients	"Session Facade" on page 291, "Business Delegate" on page 248	Pattern
Provide uniform boundary access to business tier components	"Session Facade" on page 291	Pattern
Design complex entity beans	"Composite Entity" on page 310	Pattern
Identify coarse-grained objects and dependent objects for entity bean design	"Composite Entity" on page 310	Pattern
Design for coarse-grained entity beans	"Composite Entity" on page 310	Pattern
Reduce or eliminate the entity bean clients' dependency on the database schema	"Composite Entity" on page 310	Pattern
Reduce or eliminate entity bean to entity bean relationships	"Composite Entity" on page 310, "Session Facade" on page 291	Pattern
Reduce number of entity beans and improve manageability	"Composite Entity" on page 310	Pattern
Obtain the data model for the application from various business tier components	"Value Object Assembler" on page 339	Pattern
On the fly construction of the data model	"Value Object Assembler" on page 339	Pattern

Table 6-7 Business Tier Patterns (continued)

If you are looking for this	Find it here	
Hide the complexity of data model construction from the clients	"Value Object Assembler" on page 340	**Pattern**
Provide business tier query and results list processing facility	"Value List Handler" on page 354	**Pattern**
Minimize the overhead of using enterprise bean finder methods	"Value List Handler" on page 354	**Pattern**
Provide query-results caching for clients on the server side with forward and backward navigation	"Value List Handler" on page 354	**Pattern**
Use session beans as business tier facades	"Session Beans as Business-Tier Facades" on page 57	**Design**
Trade-offs between using stateful and stateless session beans	"Session Bean—Stateless Versus Stateful" on page 56	**Design**
Provide protection to entity beans from direct client access	"Wrap Entities With Session" on page 104	**Refactoring**
Encapsulate business services to hide the implementation details of the business tier	"Introduce Business Delegate" on page 106	**Refactoring**
Coding business logic in entity beans	"Business Logic in Entity Beans" on page 60 "Move Business Logic to Session" on page 112	**Design** **Refactoring**
Provide session beans as coarse-grained business services	"Merge Session Beans" on page 108 "Wrap Entities With Session" on page 104	**Refactoring** **Refactoring**
Minimize and/or eliminate network and container overhead due to entity-bean-to-entity-bean communication	"Reduce Inter-Entity Bean Communication" on page 110	**Refactoring**
Partitioning Data Access Code	"Separate Data Access Code" on page 113	**Refactoring**

Table 6-8 shows the functions typically handled by the presentation tier patterns and indicates which pattern provides a solution.

Table 6-8 Integration Tier Patterns

If you are looking for this	Find it here	
Minimize coupling between business and resource tiers	"Data Access Object" on page 390	Pattern
Centralize access to resource tiers	"Data Access Object" on page 390	Pattern
Minimize complexity of resource access in business tier components	"Data Access Object" on page 390	Pattern
Provide asynchronous processing for enterprise bean components	"Service Activator" on page 408	Pattern
Send a message to an enterprise bean component	"Service Activator" on page 408	Pattern

Summary

So far, we have seen the basic concepts behind the J2EE patterns, understood the tiers for pattern categorization, explored the relationships between different patterns, and taken a look at the roadmap to help guide you to a particular pattern. In the following chapters, we present the patterns individually. They are grouped into chapters based on the tier into which each has been categorized.

PRESENTATION TIER PATTERNS

Topics in This Chapter

- Intercepting Filter
- Front Controller
- View Helper
- Composite View
- Service to Worker
- Dispatcher View

Chapter 7

Intercepting Filter

Context

The presentation-tier request handling mechanism receives many different types of requests, which require varied types of processing. Some requests are simply forwarded to the appropriate handler component, while other requests must be modified, audited, or uncompressed before being further processed.

Problem

Preprocessing and post-processing of a client Web request and response are required.

When a request enters a Web application, it often must pass several entrance tests prior to the main processing stage. For example,

- *Has the client been authenticated?*
- *Does the client have a valid session?*
- *Is the client's IP address from a trusted network?*
- *Does the request path violate any constraints?*
- *What encoding does the client use to send the data?*
- *Do we support the browser type of the client?*

Some of these checks are tests, resulting in a yes or no answer that determines whether processing will continue. Other checks manipulate the incoming data stream into a form suitable for processing.

The classic solution consists of a series of conditional checks, with any failed check aborting the request. Nested if/else statements are a standard strategy, but this solution leads to code fragility and a copy-and-paste style of programming, because the flow of the filtering and the action of the filters is compiled into the application.

The key to solving this problem in a flexible and unobtrusive manner is to have a simple mechanism for adding and removing processing components, in which each component completes a specific filtering action.

Forces

- Common processing, such as checking the data-encoding scheme or logging information about each request, completes per request.
- Centralization of common logic is desired.
- Services should be easy to add or remove unobtrusively without affecting existing components, so that they can be used in a variety of combinations, such as
  - Logging and authentication
  - Debugging and transformation of output for a specific client
  - Uncompressing and converting encoding scheme of input

Solution

Create pluggable filters to process common services in a standard manner without requiring changes to core request processing code. The filters intercept incoming requests and outgoing responses, allowing preprocessing and post-processing. We are able to add and remove these filters unobtrusively, without requiring changes to our existing code.

We are able, in effect, to decorate our main processing with a variety of common services, such as security, logging, debugging, and so forth. These filters are components that are independent of the main application code, and they may be added or removed declaratively. For example, a deployment configuration file may be modified to set up a chain of filters. The same configuration file might include a mapping of specific URLs to this filter chain. When a client requests a resource that matches this configured URL mapping, the filters in the chain are each processed in order before the requested target resource is invoked.

Structure

Figure 7.1 represents the Intercepting Filter pattern.

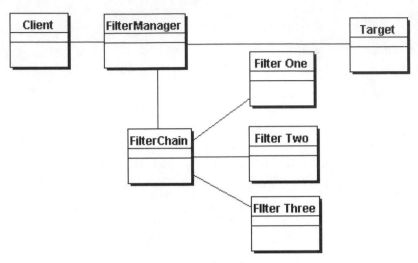

Figure 7.1 Intercepting Filter pattern class diagram

Participants and Responsibilities

Figure 7.2 represents the Intercepting Filter pattern.

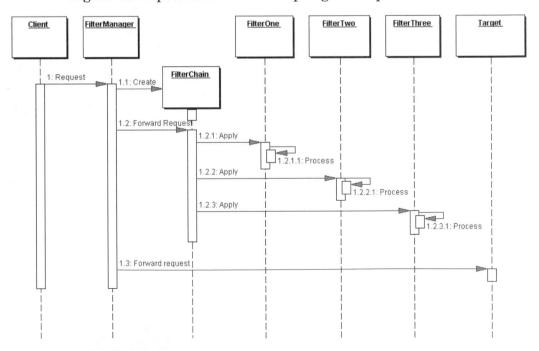

Figure 7.2 Intercepting Filter sequence diagram

FilterManager

The FilterManager manages filter processing. It creates the Filter-Chain with the appropriate filters, in the correct order, and initiates processing.

FilterChain

The FilterChain is an ordered collection of independent filters.

FilterOne, FilterTwo, FilterThree

These are the individual filters that are mapped to a target. The FilterChain coordinates their processing.

Target

The Target is the resource requested by the client.

Strategies

Custom Filter Strategy

Filter is implemented via a custom strategy defined by the developer. This is less flexible and less powerful than the preferred Standard Filter Strategy, which is presented in the next section and is only available in containers supporting the 2.3 servlet specification. The Custom Filter Strategy is less powerful because it cannot provide for the wrapping of request and response objects in a standard and portable way. Additionally, the request object cannot be modified, and some sort of buffering mechanism must be introduced if filters are to control the output stream. To implement the Custom Filter Strategy, the developer could use the Decorator pattern [GoF] to wrap filters around the core request processing logic. For example, there may be a debugging filter that wraps an authentication filter. Example 7.1 and Example 7.2 show how this mechanism might be created programmatically:

Example 7.1 Implementing a Filter – Debugging Filter

```java
public class DebuggingFilter implements Processor {
  private Processor target;

  public DebuggingFilter(Processor myTarget) {
    target = myTarget;
  }

  public void execute(ServletRequest req,
    ServletResponse res) throws IOException,
      ServletException {
    //Do some filter processing here, such as
    // displaying request parameters
    target.execute(req, res);
  }
}
```

Example 7.2 Implementing a Filter – Core Processor

```java
public class CoreProcessor implements Processor {
  private Processor target;
  public CoreProcessor()    {
    this(null);
  }

  public CoreProcessor(Processor myTarget)    {
    target = myTarget;
  }

  public void execute(ServletRequest req,
      ServletResponse res) throws IOException,
      ServletException    {
    //Do core processing here
  }
}
```

In the servlet controller, we delegate to a method called `process-Request` to handle incoming requests, as shown in Example 7.3.

Example 7.3 Handling Requests

```
public void processRequest(ServletRequest req,
   ServletResponse res)
   throws IOException, ServletException {
   Processor processors = new DebuggingFilter(
     new AuthenticationFilter(new CoreProcessor()));
   processors.execute(req, res);

   //Then dispatch to next resource, which is probably
   // the View to display
   dispatcher.dispatch(req, res);
}
```

For example purposes only, imagine that each processing component writes to standard output when it is executed. Example 7.4 shows the possible execution output.

Example 7.4 Messages Written to Standard Output

```
Debugging filter preprocessing completed...
Authentication filter processing completed...
Core processing completed...
Debugging filter post-processing completed...
```

A chain of processors is executed in order. Each processor, except for the last one in the chain, is considered a filter. The final processor component is where we encapsulate the core processing we want to complete for each request. Given this design, we will need to change the code in the CoreProcessor class, as well as in any filter classes, when we want to modify how we handle requests.

Figure 7.3 is a sequence diagram describing the flow of control when using the filter code of Example 7.1, Example 7.2, and Example 7.3.

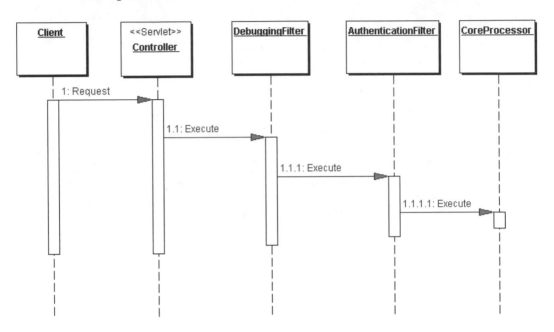

Figure 7.3 Sequence diagram for Custom Filter Strategy, decorator implementation

Notice that when we use a decorator implementation, each filter invokes on the next filter directly, though using a generic interface. Alternatively, this strategy can be implemented using a FilterManager and FilterChain. In this case, these two components coordinate and manage filter processing and the individual filters do not communicate with one another directly. This design approximates that of a servlet 2.3-compliant implementation, though it is still a custom strategy. Example 7.5 is the listing of just such a FilterManager class that creates a FilterChain, which is shown in Example 7.6. The FilterChain adds filters to the chain in the appropriate order (for the sake of brevity, this is done in the FilterChain constructor, but would normally be done in place of the comment), processes the filters, and finally processes the target resource. Figure 7.4 is a sequence diagram for this code.

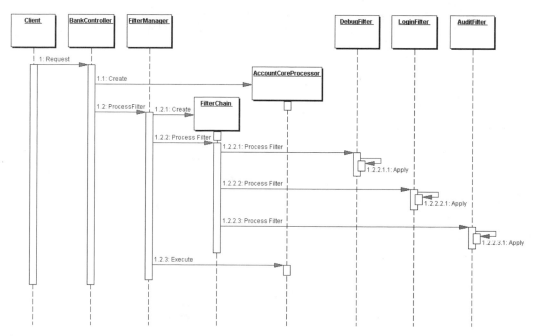

Figure 7.4 Sequence diagram for Custom Filter Strategy, nondecorator implementation

Example 7.5 FilterManager – Custom Filter Strategy

```
public class FilterManager {
  public void processFilter(Filter target,
    javax.servlet.http.HttpServletRequest request,
    javax.servlet.http.HttpServletResponse response)
    throws javax.servlet.ServletException,
      java.io.IOException {
    FilterChain filterChain = new FilterChain();

    // The filter manager builds the filter chain here
    // if necessary

    // Pipe request through Filter Chain
    filterChain.processFilter(request, response);

    //process target resource
    target.execute(request, response);
  }
}
```

Example 7.6 FilterChain – Custom Filter Strategy

```java
public class FilterChain {
  // filter chain
  private Vector myFilters = new Vector();

  // Creates new FilterChain
  public FilterChain() {
    // plug-in default filter services for example
    // only. This would typically be done in the
    // FilterManager, but is done here for example
    // purposes
    addFilter(new DebugFilter());
    addFilter(new LoginFilter());
    addFilter(new AuditFilter());
  }

  public void processFilter(
    javax.servlet.http.HttpServletRequest request,
    javax.servlet.http.HttpServletResponse response)
  throws javax.servlet.ServletException,
    java.io.IOException {
    Filter filter;

    // apply filters
    Iterator filters = myFilters.iterator();
    while (filters.hasNext())
    {
      filter = (Filter)filters.next();
      // pass request & response through various
      // filters
      filter.execute(request, response);
    }
  }

  public void addFilter(Filter filter) {
    myFilters.add(filter);
  }
}
```

This strategy does not allow us to create filters that are as flexible or as powerful as we would like. For one, filters are added and removed programmatically. While we could write a proprietary mechanism for handling adding and removing filters via a configuration file, we still would have no way of wrapping the request and response objects. Additionally, without a sophisticated buffering mechanism, this strategy does not provide flexible postprocessing.

The Standard Filter Strategy provides solutions to these issues, leveraging features of the 2.3 Servlet specification, which has provided a standard solution to the filter dilemma.

Note

As of this writing, the Servlet 2.3 specification is in final draft form.

Standard Filter Strategy

Filters are controlled declaratively using a deployment descriptor, as described in the servlet specification version 2.3, which, as of this writing, is in final draft form. The servlet 2.3 specification includes a standard mechanism for building filter chains and unobtrusively adding and removing filters from those chains. Filters are built around interfaces, and added or removed in a declarative manner by modifying the deployment descriptor for a Web application.

Our example for this strategy will be to create a filter that preprocesses requests of any encoding type such that each request may be handled similarly in our core request handling code. Why might this be necessary? HTML forms that include a file upload use a different encoding type than that of most forms. Thus, form data that accompanies the upload is not available via simple `getParameter()` invocations. So, we create two filters that preprocess requests, translating all encoding types into a single consistent format. The format we choose is to have all form data available as request attributes.

One filter handles the standard form encoding of type `application/x-www-form-urlencoded` and the other handles the less common encoding type `multipart/form-data`, which is used for forms that include file uploads. The filters translate all form data into request attributes, so the core request handling mechanism can work with every request in the same manner, instead of with special casing for different encodings.

Example 7.8 shows a filter that translates requests using the common application form encoding scheme. Example 7.9 shows the filter that handles the translation of requests that use the multipart form encoding scheme. The code for these filters is based on the final draft of the servlet specification, version 2.3. A base filter is used as well, from which both of these filters inherit (see the section "Base Filter Strategy"). The base filter, shown in Example 7.7, provides default behavior for the standard filter callback methods.

Example 7.7 Base Filter – Standard Filter Strategy

```
public class BaseEncodeFilter implements
      javax.servlet.Filter {
  private javax.servlet.FilterConfig myFilterConfig;

  public BaseEncodeFilter()      {   }

  public void doFilter(
    javax.servlet.ServletRequest servletRequest,
    javax.servlet.ServletResponse servletResponse,
    javax.servlet.FilterChain filterChain)
  throws java.io.IOException,
    javax.servlet.ServletException {
    filterChain.doFilter(servletRequest,
        servletResponse);
  }

  public javax.servlet.FilterConfig getFilterConfig()
  {
    return myFilterConfig;
  }

  public void setFilterConfig(
    javax.servlet.FilterConfig filterConfig) {
      myFilterConfig = filterConfig;
  }
}
```

Example 7.8 StandardEncodeFilter – Standard Filter Strategy

```
public class StandardEncodeFilter
  extends BaseEncodeFilter {
  // Creates new StandardEncodeFilter
  public StandardEncodeFilter()    {   }

  public void doFilter(javax.servlet.ServletRequest
    servletRequest,javax.servlet.ServletResponse
    servletResponse,javax.servlet.FilterChain
    filterChain)
  throws java.io.IOException,
    javax.servlet.ServletException {

    String contentType =
      servletRequest.getContentType();
```

Example 7.8 StandardEncodeFilter – Standard Filter Strategy

```
    if ((contentType == null) ||
      contentType.equalsIgnoreCase(
        "application/x-www-form-urlencoded"))      {
        translateParamsToAttributes(servletRequest,
          servletResponse);
    }

    filterChain.doFilter(servletRequest,
      servletResponse);
  }

  private void translateParamsToAttributes(
    ServletRequest request, ServletResponse response)
  {
    Enumeration paramNames =
        request.getParameterNames();

    while (paramNames.hasMoreElements())       {
      String paramName = (String)
          paramNames.nextElement();

      String [] values;

      values = request.getParameterValues(paramName);
      System.err.println("paramName = " + paramName);
      if (values.length == 1)
        request.setAttribute(paramName, values[0]);
      else
        request.setAttribute(paramName, values);
    }
  }
}
```

Example 7.9 MultipartEncodeFilter – Standard Filter Strategy

```
public class MultipartEncodeFilter extends
  BaseEncodeFilter {
  public MultipartEncodeFilter() { }
  public void doFilter(javax.servlet.ServletRequest
    servletRequest, javax.servlet.ServletResponse
    servletResponse,javax.servlet.FilterChain
    filterChain)
  throws java.io.IOException,
    javax.servlet.ServletException {
```

Example 7.9 MultipartEncodeFilter – Standard Filter Strategy

```
    String contentType =
      servletRequest.getContentType();
    // Only filter this request if it is multipart
    // encoding
    if (contentType.startsWith(
              "multipart/form-data")){
      try {
        String uploadFolder =
          getFilterConfig().getInitParameter(
            "UploadFolder");
        if (uploadFolder == null) uploadFolder = ".";

        /** The MultipartRequest class is:
        * Copyright (C) 2001 by Jason Hunter
        * <jhunter@servlets.com>. All rights reserved.
        **/
        MultipartRequest multi = new
          MultipartRequest(servletRequest,
                           uploadFolder,
                           1 * 1024 * 1024 );
        Enumeration params =
            multi.getParameterNames();
        while (params.hasMoreElements()) {
          String name = (String)params.nextElement();
          String value = multi.getParameter(name);
          servletRequest.setAttribute(name, value);
        }

        Enumeration files = multi.getFileNames();
        while (files.hasMoreElements()) {
          String name = (String)files.nextElement();
          String filename =
            multi.getFilesystemName(name);
          String type = multi.getContentType(name);
          File f = multi.getFile(name);
          // At this point, do something with the
          // file, as necessary
        }
      }
      catch (IOException e)
      {
        LogManager.logMessage(
          "error reading or saving file"+ e);
      }
    } // end if
    filterChain.doFilter(servletRequest,
                         servletResponse);
  } // end method doFilter()
}
```

The following excerpt in Example 7.10 is from the deployment descriptor for the Web application containing this example. It shows how these two filters are registered and then mapped to a resource, in this case a simple test servlet. Additionally, the sequence diagram for this example is shown in Figure 7.5.

Example 7.10 Deployment Descriptor – Standard Filter Strategy

```
.
.
.
<filter>
    <filter-name>StandardEncodeFilter</filter-name>
    <display-name>StandardEncodeFilter</display-name>
    <description></description>
    <filter-class> corepatterns.filters.encodefilter.
           StandardEncodeFilter</filter-class>
  </filter>
  <filter>
    <filter-name>MultipartEncodeFilter</filter-name>
    <display-name>MultipartEncodeFilter</display-name>
    <description></description>
    <filter-class>corepatterns.filters.encodefilter.
           MultipartEncodeFilter</filter-class>
    <init-param>
      <param-name>UploadFolder</param-name>
      <param-value>/home/files</param-value>
    </init-param>
 </filter>
.
.
.
<filter-mapping>
    <filter-name>StandardEncodeFilter</filter-name>
    <url-pattern>/EncodeTestServlet</url-pattern>
  </filter-mapping>
  <filter-mapping>
    <filter-name>MultipartEncodeFilter</filter-name>
    <url-pattern>/EncodeTestServlet</url-pattern>
  </filter-mapping>
.
.
.
```

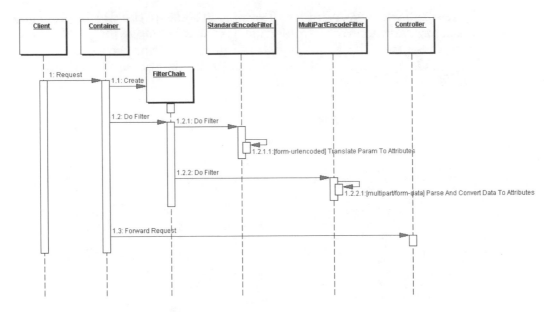

Figure 7.5 Sequence diagram for Intercepting Filter, Standard Filter Strategy – encoding conversion example

The StandardEncodeFilter and the MultiPartEncodeFilter intercept control when a client makes a request to the controller servlet. The container fulfills the role of filter manager and vectors control to these filters by invoking their `doFilter` methods. After completing its processing, each filter passes control to its containing FilterChain, which it instructs to execute the next filter. Once both of the filters have received and subsequently relinquished control, the next component to receive control is the actual target resource, in this case the controller servlet.

Filters, as supported in version 2.3 of the servlet specification, also support wrapping the request and response objects. This feature provides for a much more powerful mechanism than can be built using the custom implementation suggested by the Custom Filter Strategy. Of course, a hybrid approach combining the two strategies could be custom built as well, but would still lack the power of the Standard Filter Strategy as supported by the servlet specification.

Base Filter Strategy

A base filter serves as a common superclass for all filters. Common features can be encapsulated in the base filter and shared among all filters. For example, a base filter is a good place to include default behavior for the container callback methods in the Declared Filter Strategy. Example 7.11 shows how this can be done.

Example 7.11 Base Filter Strategy

```
public class BaseEncodeFilter implements
  javax.servlet.Filter {
  private javax.servlet.FilterConfig myFilterConfig;

  public BaseEncodeFilter() {}

  public void doFilter(javax.servlet.ServletRequest
    servletRequest,javax.servlet.ServletResponse
    servletResponse, javax.servlet.FilterChain
    filterChain) throws java.io.IOException,
    javax.servlet.ServletException {

    filterChain.doFilter(servletRequest,
      servletResponse);
  }

  public javax.servlet.FilterConfig getFilterConfig() {
    return myFilterConfig;
  }

  public void
  setFilterConfig(javax.servlet.FilterConfig
    filterConfig) {
    myFilterConfig = filterConfig;
  }
}
```

Template Filter Strategy

Using a base filter from which all others inherit (see "Base Filter Strategy" in this chapter) allows the base class to provide template method [Gof] functionality. In this case, the base filter is used to dictate the general steps that every filter must complete, while leaving the specifics of *how* to complete that step to each filter subclass. Typically, these would be coarsely defined, basic methods that simply impose a limited structure on each template. This strategy can be combined with any other filter strategy, as well. The listings in Example 7.12 and Example 7.13 show how to use this strategy with the Declared Filter Strategy.

Example 7.12 shows a base filter called TemplateFilter, as follows.

Example 7.12 Using a Template Filter Strategy

```java
public abstract class TemplateFilter implements
  javax.servlet.Filter {
  private FilterConfig filterConfig;

  public void setFilterConfig(FilterConfig fc) {
    filterConfig=fc;
  }

  public FilterConfig getFilterConfig() {
    return filterConfig;
  }

  public void doFilter(ServletRequest request,
    ServletResponse response, FilterChain chain)
    throws IOException, ServletException {
    // Common processing for all filters can go here
    doPreProcessing(request, response, chain);

    // Common processing for all filters can go here
    doMainProcessing(request, response, chain);

    // Common processing for all filters can go here
    doPostProcessing(request, response, chain);

    // Common processing for all filters can go here

    // Pass control to the next filter in the chain or
    // to the target resource
    chain.doFilter(request, response);
  }
  public void doPreProcessing(ServletRequest request,
    ServletResponse response, FilterChain chain) {
  }

  public void doPostProcessing(ServletRequest request,
    ServletResponse response, FilterChain chain) {
  }

  public abstract void doMainProcessing(ServletRequest
  request, ServletResponse response, FilterChain
  chain);
}
```

Given this class definition for TemplateFilter, each filter is implemented as a subclass that must only implement the `doMainProc-essing` method. These subclasses have the option, though, of implementing all three methods if they desire. Example 7.13 is an example of a filter subclass that implements the one mandatory method (dictated by our template filter) and the optional preprocessing method. Additionally, a sequence diagram for using this strategy is shown in Figure 7.6.

Example 7.13 Debugging Filter

```
public class DebuggingFilter extends TemplateFilter {
  public void doPreProcessing(ServletRequest req,
    ServletResponse res, FilterChain chain) {
    //do some preprocessing here
  }

  public void doMainProcessing(ServletRequest req,
    ServletResponse res, FilterChain chain) {
    //do the main processing;
  }
}
```

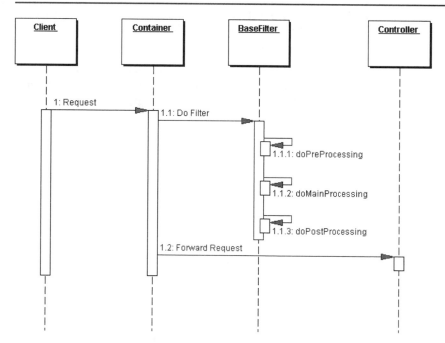

Figure 7.6 Intercepting Filter, Template Filter Strategy sequence diagram

In the sequence diagram in Figure 7.6, filter subclasses, such as DebuggingFilter, define specific processing by overriding the abstract `doMainProcessing` method and, optionally, `doPreProcessing` and `doPostProcessing`. Thus, the template filter imposes a structure to each filter's processing, as well as providing a place for encapsulating code that is common to every filter.

Consequences

- ### *Centralizes Control with Loosely Coupled Handlers*
  Filters provide a central place for handling processing across multiple requests, as does a controller. Filters are better suited to massaging requests and responses for ultimate handling by a target resource, such as a controller. Additionally, a controller often ties together the management of numerous unrelated common services, such as authentication, logging, encryption, and so forth, while filtering allows for much more loosely coupled handlers, which can be combined in various combinations.

- ### *Improves Reusability*
  Filters promote cleaner application partitioning and encourages reuse. These pluggable interceptors are transparently added or removed from existing code, and due to their standard interface, they work in any combination and are reusable for varying presentations.

- ### *Declarative and Flexible Configuration*
  Numerous services are combined in varying permutations without a single recompile of the core code base.

- ### *Information Sharing is Inefficient*
  Sharing information between filters can be inefficient, since by definition each filter is loosely coupled. If large amounts of information must be shared between filters, then this approach may prove to be costly.

Related Patterns

- ### Front Controller
  The controller solves some similar problems, but is better suited to handling core processing.

- ### Decorator [GoF]
  The Intercepting Filter pattern is related to the Decorator pattern, which provides for dynamically pluggable wrappers.

- **Template Method [GoF]**
  The Template Method pattern is used to implement the Template Filter Strategy.

- **Interceptor [POSA2]**
  The Intercepting Filter pattern is related to the Interceptor pattern, which allows services to be added transparently and triggered automatically.

- **Pipes and Filters [POSA1]**
  The Intercepting Filter pattern is related to the Pipes and Filters pattern.

Front Controller

Context

The presentation-tier request handling mechanism must control and coordinate processing of each user across multiple requests. Such control mechanisms may be managed in either a centralized or decentralized manner.

Problem

The system requires a centralized access point for presentation-tier request handling to support the integration of system services, content retrieval, view management, and navigation. When the user accesses the view directly without going through a centralized mechanism, two problems may occur:

- Each view is required to provide its own system services, often resulting in duplicate code.
- View navigation is left to the views. This may result in commingled view content and view navigation.

Additionally, distributed control is more difficult to maintain, since changes will often need to be made in numerous places.

Forces

- Common system services processing completes per request. For example, the security service completes authentication and authorization checks.
- Logic that is best handled in one central location is instead replicated within numerous views.
- Decision points exist with respect to the retrieval and manipulation of data.
- Multiple views are used to respond to similar business requests.
- A centralized point of contact for handling a request may be useful, for example, to control and log a user's progress through the site.
- System services and view management logic are relatively sophisticated.

Solution

Use a controller as the initial point of contact for handling a request. The controller manages the handling of the request, including invoking security services such as authentication and authorization, delegating business processing, managing the choice of an appropriate view, handling errors, and managing the selection of content creation strategies.

The controller provides a centralized entry point that controls and manages Web request handling. By centralizing decision points and controls, the controller also helps reduce the amount of Java code, called *scriptlets,* embedded in the JSP.

Centralizing control in the controller and reducing business logic in the view promotes code reuse across requests. It is a preferable approach to the alternative—embedding code in multiple views—because that approach may lead to a more error-prone, reuse-by-copy-and-paste environment.

Typically, a controller coordinates with a dispatcher component. Dispatchers are responsible for view management and navigation. Thus, a dispatcher chooses the next view for the user and vectors control to the resource. Dispatchers may be encapsulated within the controller directly or can be extracted into a separate component.

While the Front Controller pattern suggests centralizing the handling of all requests, it does not limit the number of handlers in the system, as does a Singleton. An application may use multiple controllers in a system, each mapping to a set of distinct services.

Structure

Figure 7.7 represents the Front Controller class diagram pattern.

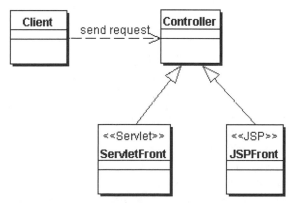

Figure 7.7 Front Controller class diagram

Participants and Responsibilities

Figure 7.8 shows the sequence diagram representing the Front Controller pattern. It depicts how the controller handles a request.

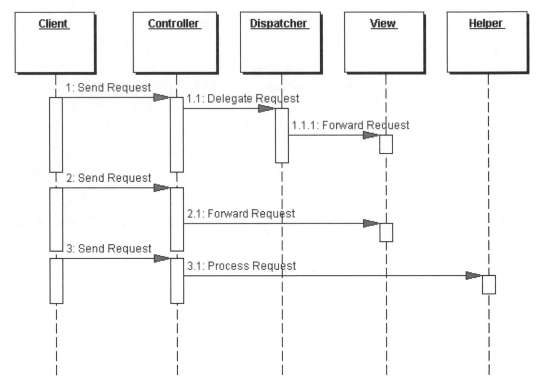

Figure 7.8 Front Controller sequence diagram

Controller

The controller is the initial contact point for handling all requests in the system. The controller may delegate to a helper to complete authentication and authorization of a user or to initiate contact retrieval.

Dispatcher

A dispatcher is responsible for view management and navigation, managing the choice of the next view to present to the user, and providing the mechanism for vectoring control to this resource.

A dispatcher can be encapsulated within a controller or can be a separate component working in coordination. The dispatcher provides either a static dispatching to the view or a more sophisticated dynamic dispatching mechanism.

The dispatcher uses the RequestDispatcher object (supported in the servlet specification) and encapsulates some additional processing.

Helper

A helper is responsible for helping a view or controller complete its processing. Thus, helpers have numerous responsibilities, including gathering data required by the view and storing this intermediate model, in which case the helper is sometimes referred to as a value bean. Additionally, helpers may adapt this data model for use by the view. Helpers can service requests for data from the view by simply providing access to the raw data or by formatting the data as Web content.

A view may work with any number of helpers, which are typically implemented as JavaBeans (JSP 1.0+) and custom tags (JSP 1.1+). Additionally, a helper may represent a Command object, a delegate (see "Business Delegate" on page 248), or an XSL Transformer, which is used in combination with a stylesheet to adapt and convert the model into the appropriate form.

View

A view represents and displays information to the client. The view retrieves information from a model. Helpers support views by encapsulating and adapting the underlying data model for use in the display.

Strategies

There are several strategies for implementing a controller.

Servlet Front Strategy

This strategy suggests implementing the controller as a servlet. Though semantically equivalent, it is preferred to the JSP Front Strategy. The controller manages the aspects of request handling that are related to business processing and control flow. These responsibilities are related to, but logically independent of, display formatting, and are more appropriately encapsulated in a servlet rather than in a JSP.

The Servlet Front Strategy does have some potential drawbacks. In particular, it does not leverage some of the JSP runtime environment utilities, such as automatic population of request parameters into helper properties. Fortunately, this drawback is minimal because it is relatively easy to create or obtain similar utilities for general use. There is also the possibility that the functionality of some of the JSP utilities may be included as standard servlet features in a future version of the servlet specification. Example 7.14 is an example of the Servlet Front Strategy.

Example 7.14 Servlet Front Strategy Sample Code

```java
public class EmployeeController extends HttpServlet {
  // Initializes the servlet.
  public void init(ServletConfig config) throws
    ServletException {
    super.init(config);
  }

  // Destroys the servlet.
  public void destroy() {
  }

  /** Processes requests for both HTTP
   * <code>GET</code> and <code>POST</code> methods.
   * @param request servlet request
   * @param response servlet response
   */
  protected void processRequest(HttpServletRequest
    request, HttpServletResponse response)
    throws ServletException, java.io.IOException {
    String page;

    /**ApplicationResources provides a simple API
     * for retrieving constants and other
     * preconfigured values**/
    ApplicationResources resource =
      ApplicationResources.getInstance();
    try {

      // Use a helper object to gather parameter
      // specific information.
      RequestHelper helper = new
        RequestHelper(request);

      Command cmdHelper= helper.getCommand();

      // Command helper perform custom operation
      page = cmdHelper.execute(request, response);

    }
    catch (Exception e) {
```

Example 7.14 Servlet Front Strategy Sample Code

```java
        LogManager.logMessage(
          "EmployeeController:exception : " +
          e.getMessage());
        request.setAttribute(resource.getMessageAttr(),
          "Exception occurred : " + e.getMessage());
        page = resource.getErrorPage(e);
      }
      // dispatch control to view
      dispatch(request, response, page);
  }

  /** Handles the HTTP <code>GET</code> method.
   * @param request servlet request
   * @param response servlet response
   */
  protected void doGet(HttpServletRequest request,
    HttpServletResponse response)
    throws ServletException, java.io.IOException {
      processRequest(request, response);
  }

  /** Handles the HTTP <code>POST</code> method.
   * @param request servlet request
   * @param response servlet response
   */
  protected void doPost(HttpServletRequest request,
    HttpServletResponse response)
    throws ServletException, java.io.IOException {
        processRequest(request, response);
  }

  /** Returns a short description of the servlet */
  public String getServletInfo() {
    return "Front Controller Pattern" +
      " Servlet Front Strategy Example";
  }

  protected void dispatch(HttpServletRequest request,
    HttpServletResponse response,
    String page)
  throws  javax.servlet.ServletException,
    java.io.IOException {
    RequestDispatcher dispatcher =
      getServletContext().getRequestDispatcher(page);
    dispatcher.forward(request, response);
  }
}
```

JSP Front Strategy

This strategy suggests implementing the controller as a JSP. Though semantically equivalent, the Servlet Front Strategy is preferred to the JSP Front Strategy. Since the controller handles processing that is not specifically related to display formatting, it is a mismatch to implement this component as a JSP.

Implementing the controller as a JSP is clearly not preferred for another reason: It requires a software developer to work with a page of markup in order to modify request handling logic. Thus, a software developer will typically find the JSP Front Strategy more cumbersome when completing the cycle of coding, compilation, testing, and debugging. Example 7.15 is an example of the JSP Front Strategy.

Example 7.15 JSP Front Strategy Sample Code

```
<%@page contentType="text/html"%>
<%@ page import="corepatterns.util.*" %>
<html>
<head><title>JSP Front Controller</title></head>
<body>

<h3><center> Employee Profile </h3>

<%
/**Control logic goes here...
   At some point in this code block we retrieve
   employee information, encapsulate it within a value
   object and place this bean in request scope with the
   key "employee". This code has been omitted.

   We either dispatch to another JSP at this point or
   simply allow the remaining portions of scriptlet
   code to execute**/
%>
   <jsp:useBean id="employee" scope="request"
     class="corepatterns.util.EmployeeVO"/>
<FORM method=POST >
<table width="60%">
<tr>
    <td>  First Name : </td>
<td>   <input type="text"
       name="<%=Constants.FLD_FIRSTNAME%>"
       value="<jsp:getProperty name="employee"
       property="firstName"/>"> </td>
</tr>
```

Example 7.15 JSP Front Strategy Sample Code

```
<tr>
    <td>  Last Name : </td>
    <td>     <input type="text"
        name="<%=Constants.FLD_LASTNAME%>"
        value="<jsp:getProperty name="employee"
        property="lastName"/>"></td>
</tr>
<tr>
    <td>  Employee ID : </td>
    <td>     <input type="text"
        name="<%=Constants.FLD_EMPID%>"
        value="<jsp:getProperty name="employee"
        property="id"/>"> </td>
</tr>
<tr>
    <td>     <input type="submit"
        name="employee_profile"> </td>
    <td> </td>
</tr>
</table>
</FORM>

</body>
</html>
```

Command and Controller Strategy

Based on the Command pattern [GoF], the Command and Controller Strategy suggests providing a generic interface to the helper components to which the controller may delegate responsibility, minimizing the coupling among these components (see "View Helper" on page 186 for more information on helper components). Adding to or changing the work that needs to be completed by these helpers does not require any changes to the interface between the controller and the helpers, but rather to the type and/or content of the commands. This provides a flexible and easily extensible mechanism for developers to add request handling behaviors.

Finally, because the command processing is not coupled to the command invocation, the command processing mechanism may be reused with various types of clients, not just with Web browsers. This strategy also facilitates the creation of composite commands (see Composite pattern [GoF]). See Example 7.16 for sample code and Figure 7.9 for a sequence diagram.

Example 7.16 Command and Controller Strategy Sample Code

```
/** This processRequest method is invoked from both
 * the servlet doGet and doPost methods **/
protected void processRequest(HttpServletRequest
  request, HttpServletResponse response)
  throws ServletException, java.io.IOException {

  String resultPage;
  try {
    RequestHelper helper = new RequestHelper(request);

    /** the getCommand() method internally uses a
     factory to retrieve command objects as follows:
     Command command = CommandFactory.create(
        request.getParameter("op"));
    **/
    Command command =  helper.getCommand();

    // delegate request to a command object helper
    resultPage = command.execute(request, response);
  }
  catch (Exception e) {
    LogManager.logMessage("EmployeeController",
      e.getMessage() );
    resultPage = ApplicationResources.getInstance().
                     getErrorPage(e);
  }

  dispatch(request, response, resultPage);
}
```

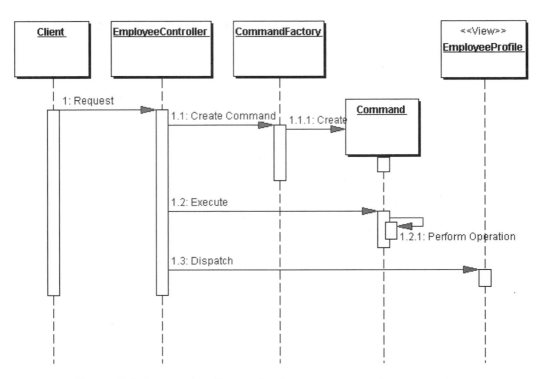

Figure 7.9 Command and Controller Strategy sequence diagram

Physical Resource Mapping Strategy

All requests are made to specific physical resource names rather than logical names. An example is the following URL: `http://some.server.com/resource1.jsp`. In the case of a controller, an example URL might be `http://some.server.com/servlet/Controller`. The Logical Resource Mapping Strategy is typically preferred over this strategy because it provides much greater flexibility. The Logical Resource Mapping Strategy lets you modify resource mappings in a declarative manner, via a configuration file. This is much more flexible than the Physical Resource Mapping Strategy, which requires that you make changes to each resource, as is necessary when implementing this strategy.

Logical Resource Mapping Strategy

Requests are made to logical resource names rather than to specific physical names. The physical resources to which these logical names refer may then be modified in a declarative manner.

For example, the URL `http://some.server.com/process` may be mapped as follows:

```
process=resource1.jsp
    OR
process=resource2.jsp
    OR
process=servletController
```

Multiplexed Resource Mapping Strategy

This is actually a substrategy of Logical Resource Naming Strategy. This strategy maps not just a single logical name, but an entire set of logical names, to a single physical resource. For example, a wildcard mapping might map all requests that end with `.ctrl` to a specific handler.

A request and mapping might look as shown in Table 7-1 .

Table 7-1

Request	Mapping
http://some.server.com/action.ctrl	*.ctrl = servletController

In fact, this is the strategy JSP engines use in order to ensure that requests for JSP resources (that is, resources whose names end in `.jsp`) are processed by a specific handler.

Additional information can also be added to a request, providing further details to leverage for this logical mapping. See Table 7-2 .

Table 7-2

Request	Mapping
http://some.server.com/profile.ctrl?usecase= create	*.ctrl = servletController

A key benefit of using this strategy is that it provides great flexibility when designing your request handling components. When combined with other strategies, such as the Command and Controller Strategy, you can create a powerful request handling framework.

Consider a controller that handles all requests ending in `.ctrl`, as described above. Also, consider the left side of this dot-delimited resource name (`profile` in the above example) to be one part of the name of a use case. Now combine this name with the query parameter value (create in the above example). We are signaling our request handler that we want to process a use case called create profile. Our multiplexed resource mapping sends the request to our servletController, which is part of the mapping shown in Table 7-2 . Our controller creates the appropriate command object, as described in the Command and Controller Strategy. How does the controller know the command object to which it should delegate? Leveraging the additional information in the request URI, the controller delegates to the command object that handles profile creation. This might be a ProfileCommand object that services requests for Profile creation and modification, or it might be a more specific ProfileCreationCommand object.

Dispatcher in Controller Strategy

When the dispatcher functionality is minimal, it can be folded into the controller, as shown in Figure 7.10.

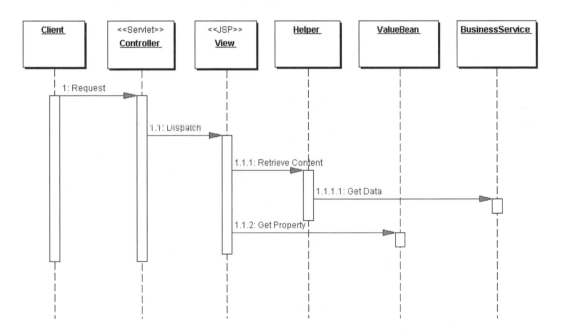

Figure 7.10 Dispatcher in the Controller sequence diagram

Base Front Strategy

Used in combination with the Servlet Front Strategy, this strategy suggests implementing a controller base class, whose implementation other controllers may extend. The base front may contain common and default implementations, while each subclass can override these implementations. The drawback of this strategy is the fact that any shared superclass, while promoting reuse and sharing, raises the issue of creating a fragile hierarchy, where changes necessary for one subclass affect all subclasses.

Filter Controller Strategy

Filters provide similar support for centralizing request processing control (see Intercepting Filter pattern). Thus, some aspects of a controller can reasonably be implemented as a filter. At the same time, filters primarily focus on request interception and decoration, not request processing and response generation. While there are overlapping responsibilities, such as managing logging or debugging, each component complements the other when used appropriately.

Consequences

- **Centralizes Control**

  A controller provides a central place to handle system services and business logic across multiple requests. A controller manages business logic processing and request handling. Centralized access to an application means that requests are easily tracked and logged. Keep in mind, though, that as control centralizes, it is possible to introduce a single point of failure. In practice, this rarely is a problem, though, since multiple controllers typically exist, either within a single server or in a cluster.

- **Improves Manageability of Security**

  A controller centralizes control, providing a choke point for illicit access attempts into the Web application. In addition, auditing a single entrance into the application requires fewer resources than distributing security checks across all pages.

- **Improves Reusability**

  A controller promotes cleaner application partitioning and encourages reuse, as code that is common among components moves into a controller or is managed by a controller.

Related Patterns

- **View Helper**
  The Front Controller pattern, in conjunction with the View Helper pattern, describes factoring business logic out of the view and providing a central point of control and dispatch. Flow logic is factored *forward* into the controller and data handling code moves *back* into the helpers.

- **Intercepting Filter**
  Both Intercepting Filter and Front Controller describe ways to centralize control of certain types of request processing, suggesting different approaches to this issue.

- **Dispatcher View and Service to Worker**
  The Dispatcher View and Service to Worker patterns are another way to name the combination of the View Helper pattern with a dispatcher, and Front Controller pattern. Dispatcher View and Service to Worker, while structurally the same, describe different divisions of labor among components.

View Helper

Context

The system creates presentation content, which requires processing of dynamic business data.

Problem

Presentation tier changes occur often and are difficult to develop and maintain when business data access logic and presentation formatting logic are interwoven. This makes the system less flexible, less reusable, and generally less resilient to change.

Intermingling the business and systems logic with the view processing reduces modularity and also provides a poor separation of roles among Web production and software development teams.

Forces

- Business data assimilation requirements are nontrivial.
- Embedding business logic in the view promotes a copy-and-paste type of reuse. This causes maintenance problems and bugs because a piece of logic is reused in the same or different view by simply duplicating it in the new location.
- It is desirable to promote a clean separation of labor by having different individuals fulfill the roles of software developer and Web production team member.
- One view is commonly used to respond to a particular business request.

Solution

A view contains formatting code, delegating its processing responsibilities to its helper classes, implemented as Java-Beans or custom tags. Helpers also store the view's intermediate data model and serve as business data adapters.

There are multiple strategies for implementing the view component. The JSP View Strategy suggests using a JSP as the view component. This is the preferred strategy, and it is the one most commonly used. The other principal strategy is the Servlet View Strategy, which utilizes a servlet as the view (see the section "Strategies" for more information).

Encapsulating business logic in a helper instead of a view makes our application more modular and facilitates component reuse. Multiple clients, such as controllers and views, may leverage the same helper to retrieve and adapt similar model state for presentation in multiple ways. The only way to reuse logic embedded in a view is by copying and pasting it elsewhere. Furthermore, copy-and-paste duplication makes a system harder to maintain, since the same bug potentially needs to be corrected in multiple places.

A signal that one may need to apply this pattern to existing code is when scriptlet code dominates the JSP view. The overriding goal when applying this pattern, then, is the partitioning of business logic outside of the view. While some logic is best encapsulated within helper objects, other logic is better placed in a centralized component that sits in front of the views and the helpers—this might include logic that is common across multiple requests, such as authentication checks or logging services, for example. Refer to the "Intercepting Filter" on page 152 and "Front Controller" on page 172 for more information on these issues.

If a separate controller is not employed in the architecture, or is not used to handle all requests, then the view component becomes the initial contact point for handling some requests. For certain requests, particularly those involving minimal processing, this scenario works fine. Typically, this situation occurs for pages that are based on static information, such as the first of a set of pages that will be served to a user to gather some information (see "Dispatcher View" on page 231). Additionally, this scenario occurs in some cases when a mechanism is employed to create composite pages (see "Composite View" on page 203).

The View Helper pattern focuses on recommending ways to partition your application responsibilities. For related discussions about issues dealing with directing client requests directly to a view, please refer to the section "Dispatcher View" on page 231.

Structure

Figure 7.11 is the class diagram representing the View Helper pattern.

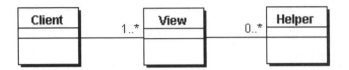

Figure 7.11 View Helper class diagram

Participants and Responsibilities

Figure 7.12 shows the sequence diagram representing the View Helper pattern. A controller typically mediates between the client and the view. In some cases, though, a controller is not used and the view becomes the initial contact point for handling the request. (Also, see Dispatcher View pattern.)

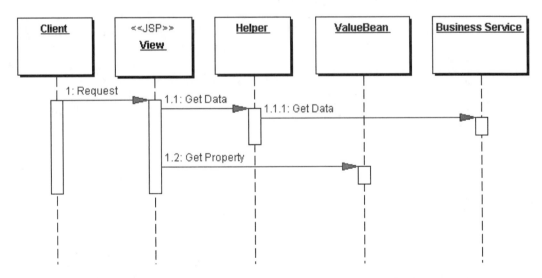

Figure 7.12 View Helper sequence diagram

As noted in the class diagram, there may be no helpers associated with a view. In this simple case, the page may be entirely static or include very small amounts of inline scriptlet code. This scenario is described in the sequence diagram in Figure 7.13.

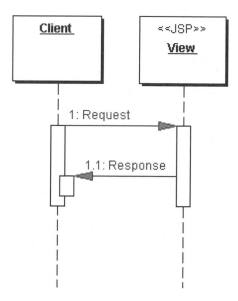

Figure 7.13 View Helper simple sequence diagram

View

A view represents and displays information to the client. The information that is used in a dynamic display is retrieved from a model. Helpers support views by encapsulating and adapting a model for use in a display.

Helper

A helper is responsible for helping a view or controller complete its processing. Thus, helpers have numerous responsibilities, including gathering data required by the view and storing this intermediate model, in which case the helper is sometimes referred to as a value bean. Additionally, helpers may adapt this data model for use by the view. Helpers can service requests for data from the view by simply providing access to the raw data or by formatting the data as Web content.

A view may work with any number of helpers, which are typically implemented as JavaBeans (JSP 1.0+) and custom tags (JSP 1.1+). Additionally, a helper may represent a Command object, a delegate (see "Business Delegate" on page 248), or an XSL Transformer, which is used in combination with a stylesheet to adapt and convert the model into the appropriate form.

ValueBean

A value bean is another name for a helper that is responsible for holding intermediate model state for use by a view. A typical case, as shown in the sequence diagram in Figure 7.12, has the business service returning a value bean in response to a request. In this case, ValueBean fulfills the role of a Value Object (see "Value Object" on page 261).

BusinessService

The business service is a role that is fulfilled by the service the client is seeking to access. Typically, the business service is accessed via a Business delegate. The business delegate's role is to provide control and protection for the business service (see the "Business Delegate" on page 248).

Strategies

JSP View Strategy

The JSP View Strategy suggests using a JSP as the view component. This is the preferred strategy to the Servlet View Strategy. While it is semantically equivalent to the Servlet View Strategy, it is a more elegant solution and is more commonly used. Views are the domain of Web designers, who prefer markup to Java code. Example 7.17 shows a code sample for this strategy. The excerpt is from a source file called `welcome.jsp`, to which a servlet controller dispatches after placing the WelcomeHelper JavaBean in request scope.

Example 7.17 JSP View Strategy Sample Code

```
<jsp:useBean id="welcomeHelper" scope="request"
  class="corepatterns.util.WelcomeHelper" />

<HTML>
<BODY bgcolor="FFFFFF">
<% if (welcomeHelper.nameExists())
{
%>
<center><H3> Welcome <b>
<jsp:getProperty name="welcomeHelper" property="name"
  />
</b><br><br> </H3></center>
<%
}
```

Example 7.17 JSP View Strategy Sample Code

```
%>

<H4><center>Glad you are visiting our
  site!</center></H4>

</BODY>
</HTML>
```

The alternative Servlet View Strategy is typically implemented by embedding HTML markup directly within Java Servlet code. Intermingling Java code and markup tags creates a poor separation of user roles within a project and increases the dependencies on the same resources among multiple members of different teams. When an individual works on a template containing unfamiliar code or tags, it increases the likelihood of an accidental change introducing problems into the system. There is also a reduction in work environment efficiency (too many people sharing the same physical resource) and an increase in source control management complexity. These problems are more likely to occur in larger enterprise environments that have more complicated system requirements and that use teams of developers. They are less likely to occur with small systems that have simple business requirements and use few developers, because the same individual may likely fill the roles mentioned above. However, keep in mind that projects often start small—with simple requirements and few developers—but may ultimately evolve to become sophisticated enough to benefit from these suggestions.

Servlet View Strategy

The Servlet View Strategy utilizes a servlet as the view. It is semantically equivalent to the preferred JSP View Strategy. However, the Servlet View Strategy, as seen in Example 7.18, is often more cumbersome for the software development and Web production teams because it embeds markup tags directly within the Java code. When tags are embedded within the code, the view template is more difficult to update and modify.

Example 7.18 Servlet View Strategy Sample Code

```java
public class Controller extends HttpServlet {
  public void init(ServletConfig config) throws
    ServletException {
    super.init(config);
  }

  public void destroy() { }

  /** Processes requests for both HTTP
   * <code>GET</code> and <code>POST</code> methods.
   * @param request servlet request
   * @param response servlet response
   */
  protected void processRequest(HttpServletRequest
    request, HttpServletResponse response)
    throws ServletException, java.io.IOException {
    String title = "Servlet View Strategy";
    try {
      response.setContentType("text/html");
      java.io.PrintWriter out = response.getWriter();
      out.println("<html><title>"+title+"</title>");
      out.println("<body>");
      out.println("<h2><center>Employees List</h2>");
      EmployeeDelegate delegate =
          new EmployeeDelegate();

      /** ApplicationResources provides a simple API
        * for retrieving constants and other
        * preconfigured values**/
      Iterator employees = delegate.getEmployees(
          ApplicationResources.getInstance().
              getAllDepartments());
      out.println("<table border=2>");
      out.println("<tr><th>First Name</th>" +
        "<th>Last Name</th>" +
          "<th>Designation</th><th>Id</th></tr>");
      while (employees.hasNext()) {
        out.println("<tr>");
        EmployeeVO emp = (EmployeeVO)employees.next();
        out.println("<td>"+emp.getFirstName()+
            "</td>");
        out.println("<td>"+emp.getLastName()+
            "</td>");
        out.println("<td>"+emp.getDesignation()+
            "</td>");
        out.println("<td>"+emp.getId()+"</td>");
        out.println("</tr>");
```

Example 7.18 Servlet View Strategy Sample Code

```java
    }
    out.println("</table>");
    out.println("<br><br>");
    out.println("</body>");
    out.println("</html>");
    out.close();
  }
  catch (Exception e) {
    LogManager.logMessage("Handle this exception",
      e.getMessage() );
  }
}

/** Handles the HTTP <code>GET</code> method.
  * @param request servlet request
  * @param response servlet response
  */
protected void doGet(HttpServletRequest request,
  HttpServletResponse response)
    throws ServletException, java.io.IOException {
      processRequest(request, response);
}

/** Handles the HTTP <code>POST</code> method.
  * @param request servlet request
  * @param response servlet response
  */
protected void doPost(HttpServletRequest request,
  HttpServletResponse response)
    throws ServletException, java.io.IOException {
      processRequest(request, response);
}

/** Returns a short description of the servlet. */
public String getServletInfo() {
  return "Example of Servlet View. " +
          "JSP View is preferable.";
}

/** dispatcher method **/
protected void dispatch(HttpServletRequest request,
    HttpServletResponse response, String page)
throws javax.servlet.ServletException,
    java.io.IOException {
  RequestDispatcher dispatcher =
    getServletContext().getRequestDispatcher(page);
  dispatcher.forward(request, response);
}
}
```

JavaBean Helper Strategy

The helper is implemented as a JavaBean. Using helpers results in a cleaner separation of the view from the business processing in an application, since business logic is factored out of the view and into the helper component. In this case the business logic is encapsulated in a JavaBean, which aids in content retrieval and adapts and stores the model for use by the view.

Using the JavaBean Helper Strategy requires less upfront work than does the Custom Tag Helper Strategy, since JavaBeans are more easily constructed and integrated into a JSP environment. Additionally, even novice developers understand JavaBeans. This strategy is also easier from a manageability standpoint, since the only resulting artifacts are the completed JavaBeans. An example of this strategy is shown in Example 7.19.

Example 7.19 JavaBean Helper Strategy Code Sample

```
<jsp:useBean id="welcomeHelper" scope="request"
  class="corepatterns.util.WelcomeHelper" />

<HTML>
<BODY bgcolor="FFFFFF">
<% if (welcomeHelper.nameExists())
{
%>
<center><H3> Welcome <b>
<jsp:getProperty name="welcomeHelper" property="name"
  />
</b><br><br> </H3></center>
<%
}
%>

<H4><center>Glad you are visiting our
  site!</center></H4>

</BODY>
</HTML>
```

Custom Tag Helper Strategy

The helper is implemented as a custom tag (JSP 1.1+ only). Using helpers results in a cleaner separation of the view from the business processing in an application, since business logic is factored out of the view and into the helper component. In this case the business logic is encapsulated in a custom tag component, which may aid in content retrieval and adapts the model for use by the view.

Using the Custom Tag Helper Strategy requires more upfront work than does the JavaBean Helper Strategy, since custom tag development is moderately complicated relative to JavaBean development. Not only is there more complexity in the development process, but there is much more complexity with respect to integrating and managing the completed tags. To use this strategy, the environment must be configured with numerous generated artifacts, including the tag itself, a tag library descriptor, and configuration files. An excerpt of a JSP View using this strategy is shown in Example 7.20.

Example 7.20 Custom Tag Helper Strategy Sample Code

```
<%@ taglib uri="/web-INF/corepatternstaglibrary.tld"
  prefix="corepatterns" %>
<html>
<head><title>Employee List</title></head>
<body>

<div align="center">
<h3> List of employees in <corepatterns:department
  attribute="id"/> department - Using Custom Tag
  Helper Strategy. </h3>
<table border="1" >
    <tr>
        <th> First Name </th>
        <th> Last Name </th>
        <th> Designation </th>
        <th> Employee Id </th>
        <th> Tax Deductibles </th>
        <th> Performance Remarks </th>
        <th> Yearly Salary</th>
    </tr>
    <corepatterns:employeelist id="employeelist_key">
    <tr>
        <td><corepatterns:employee
            attribute="FirstName"/> </td>
        <td><corepatterns:employee
            attribute= "LastName"/></td>
        <td><corepatterns:employee
            attribute= "Designation"/> </td>
        <td><corepatterns:employee
            attribute= "Id"/></td>
        <td><corepatterns:employee
            attribute="NoOfDeductibles"/></td>
        <td><corepatterns:employee
            attribute="PerformanceRemarks"/></td>
```

Example 7.20 Custom Tag Helper Strategy Sample Code

```
        <td><corepatterns:employee
            attribute="YearlySalary"/></td>
        <td>
      </tr>
    </corepatterns:employeelist>
  </table>
  </div>
  </body>
  </html>
```

Business Delegate as Helper Strategy

Helper components often make distributed invocations to the business tier. We suggest using a business delegate in order to hide the underlying implementation details of this request, such that the helper simply invokes a business service without knowing details about its physical implementation and distribution (see "Business Delegate" on page 248).

Both a helper and a business delegate may be implemented as a JavaBean. Thus, one could combine the notion of the helper component and the business delegate and implement the business delegate as a specialized type of helper. One major distinction between a helper and a business delegate, though, is as follows: A helper component is written by a developer working in the presentation tier, while the delegate is typically written by a developer working on the services in the business tier. (Note: The delegate may also be provided as part of a framework.) Thus, this strategy is as much about who actually writes the delegate as it is about the implementation. If there is some overlap in developer roles, then the business delegate as helper is a strategy to consider.

Example 7.21 Business Delegate as Helper Strategy Sample Code

```
/**A servlet delegates to a command object helper, as
   shown in the following excerpt:**/
String resultPage = command.execute(request,
   response);

/**The command object helper uses the business
   delegate, which is simply implemented as another
   JavaBean helper, as shown in the following
   excerpt:**/

AccountDelegate accountDelegate = new
   AccountDelegate();
```

Note on Helpers:

JavaBean helpers are best used for aiding in content retrieval and storing and adapting the model for the view. JavaBean helpers are often used as command objects as well.

Like JavaBean helpers, custom tag helpers may fulfill each of these roles, except for acting as a command object. Unlike Java-Bean helpers, custom tag helpers are well suited to control flow and iteration within a view. Custom tag helpers used in this way encapsulate logic that would otherwise be embedded directly within the JSP as scriptlet code. Another area where custom tag helpers are preferred is formatting raw data for display. A custom tag is able to iterate over a collection of results, format those results into an HTML table, and embed the table within a JSP View without requiring any Java Scriptlet code.

Consider an example in which a Web client is requesting account information from a system, as shown in Figure 7.14. There are five helpers shown in this diagram. The four JavaBean helpers are the AccountCommand object, Account object, AccountDAO, and AccountDetails. The sole custom tag helper is the TableFormatter object.

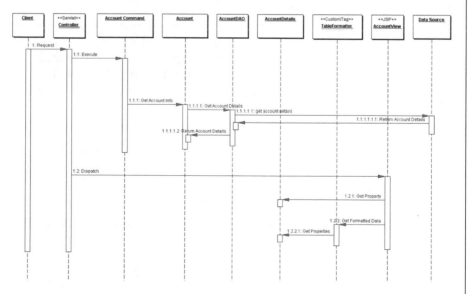

Figure 7.14 Using helpers

The controller handles the request. It creates or looks up the appropriate command object, which is implemented as a JavaBean helper. In this case, it is a command object that processes requests for account information. The controller invokes the Command object, which asks a JavaBean Account object for information about the account. The Account object invokes the business service, asking for these details, which are returned in the form of a Value object (see "Value Object" on page 261), implemented as a JavaBean.

So how does the Account object access the business services? Let us examine two cases, one simple and the other more sophisticated. In the simple case, imagine that a project is taking a phased approach, phasing Enterprise JavaBeans (EJB) into the business tier over time. Assume at the moment that the database is being accessed via JDBC calls from the presentation tier. In this case, the Account object uses a Data Access object (see "Data Access Object" on page 390), hiding the underlying implementation details of accessing the database. The Data Access object knows what SQL queries are necessary to retrieve the information. These details are hidden from the rest of the application, reducing coupling and making each component more modular and reusable. This case is described in the previous sequence diagram.

When the architecture becomes more sophisticated, and EJB is introduced in the business tier, then the Data Access object is replaced with a business delegate (see "Business Delegate" on page 248), typically written by the developers of the business service. The delegate hides the implementation details of EJB lookup, invocation, and exception handling from its client. It might also improve performance by providing caching services. Again, the object reduces coupling between tiers, improving the reusability and modularity of the various components. Regardless of the specific implementation of this object, its interface may remain unchanged during this transition. Figure 7.15 describes this scenario after the transition to the business delegate.

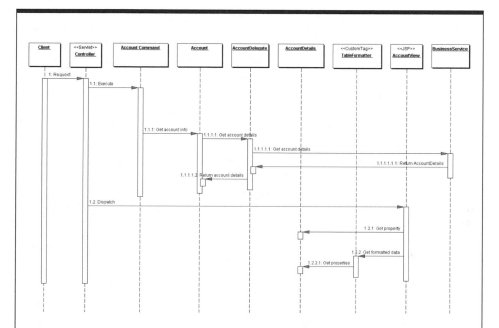

Figure 7.15 Accessing Business Services

The command object now has a handle to the AccountDetails object, which it stores before returning control to the controller. The Controller dispatches to the appropriate view, called AccountView.jsp. The view then grabs a combination of raw data and formatted data from the AccountDetails helper and the TableFormatter helper, respectively. The TableFormatter helper is implemented as a custom tag that cycles through the raw data and formats it into an HTML table for display. As stated, this conversion requires no scriptlet code in the view, which would be necessary to perform the same functionality with a JavaBean helper.

Additionally, the Account object or the AccountDetails helper could provide convenient methods to adapt the raw data in other ways. While such methods would not introduce HTML markup into the data, they might provide different combinations of data. An example is to return the full name of the user in various formats, such as "Lastname, Firstname" or "Firstname Lastname", and so forth.

The completed view is then displayed to the user.

Transformer Helper Strategy

The helper is implemented as an eXtensible Stylesheet Language Transformer. This is particularly useful with models that exist as structured markup, such as eXtensible Markup Language (XML), either natively within legacy systems or via some form of conversion. Using this strategy can help to enforce the separation of the model from the view, since much of the view markup must be factored into a separate stylesheet.

Figure 7.16 describes a potential implementation of this strategy.

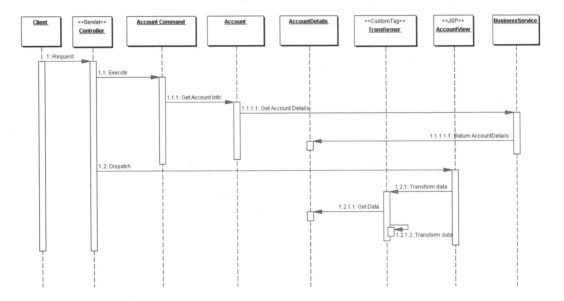

Figure 7.16 Sequence diagram for Transformer Helper Strategy

The controller handles the request and invokes a Command object, implemented as a JavaBean helper. The Command object initiates the retrieval of Account data. The Account object invokes the business service, which returns the data in the form of a Value Object (see "Value Object" on page 261), implemented as a JavaBean.

Content retrieval is complete and control is dispatched to the AccountView, which uses its custom tag transformer to manipulate the model state. The transformer relies on a stylesheet, which describes how to transform the model, typically describing how to format it with markup for display to the client. The stylesheet is usually retrieved as a static file, though it may also be dynamically generated.

An example of how the custom tag helper might look in Account-View follows:

```
<xsl:transform model="accounthelper"
  stylesheet="/transform/styles/basicaccount.xsl"/>
```

The integration of eXtensible Stylesheets and XML with JSP is evolving, as tag libraries in this area continue to mature. For now, it is a less preferred strategy, given the immature state of the supporting libraries and the additional sophisticated skills necessary to generate and maintain the stylesheets.

Consequences

- ***Improves Application Partitioning, Reuse, and Maintainability***

  Using helpers results in a cleaner separation of the view from the business processing in an application. The helpers, in the form of JavaBeans (JSP 1.0+) and custom tags (JSP 1.1+), provide a place external to the view to encapsulate business logic. Otherwise, scriptlet code clutters the JSP, a cumbersome and unwieldy situation, especially in larger projects.

  Additionally, business logic that is factored out of JSPs and into JavaBeans and custom tags is reused, reducing duplication and easing maintenance.

- ***Improves Role Separation***

  Separating formatting logic from application business logic reduces dependencies that individuals fulfilling different roles might have on the same resources. For example, a software developer might own code that is embedded within HTML markup, while a Web production team member might need to modify page layout and design components that are intermingled with business logic. Neither individual fulfilling these roles may be familiar with the implementation specifics of the other individual's work, thus raising the likelihood of accidental modifications introducing bugs into the system.

Related Patterns

- **Business Delegate**

  The helper components need to access methods in the business service API. It is also important to reduce the coupling among helpers in the presentation tier and among business services in the business tier. It is recommended that a delegate be used because these tiers may be physically distributed across a network. The delegate hides from the client the underlying details of looking up and accessing the business services, and it may also provide intermediate caching to reduce network traffic.

- **Dispatcher View and Service to Worker**

  When centralized control becomes desirable to handle such issues as security, workflow management, content retrieval, and navigation, consider the Dispatcher View or Service to Worker patterns.

- **Front Controller**

  This pattern is paired with the View Helper pattern to create the Dispatcher View pattern or Service to Worker pattern.

Composite View

Context

Sophisticated Web pages present content from numerous data sources, using multiple subviews that comprise a single display page. Additionally, a variety of individuals with different skill sets contribute to the development and maintenance of these Web pages.

Problem

Instead of providing a mechanism to combine modular, atomic portions of a view into a composite whole, pages are built by embedding formatting code directly within each view.

Modification to the layout of multiple views is difficult and error prone, due to the duplication of code.

Forces

- Atomic portions of view content change frequently.
- Multiple composite views use similar subviews, such as a customer inventory table. These atomic portions are decorated with different surrounding template text, or they appear in a different location within the page.
- Layout changes are more difficult to manage and code harder to maintain when subviews are directly embedded and duplicated in multiple views.
- Embedding frequently changing portions of template text directly into views also potentially affects the availability and administration of the system. The server may need to be restarted before clients see the modifications or updates to these template components.

Solution

Use composite views that are composed of multiple atomic subviews. Each component of the template may be included dynamically into the whole and the layout of the page may be managed independently of the content.

This solution provides for the creation of a composite view based on the inclusion and substitution of modular dynamic and static template fragments. It promotes the reuse of atomic portions of the view by encouraging modular design. It is appropriate to use a composite view to generate pages containing display components that may be combined in a variety of ways. This scenario occurs, for example, with portal sites that include numerous independent subviews, such as news feeds, weather information, and stock quotes on a single page. The layout of the page is managed and modified independent of the subview content.

Another benefit of this pattern is that Web designers can prototype the layout of a site, plugging static content into each of the template regions. As site development progresses, the actual content is substituted for these placeholders.

Figure 7.17 shows a screen capture of Sun's Java homepage, *java.sun.com*. Four regions are identified: Navigation, Search, Feature Story, and Headlines. While the content for each of these component subviews may originate from different data sources, they are laid out seamlessly to create a single composite page.

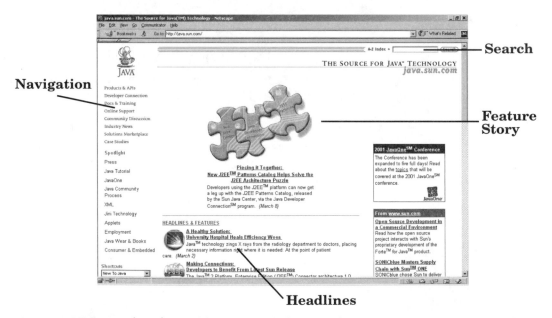

Figure 7.17 Screen shot of a modular page, including Search, Navigation, Feature Story, and Headlines regions

This pattern is not without its drawbacks. There is a runtime overhead associated with it, a tradeoff for the increased flexibility that it provides. Also, the use of a more sophisticated layout mechanism brings with it some manageability and development issues, since there are more artifacts to maintain and a level of implementation indirection to understand.

Structure

Figure 7.18 shows the class diagram that represents the Composite View pattern.

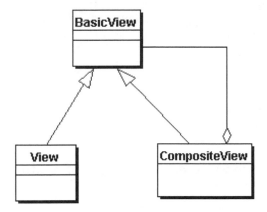

Figure 7.18 Composite View class diagram

Participants and Responsibilities

Figure 7.19 shows the sequence diagram for the Composite View pattern.

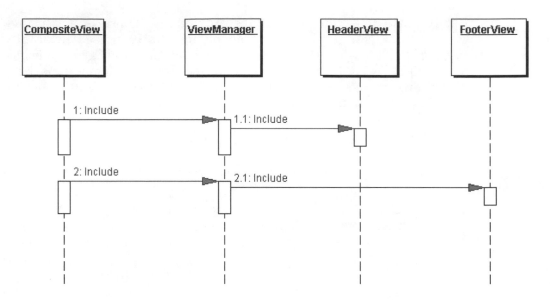

Figure 7.19 Composite View sequence diagram

Composite View

A composite view is a view that is an aggregate of multiple subviews.

View Manager

The View Manager manages the inclusion of portions of template fragments into the composite view. The View Manager may be part of a standard JSP runtime engine, in the form of the standard JSP include tag (`<jsp:include>`), or it may be encapsulated in a Java-Bean helper (JSP 1.0+) or custom tag helper (JSP 1.1+) to provide more robust functionality.

A benefit of using a mechanism other than the standard include tag is that conditional inclusion is easily done. For example, certain template fragments may be included only if the user fulfills a particular role or certain system conditions are satisfied. Furthermore, using a helper component as a View Manager allows for more sophisticated control of the page structure as a whole, which is useful for creating reusable page layouts.

Included View

An included view is a subview that is one atomic piece of a larger whole view. This included view could also potentially be a composite, itself including multiple subviews.

Strategies

JSP View Strategy

See "JSP View Strategy" on page 190.

Servlet View Strategy

See "Servlet View Strategy" on page 191.

JavaBean View Management Strategy

View management is implemented using JavaBeans, as shown in Example 7.22. The view delegates to the JavaBean, which implements the custom logic to control view layout and composition. The decisions on page layout may be based on user roles or security policies, making it much more powerful than the standard JSP include functionality. While it is semantically equivalent to the Custom Tag View Management Strategy, it is not nearly as elegant, since it introduces scriptlet code into the view.

Using the JavaBean View Management Strategy requires less up-front work than using the preferred Custom Tag View Management Strategy, since it is easier to construct JavaBeans and integrate them into a JSP environment. Additionally, even novice developers understand JavaBeans. This strategy is also easier from a manageability standpoint, because the completed JavaBeans are the only resulting artifacts to manage and configure.

Example 7.22 JavaBean View Management Strategy

```
<%@page
  import="corepatterns.compositeview.beanhelper.Conten
  tHelper" %>

<% ContentHelper personalizer = new
  ContentHelper(request); %>


<table valign="top" cellpadding="30%"  width="100%">
    <% if (personalizer.hasWorldNewsInterest() ) { %>
      <tr>
          <td><jsp:getProperty name="feeder"
             property="worldNews"/></td>
      </tr>
      <%
      }
```

Example 7.22 JavaBean View Management Strategy

```
        if ( personalizer.hasCountryNewsInterest() ) {
        %>
        <tr>
            <td><jsp:getProperty name="feeder"
                property="countryNews"/></td>
        </tr>
        <%
        }

        if ( personalizer.hasCustomNewsInterest() ) {
        %>
        <tr>
            <td><jsp:getProperty name="feeder"
                property="customNews"/></td>
        </tr>
        <%
        }

        if ( personalizer.hasAstronomyInterest() ) {
        %>

        <tr>
            <td><jsp:getProperty name="feeder"
                property="astronomyNews"/></td>
            </tr>
        <%
        }
        %>
    </table>
```

Standard Tag View Management Strategy

View management is implemented using standard JSP tags, such as the <jsp:include> tag. Using standard tags for managing the layout and composition of views is an easy strategy to implement, but does not provide the power and flexibility of the preferred Custom Tag View Management Strategy, since the layout for individual pages remains embedded within that page. Thus, while this strategy allows for the underlying content to vary dynamically, any site-wide layout changes would require individual modifications to numerous JSPs. This is shown in Example 7.23.

Example 7.23 Standard Tag View Management Strategy

```
<html>
<body>
<jsp:include
  page="/jsp/CompositeView/javabean/banner.html"
  flush="true"/>
<table width="100%">
  <tr align="left" valign="middle">
    <td width="20%">
    <jsp:include
    page="/jsp/CompositeView/javabean/ProfilePane.jsp"
      flush="true"/>
    </td>
    <td width="70%" align="center">
    <jsp:include
      page="/jsp/CompositeView/javabean/mainpanel.jsp"
      flush="true"/>
    </td>
  </tr>
</table>
<jsp:include
  page="/jsp/CompositeView/javabean/footer.html"
    flush="true"/>
</body>
</html>
```

When creating a composite display using standard tags, both static content, such as an HTML file, and dynamic content, such as a JSP, can be included. Additionally, the content can be included at translation time or at runtime. If the content is included at translation time, then the page display will remain unchanged until the JSP is recompiled, at which point any modifications to included content will be visible. In other words, the page is laid out and generated once, each time the JSP is recompiled. Example 7.24 shows an excerpt of a JSP that generates a composite page in this way, using the standard JSP include directive `<%@  include  %>`, which includes content at translation time.

Runtime inclusion of content means that changes to underlying subviews are visible in the composite page the next time a client accesses the page. This is much more dynamic and can be accomplished using the standard JSP include tag `<jsp:include>`, as shown in Example 7.25. There is of course some runtime overhead associated with this type of view generation, but it is the tradeoff for the increased flexibility of on-the-fly content modifications.

Example 7.24 Composite View with Translation-Time Content Inclusion

```
<table border=1 valign="top" cellpadding="2%"
    width="100%">
    <tr>
       <td><%@ file="news/worldnews.html" %> </td>
    </tr>
    <tr>
       <td><%@ file="news/countrynews.html" %> </td>
    </tr>
    <tr>
       <td><%@ file="news/customnews.html" %> </td>
    </tr>
    <tr>
       <td><%@ file="news/astronomy.html" %> </td>
    </tr>
</table>
```

Example 7.25 Composite View with Runtime Content Inclusion

```
<table border=1 valign="top" cellpadding="2%"
  width="100%">
    <tr>
       <td><jsp:include page="news/worldnews.jsp"
           flush="true"/> </td>
    </tr>
    <tr>
       <td><jsp:include page="news/countrynews.jsp"
           flush="true"/> </td>
    </tr>
    <tr>
       <td><jsp:include page="news/customnews.jsp"
           flush="true"/> </td>
    </tr>
    <tr>
       <td><jsp:include page="news/astronomy.jsp"
           flush="true"/> </td>
    </tr>
</table>
```

Custom Tag View Management Strategy

View management is implemented using custom tags (JSP 1.1+), which is the preferred strategy. Logic implemented within the tag controls view layout and composition. These tags are much more powerful and flexible than the standard JSP include tag, but also require a higher level of effort. Custom actions can base page layout and composition on such things as user roles or security policies.

Using this strategy requires more upfront work than do the other view management strategies, since custom tag development is more complicated than simply using JavaBeans or standard tags. Not only is there more complexity in the development process, but there is much more complexity with respect to integrating and managing the completed tags. Using this strategy requires the generation of numerous artifacts, including the tag itself, a tag library descriptor, configuration files, and configuring the environment with these artifacts.

The following JSP excerpt shows a possible implementation of this strategy and is excerpted from Example 7.26. Please refer to that code sample for more detail.

```
<region:render
    template='/jsp/CompositeView/templates/portal.jsp'>

<region:put section='banner'
    content='/jsp/CompositeView/templates/banner.jsp'
  />

<region:put section='controlpanel' content=
    '/jsp/CompositeView/templates/ProfilePane.jsp' />

<region:put section='mainpanel' content=
    '/jsp/CompositeView/templates/mainpanel.jsp' />

<region:put section='footer' content=
    '/jsp/CompositeView/templates/footer.jsp' />
</region:render>
```

Transformer View Management Strategy

View management is implemented using an XSL Transformer. This strategy would typically be combined with the Custom Tag View Management Strategy, using custom tags to implement and delegate to the appropriate components. Using this strategy can help to enforce the separation of the model from the view, since much of the view markup must be factored into a separate stylesheet. At the same time, it involves technologies that require new and sophisticated skill sets to implement correctly, an issue that makes this strategy impractical in many environments where these technologies are not already established.

The following excerpt shows the use of a custom tag from within a JSP to convert a model using a stylesheet and transformer:

```
<xsl:transform model="portfolioHelper"
    stylesheet="/transform/styles/generalPortfolio.xsl"/>
```

Early-Binding Resource Strategy

This is another name for translation-time content inclusion, as described in the Standard Tag View Management Strategy and shown in Example 7.24. It is appropriate for maintaining and updating a relatively static template and is recommended if a view includes headers and footers that change infrequently.

Late-Binding Resource Strategy

This is another name for runtime-content inclusion, as described in the Standard Tag View Management Strategy and shown in Example 7.25. It is appropriate for composite pages that may change frequently. One note: If the subview included at runtime is a dynamic resource, such as a JSP, then this subview may also be a composite view, including more runtime content. The flexibility offered by such nested composite structures should be weighed against their runtime overhead and considered in light of specific project requirements.

Consequences

- **Improves Modularity and Reuse**
  The pattern promotes modular design. It is possible to reuse atomic portions of a template, such as a table of stock quotes, in numerous views and to decorate these reused portions with different information. This pattern permits the table to be moved into its own module and simply included where necessary. This type of dynamic layout and composition reduces duplication, fosters reuse, and improves maintainability.

- **Enhances Flexibility**
  A sophisticated implementation may conditionally include view template fragments based on runtime decisions, such as user role or security policy.

- **Enhances Maintainability and Manageability**
  It is much more efficient to manage changes to portions of a template when the template is not hardcoded directly into the

view markup. When kept separate from the view, it is possible to modify modular portions of template content independent of the template layout. Additionally, these changes are available to the client immediately, depending on the implementation strategy. Modifications to the layout of a page are more easily managed as well, since changes are centralized.

- ***Reduces Manageability***
  Aggregating atomic pieces of the display together to create a single view introduces the potential for display errors, since subviews are page fragments. This is a limitation that can become a manageability issue. For example, if a JSP page is generating an HTML page using a main page that includes three subviews, and the subviews each include the HTML open and close tag (that is, <HTML> and </HTML>), then the composed page will be invalid. Thus, it is important when using this pattern to be aware that subviews must not be complete views. Tag usage must be accounted for quite strictly in order to create valid composite views, and this can become a manageability issue.

- ***Performance Impact***
  Generating a display that includes numerous subviews may slow performance. Runtime inclusion of subviews will result in a delay each time the page is served to the client. In an environment with strict Service Level Agreements that mandate specific response times, such performance slowdowns, though typically extremely minimal, may not be acceptable. An alternative is to move the subview inclusion to translation time, though this limits the subview to changing when the page is retranslated.

Sample Code

The Composite View pattern can be implemented using any number of strategies, but one of the more popular is the Custom Tag View Management Strategy. In fact, there are a number of custom tag libraries currently available for implementing composite views that separate view layout from view content and provide for modular and pluggable template subviews.

This sample will use a template library written by David Geary and featured in detail in "Advanced JavaServer Pages" [Geary].

The template library describes three basic components: *sections*, *regions*, and *templates*.

- A section is a reusable component that renders HTML or JSP.

- A region describes content by defining sections.
- A template controls the layout of regions and sections in a rendered page.

A region can be defined and rendered as shown in Example 7.26.

Example 7.26 A Region and Sections

```
<region:render template='portal.jsp'>
  <region:put section='banner' content = 'banner.jsp'
  />
  <region:put section = 'controlpanel' content =
      'ProfilePane.jsp' />
  <region:put section='mainpanel' content =
      'mainpanel.jsp' />
  <region:put section='footer' content='footer.jsp' />
</region:render>
```

A region defines its content by matching logical section names with a portion of content, such as banner.jsp.

The layout for the region and its sections is defined by a template, to which each region is associated. In this case, the template is named portal.jsp, as defined in Example 7.27.

Example 7.27 Template Definition

```
<region:render section='banner'/>
<table width="100%">
    <tr align="left" valign="middle">
        <td width="20%">
      <!-- menu region -->
      <region:render section='controlpanel' />
        </td>
        <td width="70%" align="center">
      <!-- contents -->
      <region:render section='mainpanel' />
        </td>
    </tr>
</table>
```

A site with numerous views and a single consistent layout has one JSP containing code that looks similar to the template definition in Example 7.27, and many JSPs that look similar to Example 7.26, defining alternate regions and sections.

Sections are JSP fragments that are used as subviews to build a composite whole as defined by a template. The `banner.jsp` section is shown in Example 7.28.

Example 7.28 Section Subview – banner.jsp

```
<table width="100%" bgcolor="#C0C0C0">
<tr align="left" valign="middle">
  <td width="100%">

  <TABLE ALIGN="left" BORDER=1 WIDTH="100%">
  <TR ALIGN="left" VALIGN="middle">
    <TD>Logo</TD>
    <TD><center>Sun Java Center</TD>
  </TR>
  </TABLE>

  </td>
</tr>
</table>
```

Composite views are a modular, flexible and extensible way to build JSP views for your J2EE application.

Related Patterns

- **View Helper**
  The Composite View pattern may be used as the view in the View Helper pattern.

- **Composite [GoF]**
  The Composite View pattern is based on the Composite pattern, which describes part-whole hierarchies where a composite object is comprised of numerous pieces, all of which are treated as logically equivalent.

Service to Worker

Context

The system controls flow of execution and access to business data, from which it creates presentation content.

Note

The Service to Worker pattern, like the Dispatcher View pattern, describes a common combination of other patterns from the catalog. Both of these macro patterns describe the combination of a controller and dispatcher with views and helpers. While describing this common structure, they emphasize related but different usage patterns.

Problem

The problem is a combination of the problems solved by the Front Controller and View Helper patterns in the presentation tier. There is no centralized component for managing access control, content retrieval, or view management, and there is duplicate control code scattered throughout various views. Additionally, business logic and presentation formatting logic are intermingled within these views, making the system less flexible, less reusable, and generally less resilient to change.

Intermingling business logic with view processing also reduces modularity and provides a poor separation of roles among Web production and software development teams.

Forces

- Authentication and authorization checks are completed per request.
- Scriptlet code within views should be minimized.
- Business logic should be encapsulated in components other than the view.
- Control flow is relatively complex and based on values from dynamic content.
- View management logic is relatively sophisticated, with multiple views potentially mapping to the same request.

Solution

Combine a controller and dispatcher with views and helpers (see "Front Controller" on page 172 and "View Helper" on page 186) to handle client requests and prepare a dynamic presentation as the response. Controllers delegate content retrieval to helpers, which manage the population of the intermediate model for the view. A dispatcher is responsible for view management and navigation and can be encapsulated either within a controller or a separate component.

Service to Worker describes the combination of the Front Controller and View Helper patterns with a dispatcher component.

While this pattern and the Dispatcher View pattern describe a similar structure, the two patterns suggest a different division of labor among the components. In Service to Worker, the controller and the dispatcher have more responsibilities.

Since the Service to Worker and Dispatcher View patterns represent a common combination of other patterns from the catalog, each warrants its own name to promote efficient communication among developers. Unlike the Service to Worker pattern, the Dispatcher View pattern suggests deferring content retrieval to the time of view processing.

In the Dispatcher View pattern, the dispatcher typically plays a limited to moderate role in view management. In the Service to Worker pattern, the dispatcher typically plays a moderate to large role in view management.

A limited role for the dispatcher occurs when no outside resources are utilized in order to choose the view. The information encapsulated in the request is sufficient to determine the view to dispatch the request. For example,

```
http://some.server.com/servlet/Controller?next=login.jsp
```

The sole responsibility of the dispatcher component in this case is to dispatch to the view `login.jsp`.

An example of the dispatcher playing a moderate role is the case where the client submits a request directly to a controller with a query parameter that describes an action to be completed:

```
http://some.server.com/servlet/Controller?action=login
```

The responsibility of the dispatcher component here is to translate the logical name `login` into the resource name of an appropriate view, such as `login.jsp`, and dispatch to that view. To accomplish this translation, the dispatcher may access resources such as an XML configuration file that specifies the appropriate view to display.

On the other hand, in the Service to Worker pattern, the dispatcher might be more sophisticated. The dispatcher may invoke a business service to determine the appropriate view to display.

The shared structure of Service to Worker and Dispatcher View consists of a controller working with a dispatcher, views, and helpers.

Structure

The class diagram in Figure 7.20 represents the Service to Worker pattern.

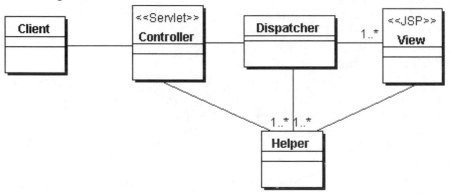

Figure 7.20 Service to Worker class diagram

Participants and Responsibilities

Figure 7.21 shows the sequence diagram that represents the Service to Worker pattern.

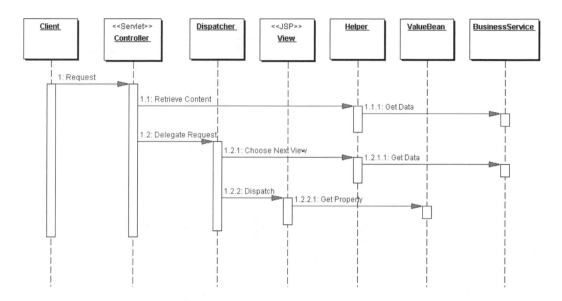

Figure 7.21 Service to Worker sequence diagram

As stated, Service to Worker and Dispatcher View represent a similar structure. The main difference is that Service to Worker describes architectures with more behavior "up front" in the controller and dispatcher, while Dispatcher View describes architectures with more behavior moved back to the time of view processing. Thus, the two patterns suggest a continuum, where behavior is either encapsulated closer to the front or moved farther back in the process flow.

Controller

The controller is typically the initial contact point for handling a request. It works with a dispatcher to complete view management and navigation. The controller manages authentication, authorization, content retrieval, validation, and other aspects of request handling. It delegates to helpers to complete portions of this work.

Dispatcher

A dispatcher is responsible for view management and navigation, managing the choice of the next view to present to the user and providing the mechanism for vectoring control to this resource.

A dispatcher can be encapsulated within a controller (see "Front Controller" on page 172) or it can be a separate component working in coordination with the controller. The dispatcher can provide static dispatching to the view or it may provide a more sophisticated dynamic dispatching mechanism.

The dispatcher uses the RequestDispatcher object (supported in the servlet specification), but it also typically encapsulates some additional processing. The more responsibilities that this component encapsulates, the more it fits into the Service to Worker pattern. Conversely, when the dispatcher plays a more limited role, it fits more closely into the Dispatcher View pattern.

View

A View represents and displays information to the client. The information that is used in a display is retrieved from a model. Helpers support views by encapsulating and adapting a model for use in a display.

Helper

A helper is responsible for helping a view or controller complete its processing. Thus, helpers have numerous responsibilities, including gathering data required by the view and storing this intermediate model, in which case the helper is sometimes referred to as a value bean. Additionally, helpers may adapt this data model for use by the view. Helpers can service requests for data from the view by simply providing access to the raw data or by formatting the data as Web content.

A view may work with any number of helpers, which are typically implemented as JavaBeans (JSP 1.0+) and custom tags (JSP 1.1+). Additionally, a helper may represent a Command object or a delegate (see "Business Delegate" on page 248).

ValueBean

A value bean is another name for a helper that is responsible for holding intermediate model state for use by a view. A typical case, as shown in the sequence diagram in Figure 7.12, has the business service returning a value bean in response to a request. In this case, ValueBean fulfills the role of a Value Object (see "Value Object" on page 261).

BusinessService

The business service is a role that is fulfilled by the service the client is seeking to access. Typically, the business service is accessed via a Business delegate. The business delegate's role is to provide control and protection for the business service (see the "Business Delegate" on page 248).

Strategies

Servlet Front Strategy

See "Servlet Front Strategy" on page 175.

JSP Front Strategy

See "JSP Front Strategy" on page 178.

JSP View Strategy

See "JSP View Strategy" on page 190.

Servlet View Strategy

See "Servlet View Strategy" on page 191.

JavaBean Helper Strategy

See "JavaBean Helper Strategy" on page 194.

Custom Tag Helper Strategy

See "Custom Tag Helper Strategy" on page 194.

Dispatcher in Controller Strategy

See "Dispatcher in Controller Strategy" on page 183.

As stated, the Service to Worker and Dispatcher View patterns suggest a continuum, where behavior is encapsulated closer to the front or moved farther back in the process flow. Figure 7.22 describes a scenario in which the controller is heavily loaded with upfront work, but the dispatcher functionality is minimal.

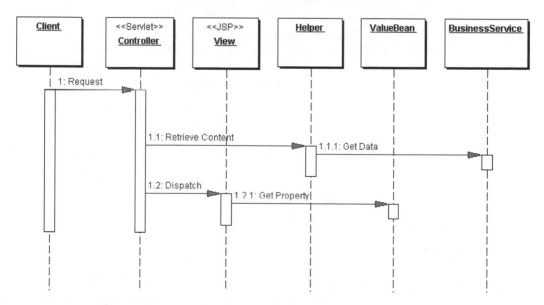

Figure 7.22 Folding the dispatcher into the controller

Transformer Helper Strategy

See "Transformer Helper Strategy" on page 200.

Consequences

- ***Centralizes Control and Improves Modularity and Reuse***
  This pattern suggests providing a central place to handle system services and business logic across multiple requests. The controller manages business logic processing and request handling. Keep in mind, though, that as control centralizes, it is possible to introduce a single point of failure.

  The pattern also promotes cleaner application partitioning and encourages reuse. Common code is moved into a controller and reused per request and moved into helper components, to which controllers and views delegate. The improved modularity and reuse means less duplication, which typically means a more bug-free environment.

- ***Improves Application Partitioning***
  Using helpers results in a cleaner separation of the view from the business processing in an application. Helpers, in the form of JavaBeans (JSP 1.0+) and Custom tags (JSP 1.1+), provide a place for business logic to be factored out of the JSP. If the business logic is left in a JSP, large projects result in cumbersome and unwieldy scriptlet code.

- ***Improves Role Separation***
  Separating the formatting logic from the application business logic also reduces dependencies on the same resources among individuals fulfilling different roles. Without this separation, for example, a software developer would own code that is embedded within HTML markup, while a Web production team member would need to modify page layout and design components that are intermingled with business logic. Because neither individual fulfilling these roles is familiar with the implementation specifics of the other individual's work, it raises the likelihood of modifications accidentally introducing bugs into the system.

Sample Code

The following sample code shows an implementation of the Service to Worker pattern, using a controller servlet, a command helper, a dispatcher component, and a view. The implementation includes the Servlet Front Strategy, Command and Controller Strategy, JSP View Strategy, and JavaBean Helper Strategy. A very basic composite view is used as well. A screen shot of the resulting display is shown in Figure 7.23.

Example 7.29 shows the controller servlet, which delegates to a Command object (Command and Controller Strategy) to complete the control processing. The Command object is retrieved via a factory invocation, which returns the generic Command type, an interface shown in Example 7.30. The sample code uses a LogManager to log messages. The screen shots in Figure 7.23 and Figure 7.28 show these messages displayed at the bottom of the page, for the purposes of this example.

Example 7.29 Controller Servlet with Command and Controller Strategy

```java
public class Controller extends HttpServlet {
  /** Processes requests for both HTTP
   * <code>GET</code> and <code>POST</code> methods.
   * @param request servlet request
   * @param response servlet response
   */
  protected void processRequest(HttpServletRequest
    request, HttpServletResponse response)
    throws ServletException, java.io.IOException {
    String next;

    try {
      // Log pattern info
      LogManager.recordStrategy(request,
        "Service To Worker",
        " ServletFront Strategy;" +
      " JSPView Strategy; JavaBean helper Strategy");

      LogManager.logMessage(request, getSignature(),
        "Process incoming request. ");

      // Use a helper object to gather parameter
      // specific information.
      RequestHelper helper = new
        RequestHelper(request, response);

      LogManager.logMessage(request, getSignature(),
          "Getting command object helper");

      // Get command object helper
      Command command = helper.getCommand();
```

Example 7.29 Controller Servlet with Command and Controller Strategy

```java
      // delegate processing to the command object,
      // passing request and response objects along
      next = command.execute(helper);

      /** If the above command returns a value, we
        * will dispatch from the controller. In this
        * example, though, the command will use a
        * separate dispatcher component to choose a
        * view and dispatch to that view. The command
        * object delegates to this dispatcher
        * component in its execute method, above, and
        * control should not return to this point **/
    }
    catch (Exception e) {
      LogManager.logMessage(
        "EmployeeController(CommandStrategy)",
        e.getMessage() );

      /** ApplicationResources provides a simple API
        * for retrieving constants and other
        * preconfigured values**/
      next = ApplicationResources.getInstance().
                  getErrorPage(e);
    }

    dispatch(request, response, next);

  }


  /** Handles the HTTP <code>GET</code> method.
   * @param request servlet request
   * @param response servlet response
   */
  protected void doGet(HttpServletRequest request,
    HttpServletResponse response)
    throws ServletException, java.io.IOException {
      processRequest(request, response);
  }

  /** Handles the HTTP <code>POST</code> method.
   * @param request servlet request
   * @param response servlet response
   */
  protected void doPost(HttpServletRequest request,
    HttpServletResponse response)
```

Example 7.29 Controller Servlet with Command and Controller Strategy

```java
   throws ServletException, java.io.IOException {
     processRequest(request, response);
   }

   /** Returns a short description of the servlet. */
   public String getServletInfo() {
     return getSignature();
   }

   /** dispatcher method */
   protected void dispatch(HttpServletRequest request,
     HttpServletResponse response,
     String page) throws
   javax.servlet.ServletException,
     java.io.IOException {
       RequestDispatcher dispatcher =
        getServletContext().getRequestDispatcher(page);
       dispatcher.forward(request, response);
   }

   public void init(ServletConfig config) throws
       ServletException {
     super.init(config);
   }

   public void destroy() { }

   private String getSignature() {
     return "ServiceToWorker-Controller";
   }
 }
```

Example 7.30 Command Interface

```java
public interface Command {

    public String execute(RequestHelper helper) throws
   javax.servlet.ServletException, java.io.IOException;
 }
```

Each Command Object helper implements this generic interface, which is an example of the GoF Command pattern. The Command object is an instance of the ViewAccountDetails class, which is shown in Example 7.31. The command instance delegates to an Accounting-Adapter to make an invocation to the business tier via business delegate. The adapter class is shown in Example 7.32. It uses a separate dispatcher component to determine the next view to which control should be dispatched and to actually dispatch to this view.

Example 7.31 ViewAccountDetailsCommand

```
public class ViewAccountDetailsCommand implements
  Command {
  public ViewAccountDetailsCommand() { }

  // view account details operation
  public String execute(RequestHelper helper)
    throws javax.servlet.ServletException,
  java.io.IOException {
    /** This will tell the user that a system error
      * has occured and will typically not be seen. It
      * should be stored in a resource file **/
    String systemerror =
      "/jspdefaultprocessingerror.jsp";

    LogManager.logMessage(helper.getRequest(),
      "ViewAccountDetailsCommand",
      "Get Account Details from an adapter object");

    /** Use an adapter to retrieve data from business
      * service, and store it in a request attribute.
      * Note: Object creation could be avoided via
      * factory, but for example purposes object
      * instantiation is shown **/
    AccountingAdapter adapter = new
                        AccountingAdapter();
    adapter.setAccountInfo(helper);

    LogManager.logMessage(helper.getRequest(),
  "ViewAccountDetailsCommand", "processing complete");

    /** Note: Object creation could be avoided via
      * factory, but for example purposes object
      * instantiation is shown**/
    Dispatcher dispatcher = new Dispatcher();
    dispatcher.dispatch(helper);
```

Example 7.31 ViewAccountDetailsCommand

```
    /** This return string will not be sent in a
      * normal execution of this scenario, because
      * control is forwarded to another resource
      * before reaching  this point. Some commands do
      * return a String,  though, so the return value
      * is included for  correctness. **/
    return systemerror;
  }
}
```

Example 7.32 AccountingAdapter

```
public class AccountingAdapter {
    public void setAccountInfo(
      RequestHelper requestHelper) {
        LogManager.logMessage(
          requestHelper.getRequest(),
          "Retrieving data from business tier");

        // retrieve data from business tier via
        // delegate. Omit try/catch block for brevity.
        AccountDelegate delegate =
                new AccountDelegate();
        AccountVO account =
          delegate.getAccount(
            requestHelper.getCustomerId(),
            requestHelper.getAccountKey());

        LogManager.logMessage(
          requestHelper.getRequest(),
  "Store account value object in request attribute");

      // transport data using request object
      requestHelper.getRequest().setAttribute(
        "account", account);
    }
}
```

The invocation on the business service via the delegate yields an Account Value object, which the adapter stores in a request attribute for use by the view. Example 7.33 shows `accountdetails.jsp`, the JSP to which the request is dispatched. The Value object is imported via the standard `<jsp:useBean>` tag and its properties accessed with the standard `<jsp:getProperty>` tag. Also, the view uses a very simple composite strategy, doing a translation-time inclusion of the `trace.jsp` subview, which is responsible for displaying log information on the display solely for example purposes.

Example 7.33 View – accountdetails.jsp

```
<html>
<head><title>AccountDetails</title></head>
<body>

<jsp:useBean id="account" scope="request"
  class="corepatterns.util.AccountVO" />


<h2><center> Account Detail for <jsp:getProperty
  name="account" property="owner" />
</h2> <br><br>
<table border=3>
<tr>
<td>
Account Number :
</td>
<td>
<jsp:getProperty name="account" property="number" />
</td>
</tr>

<tr>
<td>
Account Type:
</td>
<td>
<jsp:getProperty name="account" property="type" />
</td>
</tr>

<tr>
<td>
Account Balance:
</td>
```

Example 7.33 View – accountdetails.jsp

```
<td>
<jsp:getProperty name="account" property="balance" />
</td>
</tr>

<tr>
<td>
OverDraft Limit:
</td>
<td>
<jsp:getProperty name="account"
  property="overdraftLimit" />
</td>
</tr>

</table>


<br>
<br>

</center>
<%@ include file="/jsp/trace.jsp" %>
</body>
</html>
```

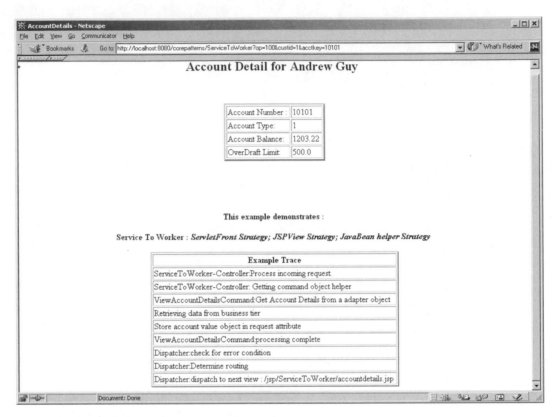

Figure 7.23 Service to Worker sample screen shot

Related Patterns

- **Front Controller and View Helper**
  The Service to Worker pattern is the result of combining the View Helper pattern with a dispatcher, in coordination with the Front Controller pattern.

- **Dispatcher View**
  The Dispatcher View pattern is another name for the combination of the Front Controller pattern with a dispatcher, and the View Helper pattern. The Service to Worker and the Dispatcher View patterns are identical with respect to the components involved, but differ in the division of labor among those components. The Dispatcher View pattern suggests deferring content retrieval to the time of view processing. Also, the dispatcher plays a more limited role in view management, as the choice of view is typically already included in the request.

Dispatcher View

Context

System controls flow of execution and access to presentation processing, which is responsible for generating dynamic content.

Note

The Dispatcher View pattern, like the Service to Worker pattern, describes a common combination of other patterns from the catalog. Both of these macro patterns describe the combination of a controller and dispatcher with views and helpers. While describing this common structure, they emphasize related but different usage patterns.

Problem

The problem is a combination of the problems solved by the Front Controller and View Helper patterns in the presentation tier. There is no centralized component for managing access control, content retrieval or view management, and there is duplicate control code scattered throughout various views. Additionally, business logic and presentation formatting logic are intermingled within these views, making the system less flexible, less reusable, and generally less resilient to change.

Intermingling business logic with view processing also reduces modularity and provides a poor separation of roles among Web production and software development teams.

Forces

- Authentication and authorization checks are completed per request.
- Scriptlet code within views should be minimized.
- Business logic should be encapsulated in components other than the view.
- Control flow is relatively simple and is typically based on values encapsulated with the request.
- View management logic is limited in complexity.

Solution

Combine a controller and dispatcher with views and helpers (see "Front Controller" on page 172 and "View Helper" on page 186) to handle client requests and prepare a dynamic presentation as the response. Controllers do not delegate content retrieval to helpers, because these activities are deferred to the time of view processing. A dispatcher is responsible for view management and navigation and can be encapsulated either within a controller, a view, or a separate component.

Dispatcher View describes the combination of the Front Controller and View Helper patterns with a dispatcher component. While this pattern and the Service to Worker pattern describe a similar structure, the two patterns suggest a different division of labor among the components. The controller and the dispatcher typically have limited responsibilities, as compared to the Service to Worker pattern, since the upfront processing and view management logic are basic. Furthermore, if centralized control of the underlying resources is considered unnecessary, then the controller is removed and the dispatcher may be moved into a view.

Since the Service to Worker and Dispatcher View patterns represent a common combination of other patterns from the catalog, each warrants its own name to promote efficient communication among developers. Unlike the Service to Worker pattern, the Dispatcher View pattern suggests deferring content retrieval to the time of view processing.

In the Dispatcher View pattern, the dispatcher typically plays a limited to moderate role in view management. In the Service to Worker pattern, the dispatcher typically plays a moderate to large role in view management.

A limited role for the dispatcher occurs when no outside resources are utilized in order to choose the view. The information encapsulated in the request is sufficient to determine the view to dispatch the request. For example:

```
http://some.server.com/servlet/Controller?next=login.jsp
```

The sole responsibility of the dispatcher component in this case is to dispatch to the view `login.jsp`.

An example of the dispatcher playing a moderate role is the case where the client submits a request directly to a controller with a query parameter that describes an action to be completed:

```
http://some.server.com/servlet/Controller?action=login
```

The responsibility of the dispatcher component here is to translate the logical name `login` into the resource name of an appropriate view, such as `login.jsp`, and dispatch to that view. To accomplish this translation, the dispatcher may access resources such as an XML configuration file that specifies the appropriate view to display.

On the other hand, in the Service to Worker pattern, the dispatcher might be more sophisticated. The dispatcher may invoke a business service to determine the appropriate view to display.

The shared structure of these two patterns, as mentioned above, consists of a controller working with a dispatcher, views, and helpers.

Structure

Figure 7.24 shows the class diagram that represents the Dispatcher View pattern.

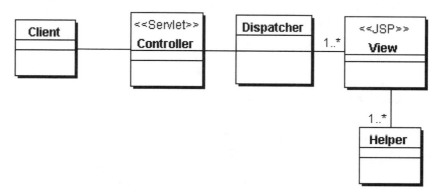

Figure 7.24 Dispatcher View class diagram

Participants and Responsibilities

Figure 7.25 shows the Dispatcher View sequence pattern.

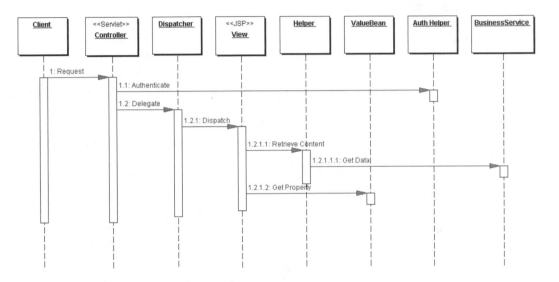

Figure 7.25 Dispatcher View sequence diagram

While the controller responsibilities are limited to system services, such as authentication and authorization, it is often still beneficial to centralize these aspects of the system. Notice also that, unlike in Service to Worker, the dispatcher does not make invocations on a business service in order to complete its view management processing.

The dispatcher functionality may be encapsulated in its own component. At the same time, when the responsibilities of the dispatcher are limited, as described by this pattern, the dispatcher functionality is often folded into another component, such as the controller or the view (see "Dispatcher in Controller Strategy" on page 183 and "Dispatcher in View Strategy" on page 237).

In fact, the dispatcher functionality may even be completed by the container, in the case where there is no extra application-level logic necessary. An example is a view called `main.jsp` that is given the alias name `first`. The container will process the following request, translate the alias name to the physical resource name, and dispatch directly to that resource:

```
http://some.server.com/first --> /mywebapp/main.jsp
```

In this case, we are left with the View Helper pattern, with the request being handled directly by the view. Since the view is the initial contact point for handling a request, custom tag helpers are typically used in these cases to perform business processing or to delegate this processing to other components. See the listing in Example 7.35 in the "Sample Code" section for an implementation sample.

Thus, the Dispatcher View pattern describes a continuum of related scenarios, moving from a scenario that is very structurally similar to Service to Worker to one that is similar to View Helper.

Controller

The controller is typically the initial contact point for handling a request. The controller manages authentication and authorization, and delegates to a dispatcher to do view management.

Dispatcher

A dispatcher is responsible for view management and navigation, managing the choice of the next view to present to the user and providing the mechanism for vectoring control to this resource.

A dispatcher can be encapsulated within a controller (see "Front Controller" on page 172) or can be a separate component working in coordination. The dispatcher can provide static dispatching to the view or may provide a more sophisticated dynamic dispatching mechanism.

View

A view represents and displays information to the client. The information that is used in a display is retrieved from a model. Helpers support views by encapsulating and adapting a model for use in a display.

Helper

A helper is responsible for helping a view or controller complete its processing. Thus, helpers have numerous responsibilities, including gathering data required by the view and storing this intermediate model, in which case the helper is sometimes referred to as a value bean. Additionally, helpers may adapt this data model for use by the view. Helpers can service requests for data from the view by simply providing access to the raw data or by formatting the data as Web content.

A view may work with any number of helpers, which are typically implemented as JavaBeans (JSP 1.0+) and custom tags (JSP 1.1+).

Additionally, a helper may represent a Command object or a Delegate (see "Business Delegate" on page 248).

ValueBean

A value bean is another name for a helper that is responsible for holding intermediate model state for use by a view. A typical case, as shown in the sequence diagram in Figure 7.12, has the business service returning a value bean in response to a request. In this case, ValueBean fulfills the role of a Value Object (see "Value Object" on page 261).

BusinessService

The business service is a role that is fulfilled by the service the client is seeking to access. Typically, the business service is accessed via a business delegate. The business delegate's role is to provide control and protection for the business service (see "Business Delegate" on page 248).

Strategies

Servlet Front Strategy

See "Servlet Front Strategy" on page 175.

JSP Front Strategy

See "JSP Front Strategy" on page 178.

JSP View Strategy

See "JSP View Strategy" on page 190.

Servlet View Strategy

See "Servlet View Strategy" on page 191.

JavaBean Helper Strategy

See "JavaBean Helper Strategy" on page 194.

Custom Tag Helper Strategy

See "Custom Tag Helper Strategy" on page 194.

Dispatcher in Controller Strategy

See "Dispatcher in Controller Strategy" on page 183.

As stated, the Service to Worker and Dispatcher View patterns suggest a continuum, where behavior is encapsulated closer to the front in Service to Worker or moved farther back in Dispatcher View.

Figure 7.26 shows the interactions for this strategy.

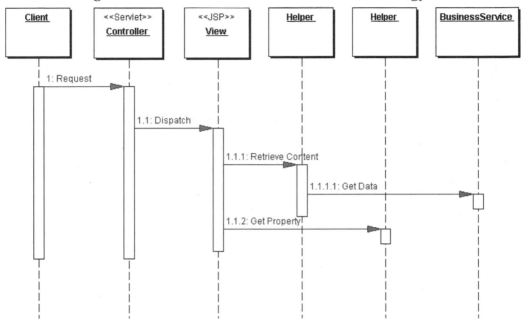

Figure 7.26 Dispatcher in Controller Strategy

The controller does not create an explicit dispatcher object. Instead, the controller takes care of dispatching to the view. Alternatively, one could implement a dispatcher to which the controller can delegate the dispatching function.

Dispatcher in View Strategy

If the controller is removed due to its limited role, the dispatcher may be moved into a view. This design can be useful in cases where there is typically one view that maps to a specific request, but where a secondary view may be used on an infrequent basis. For example, based on some information in the request or results of some processing in a view, a custom tag helper in the view might vector control to a secondary view. A typical case is when a client request is submitted to a specific view, and will be serviced by that view in almost every case. Consider the case where the user has not been authenticated, but requests access to one of the few protected JSPs on a site. Since the site has only a few protected pages, and limited dynamic content, authentication can be performed within those JSPs, instead of using a site-wide centralized controller. Those pages that need authentication include a custom tag helper at the top of the page. This helper performs the authentication check and either displays the page for the user or forwards the user to an authentication page.

Figure 7.27 represents this scenario.

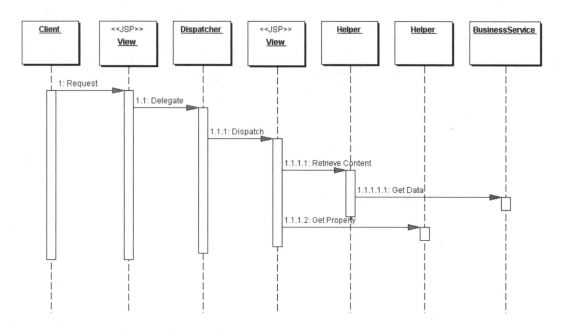

Figure 7.27 Dispatcher in View Strategy

Transformer Helper Strategy

See "Transformer Helper Strategy" on page 200.

Consequences

- ***Centralizes Control and Improves Reuse and Maintainability***
  Control processing is handled in a central place for multiple requests. It is easier to manage these activities and perform dispatching from a centralized point, since a central access point means code is reused across multiple requests, reducing duplication and easing maintenance.

- *Improves Application Partitioning*
  Use of helpers results in a cleaner separation of the view from an application's business processing. The helpers, in the form of JavaBeans (JSP 1.0+) and Custom tags (JSP 1.1+), provide a place for business logic to be factored out of the JSP, where scriptlet code quickly becomes cumbersome and unwieldy in large projects.

- *Improves Role Separation*
  Separating the formatting logic from the application business logic also reduces dependencies that individuals fulfilling different roles might have on the same resources. For example, a software developer would own code that is embedded within HTML markup, while a Web production team member would need to modify page layout and design components that are intermingled with business logic. Because neither individual fulfilling these roles may be familiar with the implementation specifics of the other individual's work, there is the likelihood of inadvertent modifications introducing bugs into the system.

Sample Code

The following sample code shows an implementation of the Dispatcher View pattern, using a controller servlet and a view with JavaBean and custom tag helpers. The implementation includes the Servlet Front Strategy, Dispatcher in Controller Strategy, JSP View Strategy, and custom tag and JavaBean helper strategies. A very basic composite view is used as well. A screen shot of the resulting display is shown in Figure 7.28.

Example 7.34 shows the controller servlet, which simply completes an authentication check and passes control to the appropriate view. Notice that the controller does not directly delegate to any helper components in order to make invocations to the business tier via a Delegate. These responsibilities are deferred to the view, which is called `accountdetails.jsp` and can be seen in Example 7.35. The sample code uses a LogManager to log messages. These messages are displayed at the bottom of the output page, for the purposes of this example, and can be seen in the screen shots in Figure 7.23 and Figure 7.28.

Example 7.34 Dispatcher View Controller Servlet

```java
public class Controller extends HttpServlet {

  /** Processes requests for both HTTP
   * <code>GET</code> and <code>POST</code> methods.
   * @param request servlet request
   * @param response servlet response
   */
  protected void processRequest(HttpServletRequest
    request, HttpServletResponse response)
    throws ServletException, java.io.IOException {
    String nextview;
    try {
      LogManager.recordStrategy(request,
        "Dispatcher View",
        " Servlet Front Strategy; " +
      "JSP View Strategy; Custom tag helper Strategy");
      LogManager.logMessage(request, getSignature(),
        "Process incoming request. ");

      // Use a helper object to gather parameter
      // specific information.
      RequestHelper helper = new
          RequestHelper(request, response);
      LogManager.logMessage(request,
        getSignature(), " Authenticate user");

      Authenticator auth = new BasicAuthenticator();
      auth.authenticate(helper);

      //This is an oversimplification for the sake of
      // simplicity. Typically, there will be a
      // mapping from logical name to resource name at
      // this point
      LogManager.logMessage(request, getSignature(),
        "Getting nextview");
      nextview = request.getParameter("nextview");

      LogManager.logMessage(request, getSignature(),
        "Dispatching to view: " + nextview);
    }
    catch (Exception e) {
      LogManager.logMessage(
        "Handle exception appropriately",
        e.getMessage() );
```

Example 7.34 Dispatcher View Controller Servlet

```java
    /** ApplicationResources provides a simple API
      * for retrieving constants and other
      * preconfigured values**/
    nextview = ApplicationResources.getInstance().
        getErrorPage(e);
  }
  dispatch(request, response, nextview);
}

/** Handles the HTTP <code>GET</code> method.
  * @param request servlet request
  * @param response servlet response
  */
protected void doGet(HttpServletRequest request,
  HttpServletResponse response)
throws ServletException, java.io.IOException {
  processRequest(request, response);
}

/** Handles the HTTP <code>POST</code> method.
  * @param request servlet request
  * @param response servlet response
  */
protected void doPost(HttpServletRequest request,
  HttpServletResponse response)
throws ServletException, java.io.IOException {
  processRequest(request, response);
}

/** Returns a short description of the servlet. */
public String getServletInfo() {
    return getSignature();
}

public void init(ServletConfig config) throws
  ServletException {
  super.init(config);
}

public void destroy() { }

/**
  * dispatcher method
  */
protected void dispatch(HttpServletRequest request,
```

Example 7.34 Dispatcher View Controller Servlet

```
    HttpServletResponse response, String page)
    throws javax.servlet.ServletException,
    java.io.IOException {
        RequestDispatcher dispatcher =
          getServletContext().
            getRequestDispatcher(page);
        dispatcher.forward(request, response);
    }

  private String getSignature() {
    return "DispatcherView-Controller";
  }
}
```

Notice that the view uses custom tag helpers to manage content retrieval, since this activity was not completed in the controller. When custom tags are used in this manner, they typically become thin facades for standalone components to which they delegate to complete this processing. This way, the general processing logic is loosely coupled to the tag implementation. If custom tags are not used with Dispatcher View, then too much scriptlet code typically ends up in the JSP, a situation to be avoided.

Example 7.35 View – accountdetails.jsp

```
<%@ taglib uri="/web-INF/corepatternstaglibrary.tld"
  prefix="corepatterns" %>

<html>
<head><title>AccountDetails</title></head>
<body>

<corepatterns:AccountQuery
  queryParams="custid,acctkey" scope="request" />

<h2><center> Account Detail for <corepatterns:Account
  attribute="owner" /></h2> <br><br>

<tr>
  <td>Account Number :</td>
  <td><corepatterns:Account attribute="number" /></td>
</tr>
```

Example 7.35 View – accountdetails.jsp

```
<tr>
  <td>Account Type:</td>
  <td><corepatterns:Account attribute="type" /></td>
</tr>

<tr>
  <td>Account Balance:</td>
  <td><corepatterns:Account attribute="balance"
  /></td>
</tr>

<tr>
  <td>OverDraft Limit:</td>
  <td><corepatterns:Account attribute="overdraftLimit"
  /></td>
</tr>
<table border=3>
</table>
</corepatterns:AccountQuery>

<br>
<br>

</center>
<%@ include file="/jsp/trace.jsp" %>
</body>
</html>
```

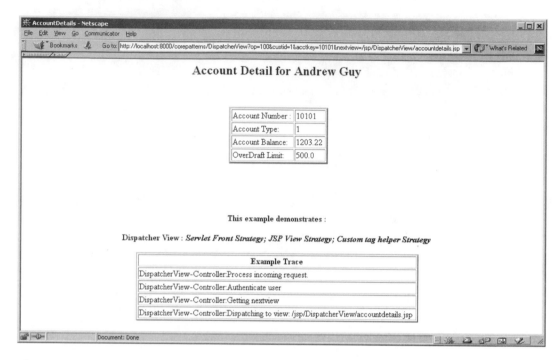

Figure 7.28 Dispatcher View sample screen shot

Related Patterns

- **Front Controller**

  The Service to Worker pattern is the result of combining the View Helper pattern with a dispatcher in coordination with the Front Controller pattern.

- **View Helper**

  The Service to Worker pattern is the result of combining the View Helper pattern with a dispatcher in coordination with the Front Controller pattern.

- **Service to Worker**

  The Service to Worker pattern is another name for the combination of the Front Controller pattern with a dispatcher and the View Helper pattern. The Service to Worker and Dispatcher View patterns are identical with respect to the components involved, but differ in the division of labor among those components. The Dispatcher View pattern suggests deferring content retrieval to the time of view processing. Also, the dispatcher plays a more limited role in view management, as the choice of view is typically already included in the request.

BUSINESS TIER PATTERNS

Chapter 8

Business Delegate

Context

A multitiered, distributed system requires remote method invocations to send and receive data across tiers. Clients are exposed to the complexity of dealing with distributed components.

Problem

Presentation-tier components interact directly with business services. This direct interaction exposes the underlying implementation details of the business service application program interface (API) to the presentation tier. As a result, the presentation-tier components are vulnerable to changes in the implementation of the business services: When the implementation of the business services change, the exposed implementation code in the presentation tier must change too.

Additionally, there may be a detrimental impact on network performance because presentation-tier components that use the business service API make too many invocations over the network. This happens when presentation-tier components use the underlying API directly, with no client-side caching mechanism or aggregating service.

Lastly, exposing the service APIs directly to the client forces the client to deal with the networking issues associated with the distributed nature of EJB technology.

Forces

- Presentation-tier clients need access to business services.
- Different clients, such as devices, Web clients, and thick clients, need access to business service.
- Business services APIs may change as business requirements evolve.
- It is desirable to minimize coupling between presentation-tier clients and the business service, thus hiding the underlying implementation details of the service, such as lookup and access.
- Clients may need to implement caching mechanisms for business service information.

- It is desirable to reduce network traffic between client and business services.

Solution

Use a Business Delegate to reduce coupling between presentation-tier clients and business services. The Business Delegate hides the underlying implementation details of the business service, such as lookup and access details of the EJB architecture.

The Business Delegate acts as a client-side business abstraction; it provides an abstraction for, and thus hides, the implementation of the business services. Using a Business Delegate reduces the coupling between presentation-tier clients and the system's business services. Depending on the implementation strategy, the Business Delegate may shield clients from possible volatility in the implementation of the business service API. Potentially, this reduces the number of changes that must be made to the presentation-tier client code when the business service API or its underlying implementation changes.

However, interface methods in the Business Delegate may still require modification if the underlying business service API changes. Admittedly, though, it is more likely that changes will be made to the business service rather than to the Business Delegate.

Often, developers are skeptical when a design goal such as abstracting the business layer causes additional upfront work in return for future gains. However, using this pattern or its strategies results in only a small amount of additional upfront work and provides considerable benefits. The main benefit is hiding the details of the underlying service. For example, the client can become transparent to naming and lookup services. The Business Delegate also handles the exceptions from the business services, such as java.rmi.Remote exceptions, JMS exceptions and so on. The Business Delegate may intercept such service level exceptions and generate application level exceptions instead. Application level exceptions are easier to handle by the clients, and may be user friendly. The Business Delegate may also tranparently perform any retry or recovery operations necessary in the event of a service failure without exposing the client to the problem until it is determined that the problem is not resolvable. These gains present a compelling reason to use the pattern.

Another benefit is that the delegate may cache results and references to remote business services. Caching can significantly improve performance, because it limits unnecessary and potentially costly round trips over the network.

A Business Delegate uses a component called the Lookup Service. The Lookup Service is responsible for hiding the underlying implementation details of the business service lookup code. The Lookup Service may be written as part of the Delegate, but we recommend that it be implemented as a separate component, as outlined in the Service Locator pattern (See "Service Locator" on page 367.).

When the Business Delegate is used with a Session Facade, typically there is a one-to-one relationship between the two. This one-to-one relationship exists because logic that might have been encapsulated in a Business Delegate relating to its interaction with multiple business services (creating a one-to-many relationship) will often be factored back into a Session Facade.

Finally, it should be noted that this pattern could be used to reduce coupling between other tiers, not simply the presentation and the business tiers.

Structure

Figure 8.1 shows the class diagram representing the Business Delegate pattern. The client requests the BusinessDelegate to provide access to the underlying business service. The BusinessDelegate uses a LookupService to locate the required BusinessService component.

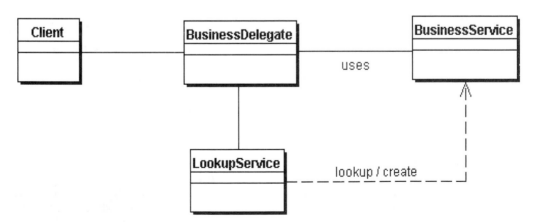

Figure 8.1 BusinessDelegate class diagram

Participants and Responsibilities

Figure 8.2 and Figure 8.3 show sequence diagrams that illustrate typical interactions for the Business Delegate pattern.

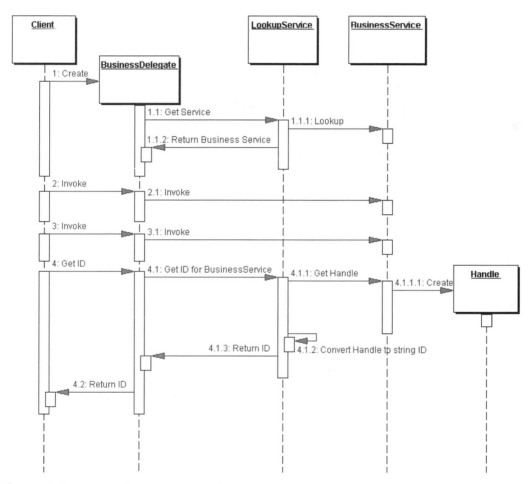

Figure 8.2 BusinessDelegate sequence diagram

The BusinessDelegate uses a LookupService for locating the business service. The business service is used to invoke the business methods on behalf of the client. The Get ID method shows that the BusinessDelegate can obtain a String version of the handle (such as EJBHandle object) for the business service and return it to the client as a String. The client can use the String version of the handle at a later time to reconnect to the business service it was using when it obtained the handle. This technique will avoid new lookups, since the handle is capable of reconnecting to its business service instance. It should be noted that handle objects are implemented by the container provider and may not be portable across containers from different vendors.

The sequence diagram in Figure 8.3 shows obtaining a BusinessService (such as a session or an entity bean) using its handle.

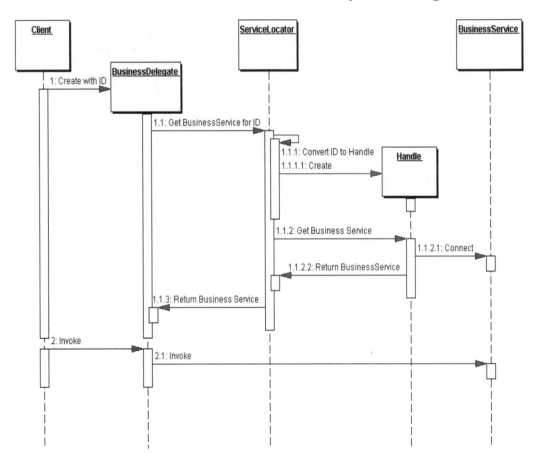

Figure 8.3 BusinessDelegate with ID sequence diagram

BusinessDelegate

The BusinessDelegate's role is to provide control and protection for the business service. The BusinessDelegate can expose two types of constructors to clients. One type of request instantiates the BusinessDelegate without an ID, while the other instantiates it with an

ID, where ID is a String version of the reference to a remote object, such as EJBHome or EJBObject.

When initialized without an ID, the BusinessDelegate requests the service from the Lookup Service, typically implemented as a Service Locator (see "Service Locator" on page 367), which returns the Service Factory, such as EJBHome. The BusinessDelegate requests that the Service Factory locate, create, or remove a BusinessService, such as an enterprise bean.

When initialized with an ID string, the BusinessDelegate uses the ID string to reconnect to the BusinessService. Thus, the Business-Delegate shields the client from the underlying implementation details of BusinessService naming and lookup. Furthermore, the presentation-tier client never directly makes a remote invocation on a BusinessSession; instead, the client uses the BusinessDelegate.

LookupService

The BusinessDelegate uses the LookupService to locate the BusinessService. The LookupService encapsulates the implementation details of BusinessService lookup.

BusinessService

The BusinessService is a business tier component, such as an enterprise bean or a JMS component, that provides the required service to the client.

Strategies

Delegate Proxy Strategy

The Business Delegate exposes an interface that provides clients access to the underlying methods of the business service API. In this strategy, a Business Delegate provides proxy function to pass the client methods to the session bean it is encapsulating. The Business Delegate may additionally cache any necessary data, including the remote references to the session bean's home or remote objects to improve performance by reducing the number of lookups. The Business Delegate may also convert such references to String versions (IDs) and vice versa, using the services of a Service Locator.

The example implementation for this strategy is discussed in the "Sample Code" section of this pattern.

Delegate Adapter Strategy

The Business Delegate proves to be a nice fit in a B2B environment when communicating with J2EE services. Disparate systems may use an XML as the integration language. Integrating one system to another typically requires an Adapter [GoF] to meld the two disparate systems. Figure 8.4 gives an example.

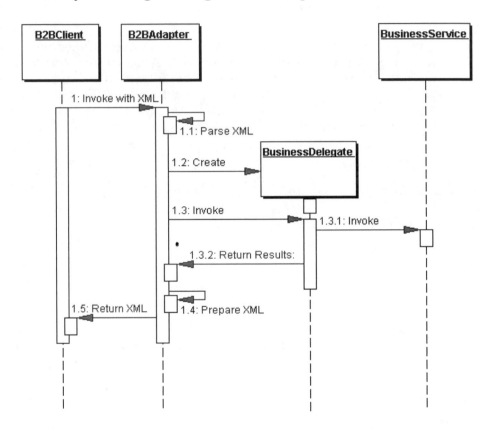

Figure 8.4 Using the Business Delegate pattern with an Adapter strategy

Consequences

- ### Reduces Coupling, Improves Manageability
  The Business Delegate reduces coupling between the presentation tier and the business tier by hiding all business-tier implementation details. It is easier to manage changes because they are centralized in one place, the Business Delegate.

- *Translates Business Service Exceptions*

  The Business Delegate is responsible for translating any network or infrastructure-related exceptions into business exceptions, shielding clients from knowledge of the underlying implementation specifics.

- *Implements Failure Recovery and Thread Synchronization*

  The Business Delegate on encountering a business service failure, may implement automatic revovery features without exposing the problem to the client. If the recovery succeeds, the client need not know about the failure. If the recovery attempt does not succeed, then the Business Delegate needs to inform the client of the failure. Additionally, the business delegate methods may be synchronized, if necessary.

- *Exposes Simpler, Uniform Interface to Business Tier*

  The Business Delegate, to better serve its clients, may provide a variant of the interface provided by the underlying enterprise beans.

- *Impacts Performance*

  The Business Delegate may provide caching services (and better performance) to the presentation tier for common service requests.

- *Introduces Additional Layer*

  The Business Delegate may be seen as adding an unnecessary layer between the client and the service, thus introducing added complexity and decreasing flexibility. Some developers may feel that it is an extra effort to develop Business Delegates with implementations that use the Delegate Proxy strategy. At the same time, the benefits of the pattern typically outweigh such drawbacks.

- *Hides Remoteness*

  While location transparency is one of the benefits of this pattern, a different problem may arise due to the developer treating a remote service as if it was a local one. This may happen if the client developer does not understand that the Business Delegate is a client side proxy to a remote service. Typically, a method invocations on the Business Delegate results in a remote method invocation under the wraps. Ignoring this, the developer may tend to make numerous method invocations to perform a single task, thus increasing the network traffic.

Sample Code

Implementing the Business Delegate Pattern

Consider a Professional Services Application (PSA), where a Web-tier client needs to access a session bean that implements the Session Facade pattern. The Business Delegate pattern can be applied to design a Delegate class ResourceDelegate, which encapsulates the complexity of dealing with the session bean ResourceSession. The ResourceDelegate implementation for this example is shown in Example 8.1, and the corresponding remote interface for the Session Facade bean ResourceSession is shown in Example 8.2.

Example 8.1 Implementing Business Delegate Pattern – ResourceDelegate

```
// imports
...

public class ResourceDelegate {

  // Remote reference for Session Facade
  private ResourceSession session;

  // Class for Session Facade's Home object
  private static final Class homeClazz =
  corepatterns.apps.psa.ejb.ResourceSessionHome.class;

  // Default Constructor. Looks up home and connects
  // to session by creating a new one
  public ResourceDelegate() throws ResourceException {
    try {
      ResourceSessionHome home = (ResourceSessionHome)
        ServiceLocator.getInstance().getHome(
          "Resource", homeClazz);
      session = home.create();
    } catch(ServiceLocatorException ex) {
      // Translate Service Locator exception into
      // application exception
      throw new ResourceException(...);
    } catch(CreateException ex) {
      // Translate the Session create exception into
      // application exception
      throw new ResourceException(...);
    } catch(RemoteException ex) {
      // Translate the Remote exception into
```

Example 8.1 Implementing Business Delegate Pattern – ResourceDelegate

```
      // application exception
      throw new ResourceException(...);
    }
  }

  // Constructor that accepts an ID (Handle id) and
  // reconnects to the prior session bean instead
  // of creating a new one
  public BusinessDelegate(String id)
    throws ResourceException {
    super();
    reconnect(id);
  }

  // Returns a String ID the client can use at a
  // later time to reconnect to the session bean
  public String getID() {
    try {
      return ServiceLocator.getId(session);
    } catch (Exception e) {
      // Throw an application exception
    }
  }

  // method to reconnect using String ID
  public void reconnect(String id)
    throws ResourceException {
    try {
      session = (ResourceSession)
             ServiceLocator.getService(id);
    } catch (RemoteException ex) {
      // Translate the Remote exception into
      // application exception
      throw new ResourceException(...);
    }
  }

  // The following are the business methods
  // proxied to the Session Facade. If any service
  // exception is encountered, these methods convert
  // them into application exceptions such as
  // ResourceException, SkillSetException, and so
  // forth.

  public ResourceVO setCurrentResource(
```

Example 8.1 Implementing Business Delegate Pattern – ResourceDelegate

```
    String resourceId)
    throws ResourceException {
    try {
      return session.setCurrentResource(resourceId);
    } catch (RemoteException ex) {
      // Translate the service exception into
      // application exception
      throw new ResourceException(...);
    }
  }

  public ResourceVO getResourceDetails()
    throws ResourceException {

    try {
      return session.getResourceDetails();
    } catch(RemoteException ex) {
      // Translate the service exception into
      // application exception
      throw new ResourceException(...);
    }
  }

  public void setResourceDetails(ResourceVO vo)
    throws ResourceException {
    try {
      session.setResourceDetails(vo);
    } catch(RemoteException ex) {
      throw new ResourceException(...);
    }
  }

  public void addNewResource(ResourceVO vo)
    throws ResourceException {
    try {
      session.addResource(vo);
    } catch(RemoteException ex) {
      throw new ResourceException(...);
    }
  }

  // all other proxy method to session bean
  ...
}
```

Example 8.2 Remote Interface for ResourceSession

```java
// imports
...
public interface ResourceSession extends EJBObject {

  public ResourceVO setCurrentResource(
    String resourceId) throws
    RemoteException, ResourceException;

  public ResourceVO getResourceDetails()
      throws RemoteException, ResourceException;
  public void setResourceDetails(ResourceVO resource)
      throws RemoteException, ResourceException;

  public void addResource(ResourceVO resource)
      throws RemoteException, ResourceException;

  public void removeResource()
      throws RemoteException, ResourceException;

  // methods for managing blockout time by the
  // resource
  public void addBlockoutTime(Collection blockoutTime)
      throws RemoteException, BlockoutTimeException;

  public void updateBlockoutTime(
    Collection blockoutTime)
      throws RemoteException, BlockoutTimeException;

  public void removeBlockoutTime(
    Collection blockoutTime)
      throws RemoteException, BlockoutTimeException;

  public void removeAllBlockoutTime()
      throws RemoteException, BlockoutTimeException;

  // methods for resource skillsets time by the
  //resource
  public void addSkillSets(Collection skillSet)
      throws RemoteException, SkillSetException;

  public void updateSkillSets(Collection skillSet)
      throws RemoteException, SkillSetException;

  public void removeSkillSet(Collection skillSet)
      throws RemoteException, SkillSetException;

  ...
}
```

Related Patterns

- **Service Locator**

  The Service Locator pattern may be used to create the Business Delegate's Service Locator, hiding the implementation details of any business service lookup and access code.

- **Proxy [GoF]**

  A Business Delegate may act as a proxy, providing a stand-in for objects in the business tier.

- **Adapter [GoF]**

  A Business Delegate may use the Adapter pattern to provide coupling for disparate systems.

- **Broker [POSA1]**

  A Business Delegate performs the role of a broker to decouple the business tier objects from the clients in other tiers.

Value Object

Context

Application clients need to exchange data with enterprise beans.

Problem

J2EE applications implement server-side business components as session beans and entity beans. Some methods exposed by the business components return data to the client. Often, the client invokes a business object's get methods multiple times until it obtains all the attribute values.

Session beans represent the business services and are not shared between users. A session bean provides coarse-grained service methods when implemented per the Session Facade pattern.

Entity beans, on the other hand, are multiuser, transactional objects representing persistent data. An entity bean exposes the values of attributes by providing an accessor method (also referred to as a *getter* or *get method*) for each attribute it wishes to expose.

Every method call made to the business service object, be it an entity bean or a session bean, is potentially remote. Thus, in an EJB application such remote invocations use the network layer regardless of the proximity of the client to the bean, creating a network overhead. Enterprise bean method calls may permeate the network layers of the system even if the client and the EJB container holding the entity bean are both running in the same JVM, OS, or physical machine. Some vendors may implement mechanisms to reduce this overhead by using a more direct access approach and bypassing the network.

As the usage of these remote methods increases, application performance can significantly degrade. Therefore, using multiple calls to get methods that return single attribute values is inefficient for obtaining data values from an enterprise bean.

Forces

- All access to an enterprise bean is performed via remote interfaces to the bean. Every call to an enterprise bean is potentially a remote method call with network overhead.

- Typically, applications have a greater frequency of read transactions than update transactions. The client requires the data from the business tier for presentation, display, and other read-only types of processing. The client updates the data in the business tier much less frequently than it reads the data.
- The client usually requires values for more than one attribute or dependent object from an enterprise bean. Thus, the client may invoke multiple remote calls to obtain the required data.
- The number of calls made by the client to the enterprise bean impacts network performance. Chattier applications—those with increased traffic between client and server tiers—often degrade network performance.

Solution

Use a Value Object to encapsulate the business data. A single method call is used to send and retrieve the value object. When the client requests the enterprise bean for the business data, the enterprise bean can construct the value object, populate it with its attribute values, and pass it by value to the client.

Clients usually require more than one value from an enterprise bean. To reduce the number of remote calls and to avoid the associated overhead, it is best to use value objects to transport the data from the enterprise bean to its client.

When an enterprise bean uses a value object, the client makes a single remote method invocation to the enterprise bean to request the value object instead of numerous remote method calls to get individual attribute values. The enterprise bean then constructs a new value object instance, copies values into the object and returns it to the client. The client receives the value object and can then invoke accessor (or getter) methods on the value object to get the individual attribute values from the value object. Or, the implementation of the value object may be such that it makes all attributes public. Because the value object is passed by value to the client, all calls to the value object instance are local calls instead of remote method invocations.

Structure

Figure 8.5 shows the class diagram that represents the Value Object pattern in its simplest form.

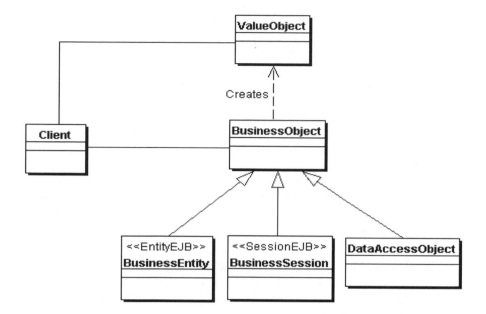

Figure 8.5 Value Object class diagram

As shown in this class diagram, the value object is constructed on demand by the enterprise bean and returned to the remote client. However, the Value Object pattern can adopt various strategies, depending on requirements. The "Strategies" section explains these approaches.

Participants and Responsibilities

Figure 8.6 contains the sequence diagram that shows the interactions for the Value Object pattern.

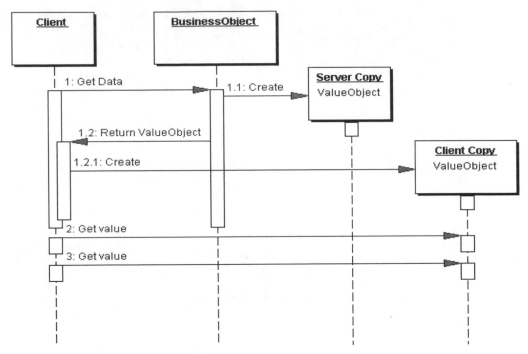

Figure 8.6 Value Object sequence diagram

Client

This represents the client of the enterprise bean. The client can be an end-user application, as in the case of a rich client application that has been designed to directly access the enterprise beans. The client can be Business Delegates (see "Business Delegate" on page 248) or a different BusinessObject.

BusinessObject

The BusinessObject represents a role in this pattern that can be fulfilled by a session bean, an entity bean, or a Data Access Object (DAO). The BusinessObject is responsible for creating the value object and returning it to the client upon request. The BusinessObject may also receive data from the client in the form of a value object and use that data to perform an update.

ValueObject

The ValueObject is an arbitrary serializable Java object referred to as a value object. A value object class may provide a constructor that accepts all the required attributes to create the value object. The constructor may accept all entity bean attribute values that the value object is designed to hold. Typically, the members in the value object are defined as public, thus eliminating the need for get and set methods. If some protection is necessary, then the members could be defined as protected or private, and methods are provided to get the values. By offering no methods to set the values, a value object is protected from modification after its creation. If only a few members are allowed to be modified to facilitate updates, then methods to set the values can be provided. Thus, the value object creation varies depending on an application's requirements. It is a design choice as to whether the value object's attributes are private and accessed via getters and setters, or all the attributes are made public.

Strategies

The first two strategies discussed are applicable when the enterprise bean is implemented as a session bean or as an entity bean. These strategies are called *Updatable Value Objects Strategy* and *Multiple Value Objects Strategy*.

The following strategies are applicable only when the BusinessObject is implemented as an entity bean: *Entity Inherits Value Object Strategy* and *Value Object Factory Strategy*.

Updatable Value Objects Strategy

In this strategy, the value object not only carries the values from the BusinessObject to the client, but also can carry the changes required by the client back to the business object.

Figure 8.7 is a class diagram showing the relationship between the BusinessObject and the value object.

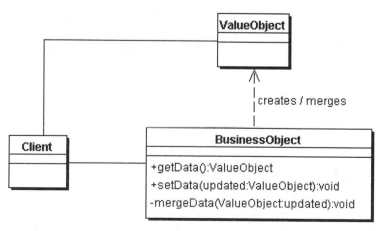

Figure 8.7 Updatable Value Object strategy – class diagram

The BusinessObject creates the value object. Recall that a client may need to access the BusinessObject values not only to read them but to modify these values. For the client to be able to modify the BusinessObject attribute values, the BusinessObject must provide mutator methods. Mutator methods are also referred to as *setters* or *set methods*.

Instead of providing fine-grained set methods for each attribute, which results in network overhead, the BusinessObject can expose a coarse-grained setData() method that accepts a value object as an argument. The value object passed to this method holds the updated values from the client. Since the value object has to be mutable, the value object class has to provide set methods for each attribute that can be modified by the client. The set methods for the value object can include field level validations and integrity checks as needed. Once the client obtains a value object from the BusinessObject, the client invokes the necessary set methods locally to change the attribute values. Such local changes do not impact the BusinessObject until the setData() method is invoked.

The setData() method serializes the client's copy of the value object and sends it to the BusinessObject. The BusinessObject receives the modified value object from the client and merges the changes into its own attributes. The merging operation may complicate the design of the BusinessObject and the value object; the "Consequences" section discusses these potential complications. One strategy to use here is to update only attributes that have changed, rather than updating all attributes. A change flag placed in the value object can be used to determine the attributes to update, rather than doing a direct comparison.

There is an impact on the design using the updatable value objects in terms of update propagation, synchronization, and version control.

Figure 8.8 shows the sequence diagram for the entire update interaction.

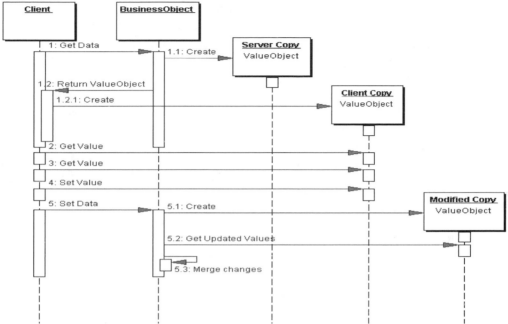

Figure 8.8 Updatable Value Object strategy – sequence diagram

Multiple Value Objects Strategy

Some application business objects can be very complex. In such cases, it is possible that a single business object produces different value objects, depending on the client request. There exists a one-to-many relationship between the business object and the many value objects it can produce. In these circumstances, this strategy may be considered.

For instance, when the business object is implemented as a session bean, typically applying the Session Facade pattern, the bean may interact with numerous other business components to provide the service. The session bean produces its value object from different sources. Similarly, when the BusinessObject is implemented as a coarse-grained entity bean, typically applying the Composite Entity pattern, the entity bean will have complex relationships with a number of dependent objects. In both these cases, it is good practice to provide mechanisms to produce value objects that actually represent parts of the underlying coarse-grained components.

For example, in a trading application, a Composite Entity that represents a customer portfolio can be a very coarse-grained complex component that can produce value objects that provide data for parts of the portfolio, like customer information, lists of stocks held, and so on. A similar example is a customer manager session bean that provides services by interacting with a number of other BusinessObjects and components to provide its service. The customer manager bean can produce discrete small value objects, like customer address, contact list, and so on, to represent parts of its model.

For both these scenarios, it is possible to adopt and apply the *Multiple Value Objects Strategy* so that the business component, whether a session bean or an entity bean, can create multiple types of value objects. In this strategy, the business entity provides various methods to get different value objects. Each such method creates and returns a different type of value object. The class diagram for this strategy is shown Figure 8.9.

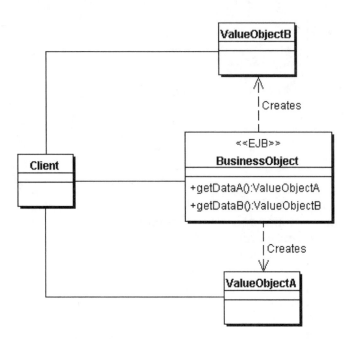

Figure 8.9 Multiple Value Objects strategy class diagram

When a client needs a value object of type ValueObjectA, it invokes the entity's getDataA() method requesting ValueObjectA. When it needs a value object of type ValueObjectB, it invokes the entity's getDataB() method requesting ValueObjectB, and so on. This is shown in the sequence diagram in Figure 8.10.

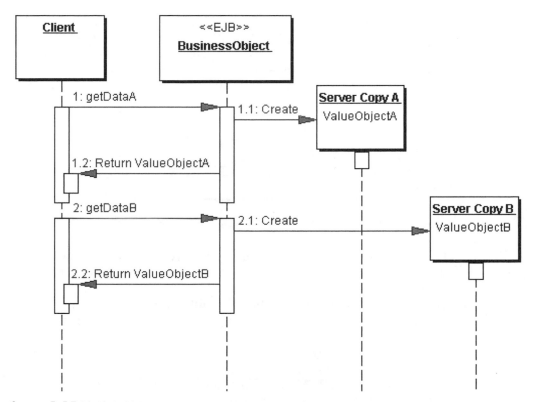

Figure 8.10 Multiple Value Objects strategy sequence diagram

Entity Inherits Value Object Strategy

When the BusinessObject is implemented as an entity bean and the clients typically need to access all the data from the entity bean, then the entity bean and the value object both have the same attributes. In this case, since there exists a one-to-one relationship between the entity bean and its value object, the entity bean may be able to use inheritance to avoid code duplication.

In this strategy, the entity bean extends (or inherits from) the value object class. The only assumption is that the entity bean and the value object share the same attribute definitions. The class diagram for this strategy is shown in Figure 8.11.

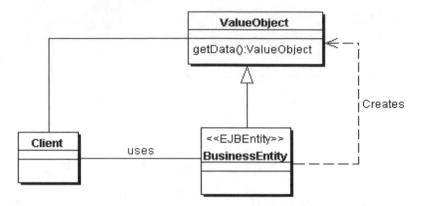

Figure 8.11 Entity Inherits Value Object strategy class diagram

The ValueObject implements one or more `getData()` methods as discussed in the *Multiple Value Objects Strategy*. When the entity inherits this value object class, the client invokes an inherited `get-Data()` method on the entity bean to obtain a value object.

Thus, this strategy eliminates code duplication between the entity and the value object. It also helps manage changes to the value object requirements by isolating the change to the value object class and preventing the changes from affecting the entity bean.

This strategy has a trade-off related to inheritance. If the value object is shared through inheritance, then changes to this value object class will affect all its subclasses, potentially mandating other changes to the hierarchy.

The sequence diagram in Figure 8.12 demonstrates this strategy.

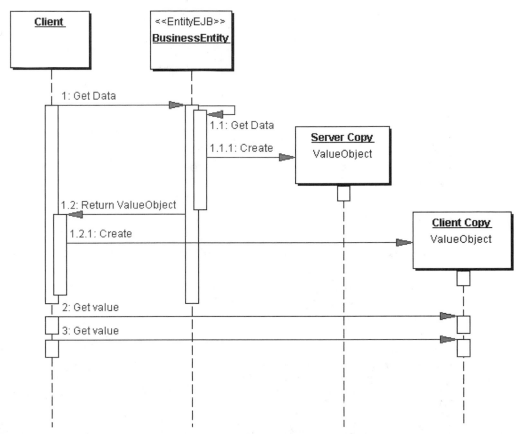

Figure 8.12 Entity Inherits Value Object strategy sequence diagram

The sample implementation for the Entity Inherits Value Object Strategy is shown in Example 8.10 (ContactVO – Value Object Class) and Example 8.11 (ContactEntity – Entity Bean Class).

Value Object Factory Strategy

The Entity Inherits Value Object Strategy can be further extended to support multiple value objects for an entity bean by employing a value object factory to create value objects on demand using reflection. This results in an even more dynamic strategy for value object creation.

To achieve this, define a different interface for each type of value object that must be returned. The entity bean implementation of value object superclass must implement all these interfaces. Furthermore, you must create a separate implementation class for each defined interface, as shown in the class diagram for this strategy in Figure 8.13.

Once all interfaces have been defined and implemented, create a method in the ValueObjectFactory that is passed two arguments:

- The entity bean instance for which a value object must be created.

- The interface that identifies the kind of value object to create.

The ValueObjectFactory can then instantiate an object of the correct class, set its values, and return the newly created value object instance.

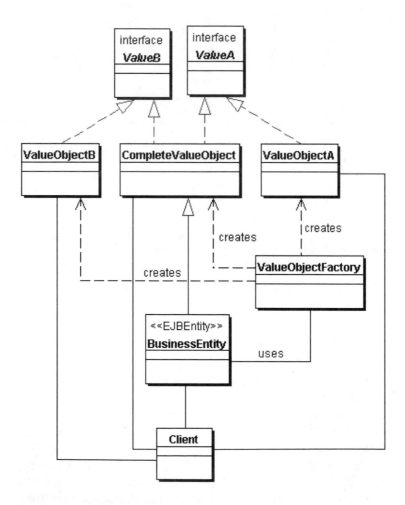

Figure 8.13 Value Object Factory strategy class diagram

The sequence diagram for this strategy is shown in Figure 8.14.

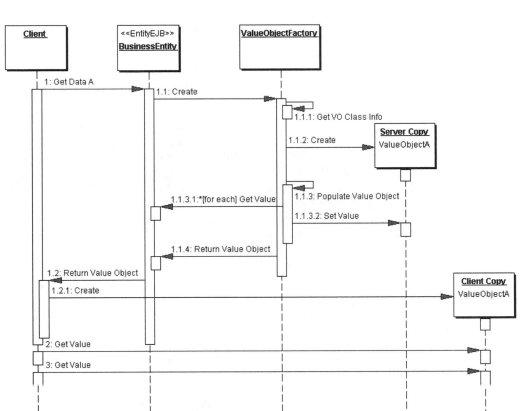

Figure 8.14 Value Object Factory strategy sequence diagram

The client requests the value object from the BusinessEntity. The BusinessEntity passes the required value object's class to the ValueObjectFactory, which creates a new value object of that given class. The ValueObjectFactory uses reflection to dynamically obtain the class information for the value object class and construct a new value object instance. Getting values from and setting values into the BusinessEntity by the ValueObjectFactory is accomplished by using dynamic invocation.

An example implementation for this strategy is shown in the "Sample Code" section for "Implementing Value Object Factory Strategy" on page 284.

The benefits of applying the Value Object Factory Strategy are as follows:

There is less code to write in order to create value objects. The same value object factory class can be reused by different enterprise beans. When a value object class definition changes, the value object factory automatically handles this change without any additional coding effort. This increases maintainability and is less error prone to changes in value object definitions.

The Value Object Factory Strategy has the following consequences:

It is based on the fact that the enterprise bean implementation extends (inherits) from the complete value object. The complete value object needs to implement all the interfaces defined for different value objects that the entity bean needs to supply. Naming conventions must be adhered to in order to make this strategy work. Since reflection is used to dynamically inspect and construct value objects, there is a slight performance loss in construction. However, when the overall communication time is considered, such loss may be negligible in comparison.

There is a trade-off associated with this strategy. Its power and flexibility must be weighed against the performance overhead associated with runtime reflection.

Consequences

- ### *Simplifies Entity Bean and Remote Interface*
  The entity bean provides a `getData()` method to get the value object containing the attribute values. This may eliminate having multiple get methods implemented in the bean and defined in the bean's remote interface. Similarly, if the entity bean provides a `setData()` method to update the entity bean attribute values in a single method call, it may eliminate having multiple set methods implemented in the bean and defined in the bean's remote interface.

- ### *Transfers More Data in Fewer Remote Calls*
  Instead of multiple client calls over the network to the BusinessObject to get attribute values, this solution provides a single method call. At the same time, this one method call returns a greater amount of data to the client than the individual accessor methods each returned. When considering this pattern, you must consider the trade-off between fewer network calls versus transmitting more data per call. Alternatively, you can provide both individual attribute

accessor methods (fine-grained get and set methods) and value object methods (coarse-grained get and set methods). The developer can choose the appropriate technique depending on the requirement.

- **Reduces Network Traffic**
  A value object transfers the values from the entity bean to the client in one remote method call. The value object acts as a data carrier and reduces the number of remote network method calls required to obtain the attribute values from the entity beans. The reduced chattiness of the application results in better network performance.

- **Reduces Code Duplication**
  By using the Entity Inherits Value Object Strategy and the Value Object Factory Strategy, it is possible to reduce or eliminate the duplication of code between the entity and its value object. However, with the use of Value Object Factory Strategy, there could be increased complexity in implementation. There is also a runtime cost associated with this strategy due to the use of dynamic reflection. In most cases, the Entity Inherits Value Object Strategy may be sufficient to meet the needs.

- **May Introduce Stale Value Objects**
  Adopting the Updatable Value Objects Strategy allows the client to perform modifications on the local copy of the value object. Once the modifications are completed, the client can invoke the entity's `setData()` method and pass the modified value object to the entity. The entity receives the modifications and merges the new (modified) values with its attributes. However, there may be a problem with stale value objects. The entity updates its values, but it is unaware of other clients that may have previously requested the same value object. These clients may be holding in their local cache value object instances that no longer reflect the current copy of the entity's data. Because the entity is not aware of these clients, it is not possible to propagate the update to the stale value objects held by other clients.

- **May Increase Complexity due to Synchronization and Version Control**
  The entity merges modified values into its own stored values when it receives a mutable value object from a client. However, the entity must handle the situation where two or more clients simultaneously request conflicting updates to the entity's values. Allowing such updates may result in data conflicts.

Version control is one way of avoiding such conflict. As one of its attributes, the entity can include a version number or a last-modified time stamp. The version number or time stamp is copied over from the entity bean into the value object. An update transaction can resolve conflicts using the time stamp or version number attribute. If a client holding a stale value object tries to update the entity, the entity can detect the stale version number or time stamp in the value object and inform the client of this error condition. The client then has to obtain the latest value object and retry the update. In extreme cases this can result in client starvation—the client might never accomplish its updates.

- ***Concurrent Access and Transactions***

    When two or more clients concurrently access the BusinessObject, the container applies the transaction semantics of the EJB architecture. If, for an Enterprise bean, the transaction isolation level is set to TRANSACTION_SERIALIZED in the deployment descriptor, the container provides the maximum protection to the transaction and ensures its integrity. For example, suppose the workflow for the first transaction involves obtaining a value object, then subsequently modifying the BusinessObject attributes in the process. The second transaction, since it is isolated to serialized transactions, will obtain the value object with the correct (most recently updated) values. However, for transactions with lesser restrictions than serialized, protection is less rigid, leading to inconsistencies in the value objects obtained by competing accesses. In addition, problems related to synchronization, stale value objects, and version control will have to be dealt with.

Sample Code

Implementing the Value Object Pattern

Consider an example where a business object called Project is modeled and implemented as an entity bean. The Project entity bean needs to send data to its clients in a value object when the client invokes its getProjectData() method. The value object class for this example, ProjectVO, is shown in Example 8.3.

Example 8.3 Implementing the Value Object Pattern – Value Object Class

```
// Value Object to hold the details for Project
public class ProjectVO implements java.io.Serializable
   {
      public String projectId;
      public String projectName;
      public String managerId;
      public String customerId;
      public Date startDate;
      public Date endDate;
      public boolean started;
      public boolean completed;
      public boolean accepted;
      public Date acceptedDate;
      public String projectDescription;
      public String projectStatus;

      // Value object constructors...
   }
```

The sample code for the entity bean that uses this value object is shown in Example 8.4.

Example 8.4 Implementing the Value Object Pattern – Entity Bean Class

```
   ...
   public class ProjectEntity implements EntityBean {
      private EntityContext context;
      public String projectId;
      public String projectName;
      public String managerId;
      public String customerId;
      public Date startDate;
      public Date endDate;
      public boolean started;
      public boolean completed;
      public boolean accepted;
      public Date acceptedDate;
      public String projectDescription;
      public String projectStatus;
      private boolean closed;

      // other attributes...
```

Example 8.4 Implementing the Value Object Pattern – Entity Bean Class

```
      private ArrayList commitments;
      ...

      // Method to get value object for Project data
      public ProjectVO getProjectData() {
        return createProjectVO();
      }

      // method to create a new value object and
      // copy data from entity bean into the value
      // object
      private ProjectVO createProjectVO() {
          ProjectVO proj = new ProjectVO();
          proj.projectId = projectId;
          proj.projectName = projectName;
          proj.managerId = managerId;
          proj.startDate = startDate;
          proj.endDate = endDate;
          proj.customerId = customerId;
          proj.projectDescription = projectDescription;
          proj.projectStatus = projectStatus;
          proj.started = started;
          proj.completed = completed;
          proj.accepted = accepted;
          proj.closed = closed;
          return proj;
      }
      ...
  }
```

Implementing the Updatable Value Objects Strategy

Example 8.4 can be extended to implement Updatable Value Objects Strategy. In this case, the entity bean would provide a `setProjectData()` method to update the entity bean by passing a value object that contains the data to be used to perform the update. The sample code for this strategy is shown in Example 8.5.

Example 8.5 Implementing Updatable Value Objects Strategy

```
...
public class ProjectEntity implements EntityBean {
    private EntityContext context;
  ...
  // attributes and other methods as in Example 8.4
  ...

  // method to set entity values with a value object
  public void setProjectData(ProjectVO updatedProj) {
    mergeProjectData(updatedProj);
  }

  // method to merge values from the value object into
  // the entity bean attributes
  private void mergeProjectData(ProjectVO updatedProj)
  {
    // version control check may be necessary here
    // before merging changes in order to
    // prevent losing updates by other clients
    projectId = updatedProj.projectId;
    projectName = updatedProj.projectName;
    managerId = updatedProj.managerId;
    startDate = updatedProj.startDate;
    endDate = updatedProj.endDate;
    customerId = updatedProj.customerId;
    projectDescription =
        updatedProj.projectDescription;
    projectStatus = updatedProj.projectStatus;
    started = updatedProj.started;
    completed = updatedProj.completed;
    accepted = updatedProj.accepted;
    closed = updatedProj.closed;
  }
  ...
}
```

Implementing the Multiple Value Objects Strategy

Consider an example where a Resource entity bean is accessed by clients to request different value objects. The first type of value object, ResourceVO, is used to transfer data for a small set of attributes. The second type of value object, ResourceDetailsVO, is used to transfer data for a larger set of attributes. The client can use the former value object if it needs only the most basic data represented by that value object, and can use the latter if it needs more detailed information. Note that this strategy can be applied in producing two or more value objects that contain different data, and not just subset-superset as shown here.

The sample code for the two value objects for this example are shown in Example 8.6 and Example 8.7. The sample code for the entity bean that produces these value objects is shown in Example 8.8, and finally the entity bean client is shown in Example 8.9.

Example 8.6 Multiple Value Objects Strategy – ResourceVO

```
// ResourceVO: This class holds basic information
// about the resource
public class ResourceVO implements
  java.io.Serializable {
  public String resourceId;
  public String lastName;
  public String firstName;
  public String department;
  public String grade;
  ...
}
```

Example 8.7 Multiple Value Objects Strategy – ResourceDetailsVO

```
// ResourceDetailsVO This class holds detailed
// information about resource
public class ResourceDetailsVO {
  public String resourceId;
  public String lastName;
  public String firstName;
  public String department;
  public String grade;
  // other data...
  public Collection commitments;
  public Collection blockoutTimes;
  public Collection skillSets;
}
```

Example 8.8 Multiple Value Objects Strategy – Resource Entity Bean

```
// imports
...
public class ResourceEntity implements EntityBean {
  // entity bean attributes
  ...

  // entity bean business methods
  ...

  // Multiple Value Object method : Get ResourceVO
  public ResourceVO getResourceData() {

    // create new ResourceVO instance and copy
    // attribute values from entity bean into VO
    ...
    return createResourceVO();
  }

  // Multiple Value Object method : Get
  // ResourceDetailsVO
  public ResourceDetailsVO getResourceDetailsData() {

    // create new ResourceDetailsVO instance and copy
    // attribute values from entity bean into VO
    ...
    return createResourceDetailsVO();
  }

  // other entity bean methods
  ...
}
```

Example 8.9 Multiple Value Objects Strategy – Entity Bean Client

```
...
private ResourceEntity resourceEntity;
private static final Class homeClazz =

corepatterns.apps.psa.ejb.ResourceEntityHome.class;
...
try {
  ResourceEntityHome home =
    (ResourceEntityHome)
      ServiceLocator.getInstance().getHome(
```

Example 8.9 Multiple Value Objects Strategy – Entity Bean Client

```
                "Resource", homeClazz);
        resourceEntity = home.findByPrimaryKey(
                            resourceId);
  } catch(ServiceLocatorException ex) {
    // Translate Service Locator exception into
    // application exception
    throw new ResourceException(...);
  } catch(FinderException ex) {
    // Translate the entity bean finder exception into
    // application exception
    throw new ResourceException(...);
  } catch(RemoteException ex) {
    // Translate the Remote exception into
    // application exception
    throw new ResourceException(...);
  }
  ...
  // retrieve basic Resource data
  ResourceVO vo = resourceEntity.getResourceData();
  ...
  // retrieve detailed Resource data
  ResourceDetailsVO =
    resourceEntity.getResourceDetailsData();
  ...
```

Implementing the Entity Inherits Value Object Strategy

Consider an example where an entity bean ContactEntity inherits all its properties from a value object ContactVO. Example 8.10 shows the code sample for an example value object ContactVO that illustrates this strategy.

Example 8.10 Entity Inherits Value Object Strategy – Value Object Class

```
// This is the value object class inherited by
// the entity bean
public class ContactVO
  implements java.io.Serializable {

  // public members
  public String firstName;
  public String lastName;
  public String address;
```

Example 8.10 Entity Inherits Value Object Strategy – Value Object Class

```java
    // default constructor
    public ContactVO() {}

    // constructor accepting all values
    public ContactVO(String firstName,
      String lastName, String address){
        init(firstName, lastName, address);
    }

    // constructor to create a new VO based
    // using an existing VO instance
    public ContactVO(ContactVO contact) {
      init (contact.firstName,
        contact.lastName, contact.address);
    }

    // method to set all the values
    public void init(String firstName, String
                lastName, String address) {
      this.firstName = firstName;
      this.lastName = lastName;
      this.address = address;
    }

    // create a new value object
    public ContactVO getData() {
      return new ContactVO(this);
    }
}
```

The entity bean sample code relevant to this pattern strategy is shown in Example 8.11.

Example 8.11 Entity Inherits Value Object Strategy – Entity Bean Class

```java
public class ContactEntity extends ContactVO
  implements javax.ejb.EntityBean {
  ...
  // the client calls the getData method
  // on the ContactEntity bean instance.
  // getData() is inherited from the value object
  // and returns the ContactVO value object
  ...
}
```

Implementing Value Object Factory Strategy

Example 8.12 demonstrates the Value Object Factory strategy.
The entity bean extends a complete value object called Customer-
ContactVO. The CustomerContactVO value object implements two
interfaces, Customer and Contact. The CustomerVO value object
implements Customer, and the ContactVO value object implements
Contact.

**Example 8.12 Value Object Factory Strategy – Value Objects and Inter-
faces**

```java
public interface Contact
  extends java.io.Serializable {
  public String getFirstName();
  public String getLastName();
  public String getContactAddress();
  public void setFirstName(String firstName);
  public void setLastName(String lastName);
  public void setContactAddress(String address);
}

public class ContactVO implements Contact {
  // member attributes
  public String firstName;
  public String lastName;
  public String contactAddress;

  // implement get and set methods per the
  // Contact interface here.
  ...
      }
public interface Customer
  extends java.io.Serializable {
  public String getCustomerName();
  public String getCustomerAddress();
  public void setCustomerName(String customerName);
  public void setCustomerAddress(String
      customerAddress);
}

public class CustomerVO implements Customer {
  public String customerName;
  public String customerAddress;

  // implement get and set methods per the
```

Example 8.12 Value Object Factory Strategy – Value Objects and Interfaces

```
// Customer interface here.
  ...
}

public class CustomerContactVO implements Customer,
  Contact {
  public String firstName;
  public String lastName;
  public String contactAddress;
  public String customerName;
  public String customerAddress;

  // implement get and set methods per the
  // Customer and Contact interfaces here.
  ...
}
```

The entity bean code sample to obtain these three different value objects is shown Example 8.13.

Example 8.13 Value Object Factory Strategy – Entity Bean Class

```
public class CustomerContactEntity extends
  CustomerContactVO implements javax.ejb.EntityBean {

  // implement other entity bean methods...not shown

  // define constant to hold class name
  // complete value object. This is required by
  // the ValueObjectFactory.createValueObject(...)
  public static final String COMPLETE_VO_CLASSNAME =
      "CustomerContactVO";

  // method to return CustomerContactVO value object
  public CustomerContactVO getCustomerContact() {
    return (CustomerContactVO)
      ValueObjectFactory.createValueObject(
        this, "CustomerContactVO",
        COMPLETE_VO_CLASSNAME);
  }

  // method to return CustomerVO value object
```

Example 8.13 Value Object Factory Strategy – Entity Bean Class

```
  public CustomerVO getCustomer() {
    return (CustomerVO)
      ValueObjectFactory.createValueObject(
        this, "CustomerVO",
        COMPLETE_VO_CLASSNAME);
  }

  // method to return ContactVO value object
  public ContactVO getContact() {
    return (ContactVO)
      ValueObjectFactory.createValueObject(
        this, "ContactVO",
        COMPLETE_VO_CLASSNAME);
  }

  // other entity bean business methods
  ...
}
```

The ValueObjectFactory class is shown in Example 8.14.

Example 8.14 Value Object Factory Strategy – Factory Class

```
import java.util.HashMap;
import java.lang.*;

/**
 * The factory class that creates a value object for a
 * given EJB.
 */
public class ValueObjectFactory {

/**
 * Use a HashMap to cache class information for
 * value object classes
 */
private static HashMap classDataInfo = new HashMap();

/**
 * Create a value object for the given object. The
 * given object must be an EJB Implementation and have
 * a superclass that acts as the class for the entity's
 * value object. Only the fields defined in this
```

Example 8.14 Value Object Factory Strategy – Factory Class

```
 * superclass are copied in to the value object.
 */
public static java.io.Serializable
  createValueObject(Object ejb,
    String whichVOType,
    String completeVOType) {
      try {
      // Get the class data for the complete
      // value object type
      ClassData cData = getClassData (completeVOType);

      // Get class data for the requested VO type
      ClassData voCData = getClassData (whichVOType);

      // Create the value object of the requested
      // value object type...
      java.lang.Object whichVO =
          Class.forName(whichVOType).newInstance();

      // get the VO fields for the requested VO
      // from the ClassData for the requested VO
      java.lang.reflect.Field[] voFields =
                voCData.arrFields;

      // get all fields for the complete VO
      // from the ClassData for complete VO
      java.lang.reflect.Field[] beanFields =
                cData.arrFields;

      // copy the common fields from the complete VO
      // to the fields of the requested VO
      for (int i = 0; i < voFields.length; i++) {
        try {
          String voFieldName = voFields[i].getName();
          for (int j=0; j < beanFields.length; j++) {
            // if the field names are same, copy value
            if ( voFieldName.equals(
                  beanFields[j].getName())) {
              // Copy value from matching field
              // from the bean instance into the new
              // value object created earlier
              voFields[i].set(whichVO,
                    beanFields[j].get(ejb));
              break;
```

Example 8.14 Value Object Factory Strategy – Factory Class

```
            }
          }
        } catch (Exception e) {
          // handle exceptions that may be thrown
          // by the reflection methods...
        }
      }
    // return the requested value object
    return (java.io.Serializable)whichVO;
  } catch (Exception ex) {
    // Handle all exceptions here...
  }
  return null;
}

/**
 * Return a ClassData object that contains the
 * information needed to create
 * a value object for the given class. This information
 * is only obtained from the
 * class using reflection once, after that it will be
 * obtained from the classDataInfo HashMap.
 */
private static ClassData getClassData(String
  className){

  ClassData cData =
    (ClassData)classDataInfo.get(className);

  try {
    if (cData == null) {
      // Get the class of the given object and the
      // value object to be created
      java.lang.reflect.Field[] arrFields ;
      java.lang.Class ejbVOClass =
          Class.forName(className);

      // Determine the fields that must be copied
      arrFields = ejbVOClass.getDeclaredFields();

      cData = new ClassData(ejbVOClass, arrFields);
      classDataInfo.put(className, cData);
    }
  } catch (Exception e) {
    // handle exceptions here...
```

Example 8.14 Value Object Factory Strategy – Factory Class

```
    }
    return cData;
    }
}

/**
 * Inner Class that contains class data for the
 * value object classes
 */
class ClassData {
  // value object Class
  public Class     clsValueObject;

  // value object fields
  public java.lang.reflect.Field[] arrFields;

  // Constructor
  public ClassData(Class cls,
      java.lang.reflect.Field[] fields) {
    clsValueObject = cls;
    arrFields = fields;
  }
}
```

Related Patterns

- **Session Facade**

  The Session Facade, which is the business interface for clients of J2EE applications, frequently uses value objects as an exchange mechanism with participating entity beans. When the facade acts as a proxy to the underlying business service, the value object obtained from the entity beans can be passed to the client.

- **Value Object Assembler**

  The Value Object Assembler is a pattern that builds composite value objects from different data sources. The data sources are usually session beans or entity beans that may be requested to provide their data to the Value Object Assembler as value objects. These value objects are considered to be parts of the composite object that the Value Object Assembler assembles.

- **Value List Handler**

  The Value List Handler is another pattern that provides lists of value objects constructed dynamically by accessing the persistent store at request time.

- **Composite Entity**

  The Value Object pattern addresses the need of getting data from BusinessObjects across tiers. This certainly is one aspect of design considerations for entity beans. The Composite Entity pattern discusses issues involved in designing coarse-grained entity beans. The Composite Entity pattern addresses complex requirements and discusses other factors and considerations involved in entity bean design.

Session Facade

Context

Enterprise beans encapsulate business logic and business data and expose their interfaces, and thus the complexity of the distributed services, to the client tier.

Problem

In a multitiered J2EE application environment, the following problems arise:

- Tight coupling, which leads to direct dependence between clients and business objects;

- Too many method invocations between client and server, leading to network performance problems;

- Lack of a uniform client access strategy, exposing business objects to misuse.

A multitiered J2EE application has numerous server-side objects that are implemented as enterprise beans. In addition, some other arbitrary objects may provide services, data, or both. These objects are collectively referred to as business objects, since they encapsulate business data and business logic.

J2EE applications implement business objects that provide processing services as session beans. Coarse-grained business objects that represent an object view of persistent storage and are shared by multiple users are usually implemented as entity beans.

Application clients need access to business objects to fulfill their responsibilities and to meet user requirements. Clients can directly interact with these business objects because they expose their interfaces. When you expose business objects to the client, the client must understand and be responsible for the business data object relationships, and must be able to handle business process flow.

However, direct interaction between the client and the business objects leads to tight coupling between the two, and such tight coupling makes the client directly dependent on the implementation of the business objects. Direct dependence means that the client must represent and implement the complex interactions regarding business object lookups and creations, and must manage the relationships between the participating business objects as well as understand the responsibility of transaction demarcation.

As client requirements increase, the complexity of interaction between various business objects increases. The client grows larger and more complex to fulfill these requirements. The client becomes very susceptible to changes in the business object layer; in addition, the client is unnecessarily exposed to the underlying complexity of the system.

Tight coupling between objects also results when objects manage their relationship within themselves. Often, it is not clear where the relationship is managed. This leads to complex relationships between business objects and rigidity in the application. Such lack of flexibility makes the application less manageable when changes are required.

When accessing the enterprise beans, clients interact with remote objects. Network performance problems may result if the client directly interacts with all the participating business objects. When invoking enterprise beans, every client invocation is potentially a remote method call. Each access to the business object is relatively fine-grained. As the number of participants increases in a scenario, the number of such remote method calls increases. As the number of remote method calls increases, the chattiness between the client and the server-side business objects increases. This may result in network performance degradation for the application, because the high volume of remote method calls increases the amount of interaction across the network layer.

A problem also arises when a client interacts directly with the business objects. Since the business objects are directly exposed to the clients, there is no unified strategy for accessing the business objects. Without such a uniform client access strategy, the business objects are exposed to clients and may reduce consistent usage.

Forces

- Provide a simpler interface to the clients by hiding all the complex interactions between business components.
- Reduce the number of business objects that are exposed to the client across the service layer over the network.
- Hide from the client the underlying interactions and interdependencies between business components. This provides better manageability, centralization of interactions (responsibility), greater flexibility, and greater ability to cope with changes.

- Provide a uniform coarse-grained service layer to separate business object implementation from business service abstraction.
- Avoid exposing the underlying business objects directly to the client to keep tight coupling between the two tiers to a minimum.

Solution

Use a session bean as a facade to encapsulate the complexity of interactions between the business objects participating in a workflow. The Session Facade manages the business objects, and provides a uniform coarse-grained service access layer to clients.

The Session Facade abstracts the underlying business object interactions and provides a service layer that exposes only the required interfaces. Thus, it hides from the client's view the complex interactions between the participants. The Session Facade manages the interactions between the business data and business service objects that participate in the workflow, and it encapsulates the business logic associated with the requirements. Thus, the session bean (representing the Session Facade) manages the relationships between business objects. The session bean also manages the life cycle of these participants by creating, locating (looking up), modifying, and deleting them as required by the workflow. In a complex application, the Session Facade may delegate this lifestyle management to a separate object. For example, to manage the lifestyle of participant session and entity beans, the Session Facade may delegate that work to a Service Locator object (see "Service Locator" on page 367).

It is important to examine the relationship between business objects. Some relationships between business objects are transient, which means that the relationship is applicable to only that interaction or scenario. Other relationships may be more permanent. Transient relationships are best modeled as workflow in a facade, where the facade manages the relationships between the business objects. Permanent relationships between two business objects should be studied to determine which business object (if not both objects) maintains the relationship.

Use Cases and Session Facades

So, how do you identify the Session Facades through studying use cases? Mapping every use case to a Session Facade will result in too many Session Facades. This defeats the intention of having fewer coarse-grained session beans. Instead, as you derive the Session Facades during your modeling, look to consolidate them into fewer numbers of session beans based on some logical partitioning.

For example, for a banking application, you may group the interactions related to managing an account into a single facade. The use cases Create New Account, Change Account Information, View Account information, and so on all deal with the coarse-grained entity object Account. Creating a session bean facade for each use case is not recommended. Thus, the functions required to support these related use cases could be grouped into a single Session Facade called AccountSessionFacade.

In this case, the Session Facade will become a highly coarse-grained controller with high-level methods that can facilitate each interaction (that is, `createNewAccount`, `changeAccount`, `getAccount`). Therefore, we recommend that you design Session Facades to aggregate a group of the related interactions into a single Session Facade. This results in fewer Session Facades for the application, and leverages the benefits of the Session Facade pattern.

Structure

Figure 8.15 shows the class diagram representing the Session Facade pattern.

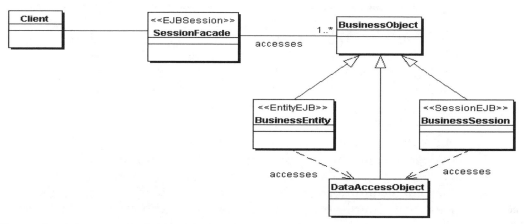

Figure 8.15 Session Facade class diagram

Participants and Collaborations

Figure 8.16 contains the sequence diagram that shows the interactions of a Session Facade with two entity beans, one session bean, and a DAO, all acting as participants in fulfilling the request from the client.

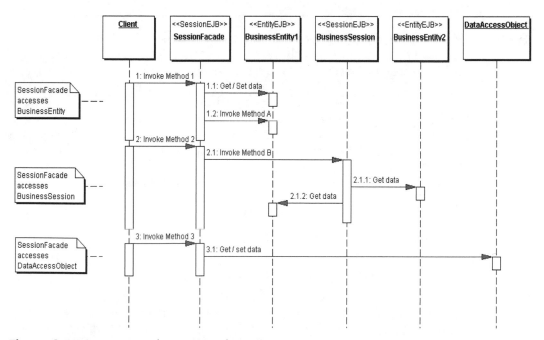

Figure 8.16 Session Facade sequence diagram

Client

This represents the client of the Session Facade, which needs access to the business service. This client can be another session bean (Session Facade) in the same business tier or a business delegate (see "Business Delegate" on page 248) in another tier.

SessionFacade

The SessionFacade is implemented as a session bean. The Session-Facade manages the relationships between numerous BusinessObjects and provides a higher level abstraction to the client. The SessionFacade offers coarse-grained access to the participating BusinessObject represented by the Invoke invocation to the session bean.

BusinessObject

The BusinessObject is a role object that facilitates applying different strategies, such as session beans entity beans and a DAO (see the next section, "Strategies"). A BusinessObject provides data and/or some service in the class diagram. The SessionFacade interacts with multiple BusinessObject instances to provide the service.

Strategies

The Session Facade is a business-tier controller object that controls the interactions between the client and the participant business data and business service objects. In a complex application, there may be numerous Session Facades that can intermediate between the client and these objects. You can identify where a Session Facade might be useful by studying the client requirements and interactions typically documented in use cases and scenarios. This analysis enables you to identify a controller layer—composed of Session Facades—that can act as facades for these scenarios.

This section explains different strategies for implementing a Session Facade.

Session Facade Strategies

Stateless Session Facade Strategy

When implementing the Session Facade, you must first decide whether the facade session bean is a stateful or a stateless session bean. Base this decision on the business process that the Session Facade is modeling.

A business process that needs only one method call to complete the service is a nonconversational business process. Such processes are suitably implemented using a stateless session bean.

A careful study of the use cases and scenarios enables you to determine the Session Facade definitions. If the use case is nonconversational, then the client initiates the use case, using a single method in the Session Facade. When the method completes, the use case completes too. There is no need to save the conversational state between one method invocation and the next. In this scenario, the Session Facade can be implemented as a stateless session bean.

Stateful Session Facade Strategy

A business process that needs multiple method calls to complete the service is a conversational business process. The conversational state must be saved between each client method invocation. In this scenario, a stateful session bean may be a more suitable approach for implementing the Session Facade.

In both the Stateless Session Facade and the Stateful Session Facade strategies, the business object's role can be fulfilled in different ways, as explained next.

Business Objects Strategies

You can implement a business object as a session bean, entity bean, DAO, or regular Java object. The following strategies discuss each of these choices.

Session Bean Strategy

The business object can be implemented as a session bean. The session bean typically provides a business service and, in some cases, it may also provide business data. When such a session bean needs access to data, it may use a DAO to manipulate the data. The Session Facade can wrap one or more such service-oriented or data-oriented session beans acting as business objects.

Entity Bean Strategy

Representing the business object by an entity bean is the most common use of the Session Facade. When multiple entity beans participate in the use case, it is not necessary to expose all the entity beans to the clients. Instead, the Session Facade can wrap these entity beans and provide a coarse-grained method to perform the required business function, thus hiding the complexity of entity bean interactions.

Data Access Object Strategy

The Session Facade can directly use one or more DAOs to represent the business data. This is done when the application is so simple that it requires no entity beans, or when the application's architecture is based only on session beans and does not use entity beans. Using DAOs inside session beans partially simulates the persistent nature of entity beans.

The application might need the services provided by an arbitrary Java object (that is, an object that is not an enterprise bean or a DAO, though a DAO can be viewed as a type of arbitrary Java object). In such cases, the Session Facade accesses this arbitrary Java object to provide the necessary functionality.

Consequences

- **Introduces Business-Tier Controller Layer**
  Session Facades can represent a control layer between clients and the business tier, as identified through analysis modeling. A Session Facade encompasses the interactions between the client and the business components. In a sophisticated application, you can identify numerous Session Facades that can intermediate between the client and the participating business-tier objects. For simpler applications, one might feel that a Session Facade is not adding much value, as it may act to mostly proxy the client requests to a single business component. However, as applications grow more complex over time, using a Session Facade up front will yield benefit at a later stage.

- **Exposes Uniform Interface**
  The underlying interactions between the business components can be very complex. A Session Facade pattern abstracts this complexity and presents the client a simpler interface that is easy to understand and to use. By applying a Session Facade, you can design a service layer that exposes simpler interfaces to the system as a whole. Thus a facade provides a uniform coarse-grained access layer to all types of clients and can protect and hide the underlying participant business components.

- **Reduces Coupling, Increases Manageability**
  Using a Session Facade decouples the business objects from the clients, thus reducing tight coupling and the client's dependency on the business objects. It is best to use a Session

Facade to manage workflow among business objects, rather than making the business objects aware of each other. A business object should only be responsible for its own (data and logic) management. Inter-business object interactions can be abstracted into a workflow in a facade. This provides better manageability, centralization of interactions (responsibility and workflow), greater flexibility, and greater ability to cope with changes.

Separating workflow into a Session Facade eliminates the direct dependency of the client on the participant objects and promotes design flexibility. Although changes to participants may require changes in the Session Facade, centralizing the workflow in the facade makes such changes more manageable. You change only the Session Facade rather than having to change all the clients. Client code is also simpler because it now delegates the workflow responsibility to the Session Facade. The client no longer manages the complex workflow interactions between business objects, nor is the client aware of interdependencies between business objects.

- ***Improves Performance, Reduces Fine-Grained Methods***
  The Session Facade also impacts performance. The Session Facade reduces network overhead between the client and the server because its use eliminates the direct interaction between the client and the business data and business service objects. Instead, all interactions are routed via the Session Facade in a coarse-grained manner. The Session Facade and its participants are closer to each other, making it more efficient for the facade to manage interactions between the participant objects. All data transfer and method invocations from the facade to the participants are presumably on a relatively high-speed network. The network performance can be further tuned to provide maximum throughput by applying the Value Object pattern for the participant objects where applicable.

- ***Provides Coarse-Grained Access***
  A Session Facade is meant to be a highly coarse-grained abstraction of the workflow. Thus, it is not desirable to have one Session Facade per entity bean interaction, which would represent a fine-grained abstraction rather than a coarse-grained one. Analyze the interaction between the client and the application services, using use cases and scenarios to determine the coarseness of the facade. Determine the optimal granularity of the Session Facade for the application by partitioning the application into logical subsystems and

providing a Session Facade for each subsystem. However, providing a single facade for the entire system can result in a very large Session Facade whose numerous methods make it inefficient. A single facade may be sufficient for very simple applications that do not warrant subsystems.

- *Centralizes Security Management*

  Security policies for the application can be managed at the Session Facade level, since this is the tier presented to the clients. Because of the Session Facade's coarse-grained access, it is easier and more manageable to define security policies at this level rather than at the participating business component level. Business components offer fine-grained control points. It is easier to manage security for Session Facades that provide coarse-grained access, because there are relatively fewer coarse-grained methods to be securely managed.

- *Centralizes Transaction Control*

  Because the Session Facade represents the workflow for the use cases, it is more logical to apply transaction management at the Session Facade level. Centralized transaction control has advantages similar to centralized security. The facade offers a central place for managing and defining transaction control in a coarse-grained fashion. It is much more work to do transaction management individually on participant business components, especially since they are more fine-grained than the facade. Also, not using a Session Facade, but rather having the client access the enterprise beans directly, puts the transaction demarcation burden on the client and can produce unwanted results.

- *Exposes Fewer Remote Interfaces to Clients*

  Clients that interact directly with the business data and business service objects cause an increase in chattiness between the client and the server. Increased chattiness may degrade network performance. All access to the business object must be via the higher level of abstraction represented by a facade. Since the facade presents a coarse-grained access mechanism to the business components, this reduces the number of business components that are exposed to the client. Thereby, the scope for application performance degradation is reduced due to the limited number of interactions between the clients and the Session Facade when compared to direct interaction by the client to the individual business components.

Sample Code

Implementing the Session Facade

Consider a Professional Services Application (PSA), where the work-flow related to entity beans (such as Project, Resource) is encapsulated in ProjectResourceManagerSession, implemented using the Session Facade pattern. Example 8.15 shows the interaction with Resource and Project entity beans, as well as other business components, like Value List Handlers (see "Value List Handler" on page 353) and Value Object Assemblers (see "Value Object Assembler" on page 339).

Example 8.15 Implementing Session Facade – Session Bean

```
package corepatterns.apps.psa.ejb;

import java.util.*;
import java.rmi.RemoteException;
import javax.ejb.*;
import javax.naming.*;
import corepatterns.apps.psa.core.*;
import corepatterns.util.ServiceLocator;
import corepatterns.util.ServiceLocatorException;

// Note: all try/catch details not shown for brevity.

public class ProjectResourceManagerSession
  implements SessionBean {

  private SessionContext context;

  // Remote references for the
  // entity Beans encapsulated by this facade
  private Resource resourceEntity = null;
  private Project projectEntity = null;
  ...

  // default create
  public void ejbCreate()
  throws CreateException {
  }

  // create method to create this facade and to
  // establish connections to the required entity
```

Example 8.15 Implementing Session Facade – Session Bean

```
// beans
// using primary key values
public void ejbCreate(
  String resourceId, String projectId, ...)
throws CreateException, ResourceException {

  try {
    // locate and connect to entity beans
    connectToEntities(resourceId, projectId, ...);
  } catch(...) {
    // Handle exceptions
  }
}

// method to connect the session facade to its
// entity beans using the primary key values
private void connectToEntities (
  String resourceId, String projectId)
throws ResourceException {
  resourceEntity = getResourceEntity(resourceId);
  projectEntity = getProjectEntity(projectId);
  ...
}

// method to reconnect the session facade to a
// different set of entity beans using primary key
// values
public resetEntities(String resourceId,
  String projectId, ...)
throws PSAException {

  connectToEntities(resourceId, projectId, ...);
}

// private method to get Home for Resource
private ResourceHome getResourceHome()
throws ServiceLocatorException {
  return ServiceLocator.getInstance().getHome(
      "ResourceEntity", ResourceHome.class);
}

// private method to get Home for Project
private ProjectHome getProjectHome()
throws ServiceLocatorException {
  return ServiceLocator.getInstance().getHome(
```

Example 8.15 Implementing Session Facade – Session Bean

```java
        "ProjectEntity", ProjectHome.class);
}

// private method to get Resource entity
private Resource getResourceEntity(
  String resourceId) throws ResourceException {
  try {
    ResourceHome home = getResourceHome();
    return (Resource)
      home.findByPrimaryKey(resourceId);
  } catch(...) {
    // Handle exceptions
  }
}

// private method to get Project entity
private Project getProjectEntity(String projectId)
throws ProjectException {
  // similar to getResourceEntity
  ...
}

// Method to encapsulate workflow related
// to assigning a resource to a project.
// It deals with Project and Resource Entity beans
public void assignResourceToProject(int numHours)
throws PSAException {

  try {
    if ((projectEntity == null) ||
        (resourceEntity == null)) {

      // SessionFacade not connected to entities
      throw new PSAException(...);
    }

    // Get Resource data
    ResourceVO resourceVO =
        resourceEntity.getResourceData();

    // Get Project data
    ProjectVO projectVO =
      projectEntity.getProjectData();
    // first add Resource to Project
    projectEntity.addResource(resourceVO);
```

Example 8.15 Implementing Session Facade – Session Bean

```
        // Create a new Commitment for the Project
        CommitmentVO commitment = new
          CommitmentVO(...);

        // add the commitment to the Resource
        projectEntity.addCommitment(commitment);

    } catch(...) {
      // Handle exceptions
    }
  }

  // Similarly implement other business methods to
  // facilitate various use cases/interactions
  public void unassignResourceFromProject()
  throws PSAException {
    ...
  }

  // Methods working with ResourceEntity
  public ResourceVO getResourceData()
  throws ResourceException {
    ...
  }

  // Update Resource Entity Bean
  public void setResourceData(ResourceVO resource)
  throws ResourceException {
    ...
  }

  // Create new Resource Entity bean
  public ResourceVO createNewResource(ResourceVO
    resource) throws ResourceException {
    ...
  }

  // Methods for managing resource's blockout time
  public void addBlockoutTime(Collection blockoutTime)
  throws RemoteException,BlockoutTimeException {
    ...
  }

  public void updateBlockoutTime(
    Collection blockoutTime)
```

Example 8.15 Implementing Session Facade – Session Bean

```
      throws RemoteException, BlockoutTimeException {
      ...
}

public Collection getResourceCommitments()
throws RemoteException, ResourceException {
   ...
}

// Methods working with ProjectEntity
public ProjectVO getProjectData()
throws ProjectException {
   ...
}

// Update Project Entity Bean
public void setProjectData(ProjectVO project)
throws ProjectException {
   ...
}

// Create new Project Entity bean
public ProjectVO createNewProject(ProjectVO project)
throws ProjectException {
   ...
}

...

// Other session facade method examples

// This proxies a call to a Value Object Assembler
// to obtain a composite value object.
// See Value Object Assembler pattern
public ProjectCVO getProjectDetailsData()
throws PSAException {
  try {
    ProjectVOAHome projectVOAHome = (ProjectVOAHome)
      ServiceLocator.getInstance().getHome(
        "ProjectVOA", ProjectVOAHome.class);
    // Value Object Assembler session bean
    ProjectVOA projectVOA =
        projectVOAHome.create(...);
    return projectVOA.getData(...);
  } catch (...) {
```

Example 8.15 Implementing Session Facade – Session Bean

```
          // Handle / throw exceptions
     }
   }

   // These method proxies a call to a ValueListHandler
   // to get a list of projects. See Value List Handler
   // pattern.
   public Collection getProjectsList(Date start,
   Date end) throws PSAException {
     try {
       ProjectListHandlerHome projectVLHHome =
         (ProjectVLHHome)
           ServiceLocator.getInstance().getHome(
             "ProjectListHandler",
             ProjectVLHHome.class);
       // Value List Handler session bean
       ProjectListHandler projectListHandler =
         projectVLHHome.create();
       return projectListHandler.getProjects(
                     start, end);
     } catch (...) {
        // Handle / throw exceptions
     }
   }

   ...

   public void ejbActivate() {
     ...
   }

   public void ejbPassivate() {
     context = null;
   }

   public void setSessionContext(SessionContext ctx) {
       this.context = ctx;
   }

   public void ejbRemove() {
     ...
   }
 }
```

The remote interface for the Session Facade is listed in Example 8.16.

Example 8.16 Implementing Session Facade – Remote Interface

```
package corepatterns.apps.psa.ejb;

import java.rmi.RemoteException;
import javax.ejb.*;
import corepatterns.apps.psa.core.*;

// Note: all try/catch details not shown for brevity.

public interface ProjectResourceManager
  extends EJBObject {

  public resetEntities(String resourceId,
  String projectId, ...)
  throws RemoteException, ResourceException ;

  public void assignResourceToProject(int numHours)
  throws RemoteException, ResourceException ;

  public void unassignResourceFromProject()
  throws RemoteException, ResourceException ;

  ...

  public ResourceVO getResourceData()
  throws RemoteException, ResourceException ;

  public void setResourceData(ResourceVO resource)
  throws RemoteException, ResourceException ;

  public ResourceVO createNewResource(ResourceVO
  resource)
  throws ResourceException ;

  public void addBlockoutTime(Collection blockoutTime)
  throws RemoteException,BlockoutTimeException ;

  public void updateBlockoutTime(Collection
  blockoutTime)
  throws RemoteException,BlockoutTimeException ;

  public Collection getResourceCommitments()
```

Example 8.16 Implementing Session Facade – Remote Interface

```
        throws RemoteException, ResourceException;

    public ProjectVO getProjectData()
    throws RemoteException, ProjectException ;

    public void setProjectData(ProjectVO project)
    throws RemoteException, ProjectException ;

    public ProjectVO createNewProject(ProjectVO project)
    throws RemoteException, ProjectException ;

    ...

    public ProjectCVO getProjectDetailsData()
    throws RemoteException, PSAException ;

    public Collection getProjectsList(Date start,
    Date end) throws RemoteException, PSAException ;

    ...
}
```

The Home interface for the Session Facade is shown in Example 8.17.

Example 8.17 Implementing Session Facade – Home Interface

```
package corepatterns.apps.psa.ejb;

import javax.ejb.EJBHome;
import java.rmi.RemoteException;
import corepatterns.apps.psa.core.ResourceException;
import javax.ejb.*;

public interface ProjectResourceManagerHome
extends EJBHome {

    public ProjectResourceManager create()
            throws RemoteException,CreateException;
    public ProjectResourceManager create(String
        resourceId, String projectId, ...)
            throws RemoteException,CreateException;
}
```

Related Patterns

- **Facade [GoF]**
  The Session Facade is based on the Facade Design pattern.

- **Data Access Object**
  One of the strategies for the business component in the Session Facade pattern is to use the DAO. This can be the case in simpler applications designed using session beans and DAOs instead of entity beans.

- **Service Locator**
  The Session Facade is a coarse-grained object that allows encapsulation of the workflow by managing business data and business service objects interactions. Business data objects can be entity beans or DAOs, and the business service objects can be session beans and other objects that provide service. The Session Facade can use the Service Locator pattern to reduce the code complexity and to exploit the benefits offered by the Service Locator.

- **Business Delegate**
  The Session Facade is used by the Business Delegate when the client requests access to business services. The Business Delegate proxies or adapts the client request to a Session Facade that provides the requested service.

- **Broker [POSA1]**
  The Session Facade performs the role of a broker to decouple the entity beans from their clients.

Composite Entity

Context

Entity beans are not intended to represent every persistent object in the object model. Entity beans are better suited for coarse-grained persistent business objects.

Problem

In a J2EE application, clients (applications, JSPs, servlets, Java-Beans) access entity beans via their remote interfaces. Thus, every client invocation potentially routes through network stubs and skeletons, even if the client and the enterprise bean are in the same JVM, OS, or machine. When entity beans are fine-grained objects, clients tend to invoke more individual entity bean methods, resulting in high network overhead.

Entity beans represent distributed persistent business objects. Whether developing or migrating an application to the J2EE platform, object granularity is very important when deciding what to implement as an entity bean. Entity beans should represent coarse-grained business objects, such as those that provide complex behavior beyond simply getting and setting field values. These coarse-grained objects typically have dependent objects. A dependent object is an object that has no real domain meaning when not associated with its coarse-grained parent.

A recurring problem is the direct mapping of the object model to an EJB model (specifically entity beans). This creates a relationship between the entity bean objects without consideration of coarse-grained versus fine-grained (or dependent) objects. Determining what to make coarse-grained versus fine-grained is typically difficult and can best be done via modeling relationships in Unified Modeling Language (UML) models.

There are a number of areas impacted by the fine-grained entity bean design approach:

- **_Entity Relationships_**—Directly mapping an object model to an EJB model does not take into account the impact of relationships between the objects. The inter-object relationships are directly transformed into inter-entity bean relationships. As a result, an entity bean might contain or hold a remote reference to another entity bean. However, maintaining remote references to distributed objects involves different techniques and semantics than maintaining references to local objects. Besides increasing the complexity of the code, it reduces flexibility, because the entity bean must change if there are any changes in its relationships.

Also, there is no guarantee as to the validity of the entity bean references to other entity beans over time. Such references are established dynamically using the entity's home object and the primary key for that entity bean instance. This implies a high maintenance overhead of reference validity checking for each such entity-bean-to-entity-bean reference.

- *Manageability*—Implementing fine-grained objects as entity beans results in a large number of entity beans in the system. An entity bean is defined using several classes. For each entity bean component, the developer must provide classes for the home interface, the remote interface, the bean implementation, and the primary key.

  In addition, the container may generate classes to support the entity bean implementation. When the bean is created, these classes are realized as real objects in the container. In short, the container creates a number of objects to support each entity bean instance. Large numbers of entity beans result in more classes and code to maintain for the development team. It also results in a large number of objects in the container. This can negatively impact the application performance.

- *Network Performance*—Fine-grained entity beans potentially have more inter-entity bean relationships. Entity beans are distributed objects. When one entity bean invokes a method on another entity bean, the call is potentially treated as a remote call by the container, even if both entity beans are in the same container or JVM. If the number of entity-bean-to-entity-bean relationships increases, then this decreases system scalability due to heavy network overhead.

- *Database Schema Dependency*—When the entity beans are fine-grained, each entity bean instance usually represents a single row in a database. This is not a proper application of the entity bean design, since entity beans are more suitable for coarse-grained components. Fine-grained entity bean implementation typically is a direct representation of the underlying database schema in the entity bean design. When clients use these fine-grained entity beans, they are essentially operating at the row level in the database, since each entity bean is effectively a single row. Because the entity bean directly models a single database row, the clients become dependent on the database schema. When the schema changes, the entity bean definitions must change as well. Further, since the clients are operating at the same granularity, they must observe and react to this change. This schema dependency causes a loss of flexibility and increases the maintenance overhead whenever schema changes are required.

- **Object Granularity (Coarse-Grained versus Fine-Grained)**—Object granularity impacts data transfer between the enterprise bean and the client. In most applications, clients typically need a larger chunk of data than one or two rows from a table. In such a case, implementing each of these fine-grained objects as an entity bean means that the client would have to manage the relationships between all these fine-grained objects. Depending on the data requirements, the client might have to perform many lookups of a number of entity beans to obtain the required information.

Forces

- Entity beans are best implemented as coarse-grained objects due to the high overhead associated with each entity bean. Each entity bean is implemented using several objects, such as EJB home object, remote object, bean implementation, and primary key, and each is managed by the container services.
- Applications that directly map relational database schema to entity beans (where each row in a table is represented by an entity bean instance) tend to have a large number of fine-grained entity beans. It is desirable to keep the entity beans coarse-grained and reduce the number of entity beans in the application.
- Direct mapping of object model to EJB model yields fine-grained entity beans. Fine-grained entity beans usually map to the database schema. This entity-to-database row mapping causes problems related to performance, manageability, security, and transaction handling. Relationships between tables are implemented as relationships between entity beans, which means that entity beans hold references to other entity beans to implement the fine-grained relationships. It is very expensive to manage inter-entity bean relationships, because these relationships must be established dynamically, using the entity home objects and the enterprise beans' primary keys.

- Clients do not need to know the implementation of the database schema to use and support the entity beans. With fine-grained entity beans, the mapping is usually done so that each entity bean instance maps to a single row in the database. This fine-grained mapping creates a dependency between the client and the underlying database schema, since the clients deal with the fine-grained beans and they are essentially a direct representation of the underlying schema. This results in tight coupling between the database schema and entity beans. A change to the schema causes a corresponding change to the entity bean, and in addition requires a corresponding change to the clients.
- There is an increase in chattiness of applications due to inter-communication among fine-grained entity beans. Excessive inter-entity bean communication often leads to a performance bottleneck. Every method call to the entity bean is made via the network layer, even if the caller is in the same address space as the called bean (that is, both the client, or caller entity bean, and the called entity bean are in the same container). While some container vendors optimize for this scenario, the developer cannot rely on this optimization in all containers.
- Additional chattiness can be observed between the client and the entity beans because the client may have to communicate with many fine-grained entity beans to fulfill a requirement. It is desirable to reduce the communication between or among entity beans and to reduce the chattiness between the client and the entity bean layer.

Solution

Use Composite Entity to model, represent, and manage a set of interrelated persistent objects rather than representing them as individual fine-grained entity beans. A Composite Entity bean represents a graph of objects.

In order to understand this solution, let us first define what is meant by persistent objects and discuss their relationships.

A persistent object is an object that is stored in some type of data store. Multiple clients usually share persistent objects. Persistent objects can be classified into two types: coarse-grained objects and dependent objects.

A coarse-grained object is self-sufficient. It has its own life cycle and manages its relationships to other objects. Each coarse-grained object may reference or contain one or more other objects. The coarse-grained object usually manages the lifecycles of these objects. Hence, these objects are called dependent objects. A dependent object can be a simple self-contained object or may in turn contain other dependent objects.

The life cycle of a dependent object is tightly coupled to the life cycle of the coarse-grained object. A client may only indirectly access a dependent object through the coarse-grained object. That is, dependent objects are not directly exposed to clients because their parent (coarse-grained) object manages them. Dependent objects cannot exist by themselves. Instead, they always need to have their coarse-grained (or parent) object to justify their existence.

Typically, you can view the relationship between a coarse-grained object and its dependent objects as a tree. The coarse-grained object is the root of the tree (the root node). Each dependent object can be a standalone dependent object (a leaf node) that is a child of the coarse-grained object. Or, the dependent object can have parent-child relationships with other dependent objects, in which case it is considered a branch node.

A Composite Entity bean can represent a coarse-grained object and all its related dependent objects. Aggregation combines interrelated persistent objects into a single entity bean, thus drastically reducing the number of entity beans required by the application. This leads to a highly coarse-grained entity bean that can better leverage the benefits of entity beans than can fine-grained entity beans.

Without the Composite Entity approach, there is a tendency to view each coarse-grained and dependent object as a separate entity bean, leading to a large number of entity beans.

Structure

While there are many strategies in implementing the Composite Entity pattern, the first one we discuss is represented by the class diagram in Figure 8.17. Here the Composite Entity contains the coarse-grained object, and the coarse-grained object contains dependent objects.

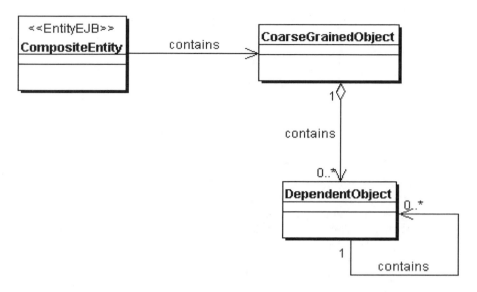

Figure 8.17 Composite Entity class diagram

The sequence diagram in Figure 8.18 shows the interactions for this pattern.

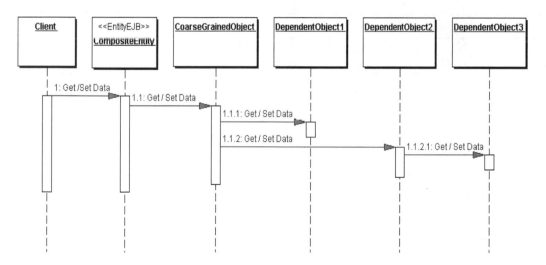

Figure 8.18 Composite Entity sequence diagram

Participants and Responsibilities

CompositeEntity

CompositeEntity is the coarse-grained entity bean. The Composi-teEntity may be the coarse-grained object, or it may hold a reference to the coarse-grained object. The "Strategies" section explains the different implementation strategies for a Composite Entity.

Coarse-Grained Object

A coarse-grained object is an object that has its own life cycle and manages its own relationships to other objects. A coarse-grained object can be a Java object contained in the Composite Entity. Or, the Composite Entity itself can be the coarse-grained object that holds dependent objects. These strategies are explained in the "Strategies" section.

DependentObject1, DependentObject2, and DependentObject3

A dependent object is an object that depends on the coarse-grained object and has its life cycle managed by the coarse-grained object. A dependent object can contain other dependent objects; thus there may be a tree of objects within the Composite Entity.

Strategies

This section explains different strategies for implementing a Composite Entity. The strategies consider possible alternatives and options for persistent objects (coarse-grained and dependent) and the use of value objects.

Composite Entity Contains Coarse-Grained Object Strategy

In this strategy, the Composite Entity holds or contains the coarse-grained object. The coarse-grained object continues to have relationships with its dependent objects. The structure section of this pattern describes this as the main strategy.

Composite Entity Implements Coarse-Grained Object Strategy

In this strategy, the Composite Entity itself is the coarse-grained object and it has the coarse-grained object's attributes and methods. The dependent objects are attributes of the Composite Entity. Since the Composite Entity is the coarse-grained object, the entity bean expresses and manages all relationships between the coarse-grained object and the dependent objects.

Figure 8.19 is the class diagram for this strategy.

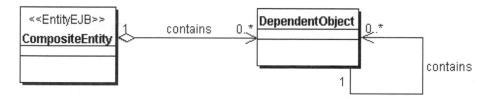

Figure 8.19 Composite Entity Implements Coarse-Grained Object class diagram

The sequence diagram for this strategy is shown in Figure 8.20.

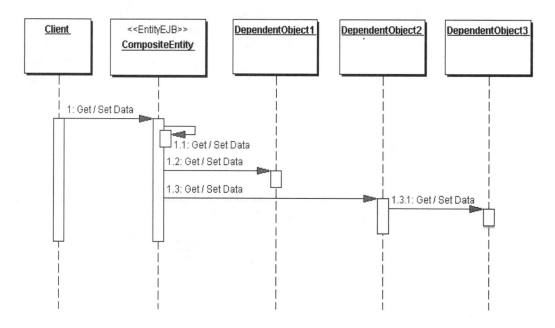

Figure 8.20 Composite Entity Implements Coarse-Grained Object sequence diagram

Lazy Loading Strategy

A Composite Entity can be composed of many levels of dependent objects in its tree of objects. Loading all the dependent objects when the Composite Entity's `ejbLoad()` method is called by the EJB Container may take considerable time and resources. One way to optimize this is by using a lazy loading strategy for loading the dependent objects. When the `ejbLoad()` method is called, at first only load those dependent objects that are most crucial to the Composite Entity clients. Subsequently, when the clients access a dependent object that has not yet been loaded from the database, the

Composite Entity can perform a load on demand. Thus, if some dependent objects are not used, they are not loaded on initialization. However, when the clients subsequently need those dependent objects, they get loaded at that time. Once a dependent object is loaded, subsequent container calls to the `ejbLoad()` method must include those dependent objects for reload to synchronize the changes with the persistent store.

Store Optimization (Dirty Marker) Strategy

A common problem with bean-managed persistence occurs when persisting the complete object graph during an `ejbStore()` operation. Since the EJB Container has no way of knowing what data has changed in the entity bean and its dependent objects, it puts the burden on the developer to determine what and how to persist the data. Some EJB containers provide a feature to identify what objects in Composite Entity's graph need to be stored due to a prior update. This may be done by having the developers implement a special method in the dependent objects, such as `isDirty()`, that is called by the container to check if the object has been updated since the previous `ejbStore()` operation.

A generic solution may be to use an interface, DirtyMarker, as shown in the class diagram in Figure 8.21. The idea is to have dependent objects implement the DirtyMarker interface to let the caller (typically the `ejbStore()` method) know if the state of the dependent object has changed. This way, the caller can choose to obtain the data for subsequent storage.

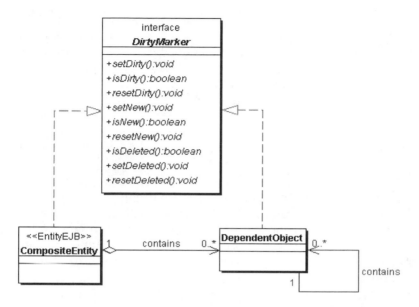

Figure 8.21 Store Optimization Strategy class diagram

Figure 8.22 contains a sequence diagram showing an example interaction for this strategy.

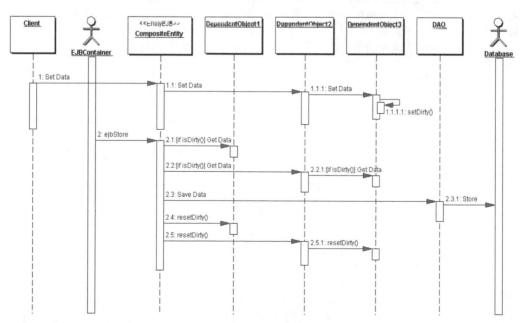

Figure 8.22 Store Optimization Strategy sequence diagram

The client performs an update to the Composite Entity, which results in a change to DependentObject3. DependentObject3 is accessed via its parent DependentObject2. The Composite Entity is the parent of DependentObject2. When this update is performed, the setDirty() method is invoked in the DependentObject3. Subsequently, when the container invokes the ejbStore() method on this Composite Entity instance, the ejbStore() method can check which dependent objects have gone dirty and selectively save those changes to the database. The dirty marks are reset once the store is successful.

The DirtyMarker interface can also include methods that can recognize other persistence status of the dependent object. For example, if a new dependent object is included into the Composite Entity, the ejbStore() method should be able to recognize what operation to use—in this case, the dependent object is not dirty, but is a new object. By extending the DirtyMarker interface to include a method called isNew(), the ejbStore() method can invoke an insert operation instead of an update operation. Similarly, by including a method called isDeleted(), the ejbStore() method can invoke delete operation as required.

In cases where ejbStore() is invoked with no intermediate updates to the Composite Entity, none of the dependent objects have been updated.

This strategy avoids the huge overhead of having to persist the entire dependent objects graph to the database whenever the ejbStore() method is invoked by the container.

Note

The EJB 2.0 specification addresses the Lazy Loading strategy and the Store Optimization strategy. The 2.0 specification is in final draft at the time of this writing. However, it is possible to use these strategies in pre-EJB 2.0 implementations. Please follow the EJB 2.0 developments to understand how these strategies will be finalized in the specification.

Composite Value Object Strategy

With a Composite Entity, a client can obtain all required information with just one remote method call. Because the Composite Entity either implements or holds the coarse-grained object and the hierarchy (or tree) of dependent objects, it can create the required value object and return it to the client by applying the Value Object pattern (see "Value Object" on page 261). The sequence diagram for this strategy is shown in Figure 8.23.

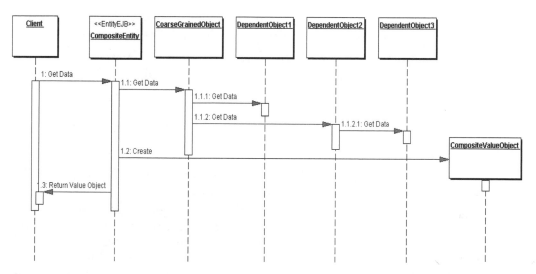

Figure 8.23 Composite Value Object Strategy sequence diagram

The value object can be a simple object or a composite object that has subobjects (a graph), depending on the data requested by the client. The value object is serializable and it is passed by value to the client. The value object functions only as a data transfer object; it has no responsibility with respect to security, transaction, and business logic. The value object packages all information into one object, obtaining the information with one remote call rather than multiple remote calls. Once the client receives the value object, all further calls from the client to the value object are local to the client.

This discussion points to how the entity can package all its data into a composite value object and return it to the client. However, this strategy also allows the entity bean to return only the required data to the client. If the client needs data only from a subset of dependent objects, then the composite value object returned can contain data derived from only those required parts and not from all the dependent objects. This would be an application of the Multiple Value Objects Strategy from the Value Object pattern (see "Value Object" on page 261).

Consequences

- ### *Eliminates Inter-Entity Relationships*
  Using the Composite Entity pattern, the dependent objects are composed into a single entity bean, eliminating all

inter-entity-bean relationships. This pattern provides a central place to manage both relationships and object hierarchy.

- ***Improves Manageability by Reducing Entity Beans***

  As discussed, implementing persistent objects as fine-grained entity beans results in a large number of classes that need to be developed and maintained. Using a Composite Entity reduces the number of EJB classes and code, and makes maintenance easier. It improves the manageability of the application by having fewer coarse-grained components instead of many more fine-grained components.

- ***Improves Network Performance***

  Aggregation of the dependent objects improves overall performance. Aggregation eliminates all fine-grained communications between dependent objects across the network. If each dependent object were designed as a fine-grained entity bean, a huge network overhead would result due to inter-entity bean communications.

- ***Reduces Database Schema Dependency***

  When the Composite Entity pattern is used, it results in coarse-grained entity bean implementations. The database schema is hidden from the clients, since the mapping of the entity bean to the schema is internal to the coarse-grained entity bean. Changes to the database schema may require changes to the Composite Entity beans. However, the clients are not affected since the Composite Entity beans do not expose the schema to the external world.

- ***Increases Object Granularity***

  With a Composite Entity, the client typically looks up a single entity bean instead of a large number of fine-grained entity beans. The client requests the Composite Entity for data. The Composite Entity can create a composite value object that contains all the data from the entity bean and return the value object to the client in a single remote method call. This reduces the chattiness between the client and the business tier.

- ***Facilitates Composite Value Object Creation***

  By using this strategy, chattiness of the communication between the client and the entity bean is reduced, since the Composite Entity bean can return a composite value object by providing a mechanism to send serialized value objects from the Composite Entity bean. Although a value object returns all data in one remote call, the amount of data returned with this one call is much larger than the amount of data returned by separate remote calls to obtain individual entity bean properties. This trade-off works well when the goal is to avoid repeated remote calls and multiple lookups.

*   ***Overhead of Multi-level Dependent Object Graphs***
    If the dependent objects graph managed by the Composite Entity has many levels, then the overhead of loading and storing the dependent objects increases. This can be reduced by using the optimization strategies for load and store, but then there may be an overhead associated with checking the dirty objects to store and loading the required objects.

Sample Code

Consider a Professional Service Automation application (PSA) where a Resource business object is implemented using the Composite Entity pattern. The Resource represents the employee resource that is assigned to projects. Each Resource object can have different dependent objects as follows:

*   BlockOutTime—This dependent object represents the time period the Resource is unavailable for reasons such as training, vacation, timeoffs, etc. Since each resource can have multiple blocked out times, the Resource-to-BlockOutTime relationship is a one-to-many relationship.
*   SkillSet—This dependent object represents the Skill that a Resource possesses. Since each resource can have multiple skills, the Resource-to-SkillSet relationship is a one-to-many relationship.

Implementing the Composite Entity Pattern

The pattern for the Resource business object is implemented as a Composite Entity (ResourceEntity), as shown in Example 8.18. The one-to-many relationship with its dependent objects (BlockOutTime and SkillSet objects) are implemented using collections.

Example 8.18 Entity Implements Coarse-Grained Object

```
package corepatterns.apps.psa.ejb;

import corepatterns.apps.psa.core.*;
import corepatterns.apps.psa.dao.*;
import java.sql.*;
```

Example 8.18 Entity Implements Coarse-Grained Object

```
import javax.sql.*;
import java.util.*;
import javax.ejb.*;
import javax.naming.*;

public class ResourceEntity implements EntityBean {
  public String employeeId;
  public String lastName;
  public String firstName;
  public String departmentId;
  public String practiceGroup;
  public String title;
  public String grade;
  public String email;
  public String phone;
  public String cell;
  public String pager;
  public String managerId;

  // Collection of BlockOutTime Dependent objects
  public Collection blockoutTimes;

  // Collection of SkillSet Dependent objects
  public Collection skillSets;

  ...

  private EntityContext context;
// Entity Bean methods implementation
public String ejbCreate(ResourceVO resource) throws
  CreateException {
    try {
      this.employeeId = resource.employeeId;
      setResourceData(resource);
      getResourceDAO().create(resource);
    } catch(Exception ex) {
      throw new EJBException("Reason:" + ...);
    }
    return this.employeeId;
}

public String ejbFindByPrimaryKey(String primaryKey)
  throws FinderException {
    boolean result;
    try {
```

Example 8.18 Entity Implements Coarse-Grained Object

```
      ResourceDAO resourceDAO = getResourceDAO();
      result =
        resourceDAO.selectByPrimaryKey(primaryKey);
    } catch(Exception ex) {
      throw new EJBException("Reason:" + ...);
    }
    if(result) {
      return primaryKey;
    }
    else {
      throw new ObjectNotFoundException(...);
    }
  }

  public void ejbRemove() {
    try {
      // Remove dependent objects
      if(this.skillSets != null) {

        SkillSetDAO skillSetDAO = getSkillSetDAO();
        skillSetDAO.setResourceID(employeeId);
        skillSetDAO.deleteAll();
        skillSets = null;
      }
      if(this.blockOutTime != null) {
        BlockOutTimeDAO blockouttimeDAO =
            getBlockOutTimeDAO();
        blockouttimeDAO.setResourceID(employeeId);
        blockouttimeDAO.deleteAll();
        blockOutTimes = null;
      }

      // Remove the resource from the persistent store
      ResourceDAO resourceDAO = new
        ResourceDAO(employeeId);
      resourceDAO.delete();
    } catch(ResourceException ex) {
      throw new EJBException("Reason:"+...);
    } catch(BlockOutTimeException ex) {
      throw new EJBException("Reason:"+...);
    } catch(Exception exception) {
      ...
    }
  }
}
```

Example 8.18 Entity Implements Coarse-Grained Object

```java
public void setEntityContext(EntityContext context)
{
  this.context = context;
}

public void unsetEntityContext() {
  context = null;
}

public void ejbActivate() {
  employeeId = (String)context.getPrimaryKey();
}

public void ejbPassivate() {
  employeeId = null;
}

public void ejbLoad() {
  try {
    // load the resource info from
    ResourceDAO resourceDAO = getResourceDAO();
    setResourceData((ResourceVO)
      resourceDAO.load(employeeId));

    // Load other dependent objects, if necessary
    ...
  } catch(Exception ex) {
    throw new EJBException("Reason:" + ...);
  }
}

public void ejbStore() {
  try {
    // Store resource information
    getResourceDAO().update(getResourceData());

    // Store dependent objects as needed
    ...
  } catch(SkillSetException ex) {
    throw new EJBException("Reason:" + ...);
  } catch(BlockOutTimeException ex) {
    throw new EJBException("Reason:" + ...);
  }
  ...
}
```

Example 8.18 Entity Implements Coarse-Grained Object

```java
public void ejbPostCreate(ResourceVO resource) {
}

// Method to Get Resource value object
public ResourceVO getResourceVO() {
  // create a new Resource value object
  ResourceVO resourceVO = new
      ResourceVO(employeeId);

  // copy all values
  resourceVO.lastName = lastName;
  resourceVO.firstName = firstName;
  resourceVO.departmentId = departmentId;
  ...
  return resourceVO;
}

public void setResourceData(ResourceVO resourceVO) {
  // copy values from value object into entity bean
  employeeId = resourceVO.employeeId;
  lastName = resourceVO.lastName;
  ...
}

// Method to get dependent value objects
public Collection getSkillSetsData() {
  // If skillSets is not loaded, load it first.
  // See Lazy Load strategy implementation.

  return skillSets;
}
...

// other get and set methods as needed
...

// Entity bean business methods
public void addBlockOutTimes(Collection moreBOTs)
throws BlockOutTimeException {
  // Note: moreBOTs is a collection of
  // BlockOutTimeVO objects
  try {
    Iterator moreIter = moreBOTs.iterator();
    while(moreIter.hasNext()) {
```

Example 8.18 Entity Implements Coarse-Grained Object

```
          BlockOutTimeVO botVO = (BlockOutTimeVO)
                          moreIter.next();
        if (! (blockOutTimeExists(botVO))) {
          // add BlockOutTimeVO to collection
          botVO.setNew();
          blockOutTime.add(botVO);
        } else {
          // BlockOutTimeVO already exists, cannot add
          throw new BlockOutTimeException(...);
        }
      }
    } catch(Exception exception) {
      throw new EJBException(...);
    }
}

public void addSkillSet(Collection moreSkills)
throws SkillSetException {
  // similar to addBlockOutTime() implementation
  ...
}

...

public void updateBlockOutTime(Collection updBOTs)
throws BlockOutTimeException {
  try {
    Iterator botIter = blockOutTimes.iterator();
    Iterator updIter = updBOTs.iterator();
    while (updIter.hasNext()) {
      BlockOutTimeVO botVO = (BlockOutTimeVO)
        updIter.next();
      while (botIter.hasNext()) {
        BlockOutTimeVO existingBOT =
          (BlockOutTimeVO) botIter.next();
        // compare key values to locate BlockOutTime
        if (existingBOT.equals(botVO)) {
          // Found BlockOutTime in collection
          // replace old BlockOutTimeVO with new one
          botVO.setDirty(); //modified old dependent
          botVO.resetNew(); //not a new dependent
          existingBOT = botVO;
        }
      }
    }
```

Example 8.18 Entity Implements Coarse-Grained Object

```
    } catch (Exception exc) {
      throw new EJBException(...);
    }
  }

  public void updateSkillSet(Collection updSkills)
  throws CommitmentException {
    // similar to updateBlockOutTime...
    ...
  }

  ...

}
```

Implementing the Lazy Loading Strategy

When the Composite Entity is first loaded in the `ejbLoad()` method
by the container, let us assume that only the resource data is to be
loaded. This includes the attributes listed in the ResourceEntity
bean, excluding the dependent object collections. The dependent
objects can then be loaded only if the client invokes a business
method that needs these dependent objects to be loaded. Subsequently, the `ejbLoad()` needs to keep track of the dependent objects
loaded in this manner and include them for reloading.

The relevant methods from the ResourceEntity class are shown in
Example 8.19.

Example 8.19 Implementing Lazy Loading Strategy

```
  ...
  public Collection getSkillSetsData() {
  throws SkillSetException {
    checkSkillSetLoad();
    return skillSets;
  }

  private void checkSkillSetLoad()
  throws SkillSetException {
    try {
      // Lazy Load strategy...Load on demand
      if (skillSets == null)
```

Example 8.19 Implementing Lazy Loading Strategy

```
          skillSets =
            getSkillSetDAO(resourceId).loadAll();
    } catch(Exception exception) {
      // No skills, throw an exception
      throw new SkillSetException(...);
    }
  }

  ...

  public void ejbLoad() {
    try {
      // load the resource info from
      ResourceDAO resourceDAO = new
        ResourceDAO(employeeId);
      setResourceData((ResourceVO)resourceDAO.load());

      // If the lazy loaded objects are already
      // loaded, they need to be reloaded.
      // If there are not loaded, do not load them
      // here...lazy load will load them later.
      if (skillSets != null) {
        reloadSkillSets();
      }
      if (blockOutTimes != null) {
        reloadBlockOutTimes();
      }
      ...
      throw new EJBException("Reason:"+...);
    }
  }

  ...
```

Implementing the Store Optimization (Dirty Marker) Strategy

To use the Store Optimization strategy, the dependent objects need to have implemented the DirtyMarker interface, as shown in Example 8.20. The `ejbStore()` method to optimize using this strategy is listed in Example 8.21.

Example 8.20 SkillSet Dependent Object Implements DirtyMarker Interface

```
public class SkillSetVO implements DirtyMarker,
  java.io.Serializable {
  private String skillName;
  private String expertiseLevel;
  private String info;
  ...

  // dirty flag
  private boolean dirty = false;

  // new flag
  private boolean isnew = true;

  // deleted flag
  private boolean deleted = false;

  public SkillSetVO(...) {
    // initialization
    ...
    // is new VO
    setNew();
  }

  // get, set and other methods for SkillSet
  // all set methods and modifier methods
  // must call setDirty()
  public setSkillName(String newSkillName) {
    skillName = newSkillName;
    setDirty();
  }
  ...

  // DirtyMarker methods
  // used for modified value objects only
```

Example 8.20 SkillSet Dependent Object Implements DirtyMarker Interface

```
public void setDirty() {
  dirty = true;
}
public void resetDirty() {
  dirty = false;
}
public boolean isDirty() {
  return dirty;
}

// used for new value objects only
public void setNew() {
  isnew = true;
}
public void resetNew() {
  isnew = false;
}
public boolean isNew() {
  return isnew;
}

// used for deleted objects only
public void setDeleted() {
  deleted = true;
}
public boolean isDeleted() {
  return deleted;
}
public void resetDeleted() {
  deleted = false;
}

}
```

Example 8.21 Implementing Store Optimization

```
...

public void ejbStore() {
  try {
    // Load the mandatory data
    getResourceDAO().update(getResourceData());

    // Store optimization for dependent objects
    // check dirty and store
    // Check and store commitments
    if (skillSets != null) {
      // Get the DAO to use to store
      SkillSetDAO skillSetDAO = getSkillSetDAO();
      Iterator skillIter = skillSet.iterator();
      while(skillIter.hasNext()) {
        SkillSetVO skill =
          (SkillSetVO) skillIter.next();
        if (skill.isNew()) {
          // This is a new dependent, insert it
          skillSetDAO.insert(skill);
          skill.resetNew();
          skill.resetDirty();
        }
        else if (skill.isDeleted()) {
          // delete Skill
          skillSetDAO.delete(skill);
          // Remove from dependents list
          skillSets.remove(skill);
        }
        else if (skill.isDirty()) {
          // Store Skill, it has been modified
          skillSetDAO.update(skill);
          // Saved, reset dirty.
          skill.resetDirty();
          skill.resetNew();
        }
      }
    }

    // Similarly, implement store optimization
    // for other dependent objects such as

    // BlockOutTime, ...
    ...
  } catch(SkillSetException ex) {
```

Example 8.21 Implementing Store Optimization

```
        throw new EJBException("Reason:"+...);
    } catch(BlockOutTimeException ex) {
        throw new EJBException("Reason:"+...);
    } catch(CommitmentException ex) {
        throw new EJBException("Reason:"+...);
    }
}

...
```

Implementing the Composite Value Object Strategy

Now consider the requirement where the client needs to obtain all the data from the ResourceEntity, and not just one part. This can be done using the Composite Value Object Strategy, as shown in Example 8.22.

Example 8.22 Implementing the Composite Value Object

```
public class ResourceCompositeVO {
    private ResourceVO resourceData;
    private Collection skillSets;
    private Collection blockOutTimes;

    // value object constructors
    ...

    // get and set methods
    ...
}
```

The ResourceEntity provides a `getResourceDetailsData()` method to return the ResourceCompositeVO composite value object, as shown in Example 8.23.

Example 8.23 Creating the Composite Value Object

```
...
public ResourceCompositeVO getResourceDetailsData() {
    ResourceCompositeVO compositeVO =
        new ResourceCompositeVO (getResourceData(),
            getSkillsData(), getBlockOutTimesData());
    return compositeVO;
}
...
```

Related Patterns

- **Value Object**

  The Composite Entity pattern uses the Value Object pattern for creating the value object and returning it to the client. The Value Object pattern is used to serialize the coarse-grained and dependent objects tree, or part of the tree, as required.

- **Session Facade**

  If dependent objects tend to be entity beans rather than the arbitrary Java objects, try to use the Session Facade pattern to manage the inter-entity-bean relationships.

- **Value Object Assembler**

  When it comes to obtaining a composite value object from the Composite Entity (see the "Facilitates Composite Value Object Creation" under the "Consequences" section), this pattern is similar to the Value Object Assembler pattern. However, in this case, the data sources for all the value objects in the composite are parts of the Composite Entity itself, whereas for the Value Object Assembler, the data sources can be different entity beans, session beans, DAOs, Java objects, and so on.

Entity Bean as a Dependent Object: Issues and Recommendations

Typically, we design dependent objects as Java objects that have a direct relationship with the parent coarse-grained object. However, there may be situations when a dependent object may appear as an entity bean itself. This can happen

1. If the dependent object appears to be depending on two different parent objects (as is the case with association classes).
2. If the dependent object already exists as an entity bean in the same application or is imported from a different application.

In these cases, the lifestyle of the dependent object may not appear to be directly related to and managed by a single parent coarse-grained object. So, what do you do when a dependent object is an entity bean? When you see a dependent object that is not totally dependent on its parent object? Or when you cannot identify its sole parent object?

Let's consider each case in a little more detail.

Case 1: The Dependent Object Depends on Two Parent Objects

Let us explore this with the following example. A Commitment represents an association between a Resource and a Project.

Figure 8.24 shows an example class diagram with relationships between Project, Resource and Commitment.

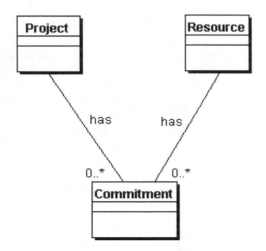

Figure 8.24 Example: Dependent object with two parent objects

Commitment is a dependent object. Both Projects and Resources are coarse-grained objects. Each Project has a one-to-many relationship with Commitment objects. Each Resource also has a one-to-many relationship with Commitment objects. So, is Commitment a dependent object of Project or of Resource? The answer lies in analyzing the interactions for the use cases that involve these three objects. If you make the Commitment a dependent of the Project, then when the Resource accesses its list Commitment objects, it has to do so through the Project object. On the other hand, if the Commitment is a dependent of a Resource, when the Project accesses its list of Commitment objects, it has to do so via the Resource. Both these choices will introduce entity-bean-to-entity-bean relationships in the design.

But, what if the Commitment is made an entity bean instead of a dependent object? Then the relationships between the Project and its list of Commitment objects, and between a Resource and its list of Commitment objects, will be entity-to-entity bean relationships. This just worsens the problem in that now there are two entity-bean-to-entity-bean relationships.

Entity-bean-to-entity-bean relationships are not recommended due to the overhead associated with managing and sustaining such a relationship.

Case 2: The Dependent Object Already Exists as an Entity Bean

In this case, it may seem that one way to model this relationship is to store the primary key of the dependent object in the coarse-grained object. When the coarse-grained object needs to access the dependent object, it results in an entity-bean-to-entity-bean invocation. The class diagram for this example is shown in Figure 8.25.

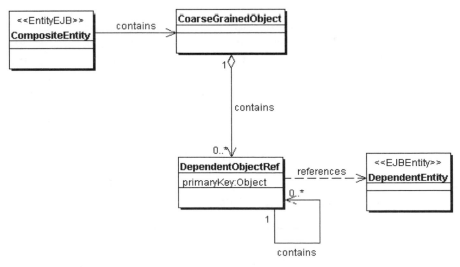

Figure 8.25 Dependent Object is an Entity Bean class diagram

The sequence diagram for this scenario is shown in Figure 8.26. The Composite Entity uses the dependent object references to look up the required dependent entity beans. The dependent object in this case is a proxy to the dependent entity bean, as shown.

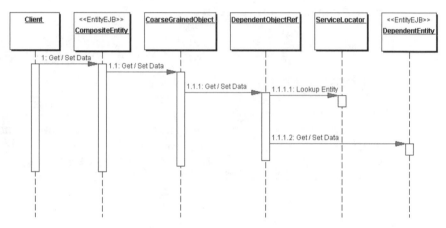

Figure 8.26 Dependent Object is an Entity Bean sequence diagram

While this may address the requirement of using a dependent entity bean from a parent entity bean, it is not an elegant solution. Instead, to avoid the complexity of designing and managing inter-entity relationships, consider using a session bean to help manage the relationships among entity beans. In our experience, we have found that the Session Facade pattern helps us to avoid this problem and provides a better way of managing entity-bean-to-entity-bean relationships.

So, we recommend avoiding entity-bean-to-entity-bean relationships as a best practice and to factor out such relationships into a session bean, using the Session Facade pattern (see "Session Facade" on page 291).

Value Object Assembler

Context

In a J2EE application, the server-side business components are implemented using session beans, entity beans, DAOs, and so forth. Application clients frequently need to access data that is composed from multiple objects.

Problem

Application clients typically require the data for the model or parts of the model to present to the user or to use for an intermediate processing step before providing some service. The application model is an abstraction of the business data and business logic implemented on the server side as business components. A model may be expressed as a collection of objects put together in a structured manner (tree or graph). In a J2EE application, the model is a distributed collection of objects such as session beans, entity beans, or DAOs and other objects. For a client to obtain the data for the model, such as to display to the user or to perform some processing, it must access individually each distributed object that defines the model. This approach has several drawbacks:

- Because the client must access each distributed component individually, there is a tight coupling between the client and the distributed components of the model over the network

- The client accesses the distributed components via the network layer, and this can lead to performance degradation if the model is complex with numerous distributed components. Network and client performance degradation occur when a number of distributed business components implement the application model and the client directly interacts with these components to obtain model data from that component. Each such access results in a remote method call that introduces network overhead and increases the chattiness between the client and the business tier.

- The client must reconstruct the model after obtaining the model's parts from the distributed components. The client therefore needs to have the necessary business logic to construct the model. If the model construction is complex and numerous objects are involved in its definition, then there may be an additional performance overhead on the client due to the construction process. In addition, the client must contain the business logic to manage the relationships between the components, which results in a more complex, larger client. When the client constructs the application model, the construction happens on the client side. Complex model construction can result in a significant performance overhead on the client side for clients with limited resources.

- Because the client is tightly coupled to the model, changes to the model require changes to the client. Furthermore, if there are different types of clients, it is more difficult to manage the changes across all client types. When there is tight coupling between the client and model implementation, which occurs when the client has direct knowledge of the model and manages the business component relationships, then changes to the model necessitate changes to the client. There is the further problem of code duplication for model access, which occurs when an application has many types of clients. This duplication makes client (code) management difficult when the model changes.

Forces

- Separation of business logic is required between the client and the server-side components.
- Because the model consists of distributed components, access to each component is associated with a network overhead. It is desirable to minimize the number of remote method calls over the network.
- The client typically needs only to obtain the model to present it to the user. If the client must interact with multiple components to construct the model on the fly, the chattiness between the client and the application increases. Such chattiness may reduce the network performance.
- Even if the client wants to perform an update, it usually updates only certain parts of the model and not the entire model.
- Clients do not need to be aware of the intricacies and dependencies in the model implementation. It is desirable to have loose coupling between the clients and the business components that implement the application model.
- Clients do not otherwise need to have the additional business logic required to construct the model from various business components.

Solution

Use a Value Object Assembler to build the required model or submodel. The Value Object Assembler uses value objects to retrieve data from various business objects and other objects that define the model or part of the model.

The Value Object Assember constructs a composite value object that represents data from different business components. The value object caries the data for the model to the client in a single method call. Since the model data can be complex, it is recommended that this value object be immutable. That is, the client obtains such value objects with the sole purpose of using them for presentation and processing in a read-only manner. Clients are not allowed to make changes to the value objects.

When the client needs the model data, and if the model is represented by a single coarse-grained component (such as a Composite Entity), then the process of obtaining the model data is simple. The client simply requests the coarse-grained component for its composite value object. However, most real-world applications have a model composed of a combination of many coarse-grained and fine-grained components. In this case, the client must interact with numerous such business components to obtain all the data necessary to represent the model. The immediate drawbacks of this approach can be seen in that the clients become tightly coupled to the model implementation (model elements) and that the clients tend to make numerous remote method invocations to obtain the data from each individual component.

In some cases, a single coarse-grained component provides the model or parts of the model as a single value object (simple or composite). However, when multiple components represent the model, a single value object (simple or composite) may not represent the entire model. To represent the model, it is necessary to obtain value objects from various components and assemble them into a new composite value object. The server, not the client, should perform such "on-the-fly" construction of the model.

Structure

Figure 8.27 shows the class diagram representing the relationships for the Value Object Assembler pattern.

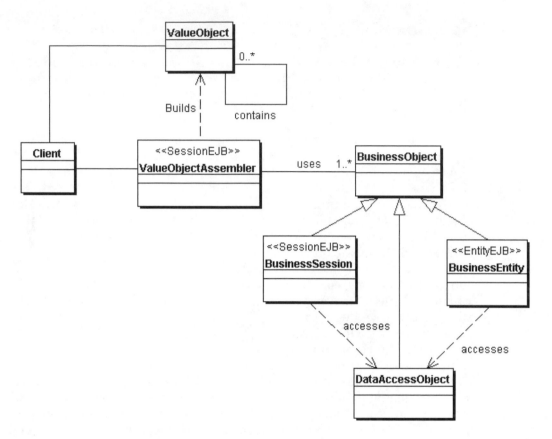

Figure 8.27 Value Object Assembler class diagram

Participants and Responsibilities

The sequence diagram in Figure 8.28 shows the interaction between the various participants in the Value Object Assembler pattern.

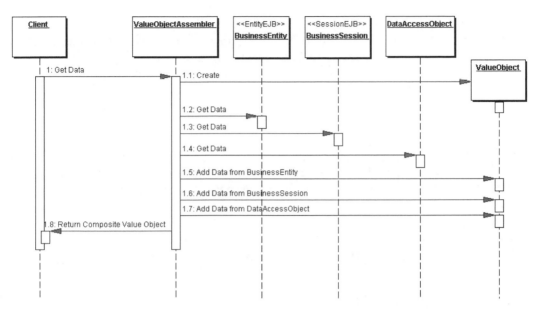

Figure 8.28 Value Object Assembler sequence diagram

ValueObjectAssembler

The ValueObjectAssembler is the main class of this pattern. The ValueObjectAssembler constructs a new value object based on the requirements of the application when the client requests a composite value object. The ValueObjectAssembler then locates the required BusinessObject instances to retrieve data to build the composite value object. BusinessObjects are business-tier components such as entity beans and session beans, DAOs, and so forth.

Client

If the ValueObjectAssembler is implemented as an arbitrary Java object, then the client is typically a Session Facade that provides the controller layer to the business tier. If the ValueObjectAssembler is implemented as a session bean, then the client can be a Session Facade or a Business Delegate.

BusinessObject

The BusinessObject participates in the construction of the new value object by providing the required data to the ValueObjectAssembler. Therefore, the BusinessObject is a role that can be fulfilled by a session bean, an entity bean, a DAO, or a regular Java object.

ValueObject

The ValueObject is a composite value object that is constructed by the ValueObjectAssembler and returned to the client. This represents the complex data from various components that define the application model.

BusinessObject

BusinessObject is a role that can be fulfilled by a session bean, entity bean, or DAO. When the assembler needs to obtain data directly from the persistent storage to build the value object, it can use a DAO. This is shown as the DataAccessObject object in the diagrams.

Strategies

This section explains different strategies for implementing a Value Object Assembler pattern.

Java Object Strategy

The ValueObjectAssembler can be an arbitrary Java object and need not be an enterprise bean. In such implementations, a session bean usually fronts the ValueObjectAssembler. This session bean is typically a Session Facade that performs its other duties related to providing business services. The ValueObjectAssembler runs in the business tier, regardless of the implementation strategies. The motivation for this is to prevent the remote invocations from the ValueObjectAssembler to the source objects from crossing the tier.

Session Bean Strategy

This strategy implements the ValueObjectAssembler as a session bean (as shown in the class diagram). If a session bean implementation is preferred to provide the ValueObjectAssembler as a business service, it is typically implemented as a stateless session bean. The business components that make up the application model are constantly involved in transactions with various clients. As a result, when a ValueObjectAssembler constructs a new composite value object from various business components, it produces a snapshot of the model at the time of construction. The model could change immediately thereafter if another client changes one or more business components, effectively changing the business application model.

Therefore, implementing ValueObjectAssembler as a stateful session bean provides no benefits over implementing it as a stateless session bean, as preserving the state of the composite model data value when the underlying model is changing is futile. If the underlying model changes, it causes the value object held by the assembler to become stale. The ValueObjectAssembler, when next asked for the value object, either returns a stale state or reconstructs the value object to obtain the most recent snapshot. Therefore, it is recommended that the assembler be a stateless session bean to leverage the benefits of stateless over stateful session beans.

However, if the underlying model rarely changes, then the assembler may be a stateful session bean and retain the newly constructed value object. In this case, the ValueObjectAssembler must include mechanisms to recognize changes to the underlying model and to reconstruct the model for the next client request.

Business Object Strategy

The BusinessObject role in this pattern can be supported by different types of objects, as explained below.

- The BusinessObject can be a session bean. The Value Object Assembler may use a Service Locator (see "Service Locator" on page 367) to locate the required session bean. The Value Object Assembler requests this session bean to provide the data to construct the composite value object.

- The BusinessObject can be an entity bean. The Value Object Assembler may use a Service Locator to locate the required entity bean. The Value Object Assembler requests this entity bean to provide the data to construct the composite value object.

- The BusinessObject can be a DAO. The Value Object Assembler requests this DAO to provide the data to construct the composite value object.

- The BusinessObject can be an arbitrary Java object. The Value Object Assembler requests this Java object to provide the data to construct the composite value object.

- The BusinessObject can be another Value Object Assembler. The first Value Object Assembler requests the second Value Object Assembler to provide the data to construct the composite value object.

Consequences

- **Separates Business Logic**
  When the client includes logic to manage the interactions with distributed components, it becomes difficult to clearly separate business logic from the client tier. The Value Object Assembler contains the business logic to maintain the object relationships

and to construct the composite value object representing the model. The client needs no knowledge of how to construct the model or the different components that provide data to assemble the model.

- ***Reduces Coupling Between Clients and the Application Model***
  The Value Object Assembler hides the complexity of the construction of model data from the clients and establishes a loose coupling between clients and the model. With loose coupling, if the model changes, then the Value Object Assembler requires a corresponding change. However, the client is not dependent on the model construction and interrelationships between model business components, so model changes do not directly affect the client. In general, loose coupling is preferred to tight coupling.

- ***Improves Network Performance***
  The Value Object Assembler drastically reduces the network overhead of remote method calls and chattiness. The client can request the data for the application model from the Value Object Assembler in a single remote method call. The assembler constructs and returns the composite value object for the model. However, the composite value object may contain a large amount of data. Thus, while use of the Value Object Assembler reduces the number of network calls, there is an increase in the amount of data transported in a single call. This trade-off should be considered in applying this pattern.

- ***Improves Client Performance***
  The server-side Value Object Assembler constructs the model as a composite value object without using any client resources. The client spends no time assembling the model.

- ***Improves Transaction Performance***
  Typically, updates are isolated to a very small part of the model and can be performed by fine-grained transactions. These transactions focus on isolated parts of the model instead of locking up the coarse-grained object (model). After the client obtains the model and displays or processes it locally, the user (or the client) may need to update or otherwise modify the model. The client can interact directly with a Session Facade to accomplish this at a suitable granularity level. The Value Object Assembler is not involved in the transaction to update or modify the model. There is better performance control because transactional work with the model happens at the appropriate level of granularity.

- *May Introduce Stale Value Objects*

  The Value Object Assembler constructs value objects on demand. These value objects are snapshots of the current state of the model, represented by various business components. Once the client obtains a value object from the assembler, that value object is entirely local to the client. Since the value objects are not network-aware, other changes made to the business components used to construct the value object are not reflected in the value objects. Therefore, after the value object is obtained, it can quickly become stale if there are transactions on the business components.

Sample Code

Implementing the Value Object Assembler

Consider a Project Management application where a number of business-tier components define the complex model. Suppose a client wants to obtain the model data composed of data from various business objects, such as:

- Project Information from the Project component
- Project Manager information from the ProjectManager component
- List of Project Tasks from the Project component
- Resource Information from the Resource component

A composite value object to contain this data can be defined as shown in Example 8.24. A Value Object Assembler pattern can be implemented to assemble this composite value object. The Value Object Assembler sample code is listed in Example 8.28.

Example 8.24 Composite Value Object Class

```
public class ProjectDetailsData {
  public ProjectVO projectData;
  public ProjectManagerVO projectManagerData;
  public Collection listOfTasks;
  ...
}
```

The list of tasks in the ProjectDetailsData is a collection of TaskResourceVO objects. The TaskResourceVO is a combination of TaskVO and ResourceVO. These classes are shown in Example 8.25, Example 8.26, and Example 8.27.

Example 8.25 TaskResourceVO Class

```
public class TaskResourceVO {
  public String projectId;
  public String taskId;
  public String name;
  public String description;
  public Date startDate;
  public Date endDate;
  public ResourceVO assignedResource;
  ...

  public TaskResourceVO(String projectId,
    String taskId, String name, String description,
    Date startDate, Date endDate, ResourceVO
    assignedResource) {
      this.projectId = projectId;
      this.taskId = taskId;
      ...
      this.assignedResource = assignedResource;
  }
  ...
}
```

Example 8.26 TaskVO Class

```
public class TaskVO {
  public String projectId;
  public String taskId;
  public String name;
  public String description;
  public Date startDate;
  public Date endDate;
  public assignedResourceId;

  public TaskVO(String projectId, String taskId,
      String name, String description, Date startDate,
      Date endDate, String assignedResourceId) {
        this.projectId = projectId;
        this.taskId = taskId;
        ...
        this.assignedResource = assignedResource;
  }
  ...
}
```

Example 8.27 ResourceVO Class

```
public class ResourceVO {
  public String resourceId;
  public String resourceName;
  public String resourceEmail;
  ...

  public ResourceVO (String resourceId, String
    resourceName, String resourceEmail, ...) {
      this.resourceId = resourceId;
      this.resourceName = resourceName;
      this.resourceEmail = resourceEmail;
      ...
  }
}
```

The ProjectDetailsAssembler class that assembles the ProjectDetailsData object is listed in Example 8.28.

Example 8.28 Implementing the Value Object Assembler

```
public class ProjectDetailsAssembler
  implements javax.ejb.SessionBean {

  ...

  public ProjectDetailsData getData(String projectId){

    // Construct the composite value object
    ProjectDetailsData pData - new
                      ProjectDetailsData();

    //get the project details;
    ProjectHome projectHome =
        ServiceLocator.getInstance().getHome(
          "Project", ProjectEntityHome.class);
    ProjectEntity project =
      projectHome.findByPrimaryKey(projectId);
    ProjectVO projVO = project.getData();

    // Add Project Info to ProjectDetailsData
    pData.projectData = projVO;

    //get the project manager details;
    ProjectManagerHome projectManagerHome =
```

Example 8.28 Implementing the Value Object Assembler

```
ServiceLocator.getInstance().getHome(
  "ProjectManager", ProjectEntityHome.class);

ProjectManagerEntity projectManager =
  projectManagerHome.findByPrimaryKey(
    projVO.managerId);

ProjectManagerVO projMgrVO =
  projectManager.getData();

// Add ProjectManager info to ProjectDetailsData
pData.projectManagerData = projMgrVO;

// Get list of TaskVOs from the Project
Collection projTaskList = project.getTasksList();

// construct a list of TaskResourceVOs
ArrayList listOfTasks = new ArrayList();

Iterator taskIter = projTaskList.iterator();
while (taskIter.hasNext()) {
  TaskVO task = (TaskVO) taskIter.next();

  //get the Resource details;
  ResourceHome resourceHome =
  ServiceLocator.getInstance().getHome(
    "Resource", ResourceEntityHome.class);

  ResourceEntity resource =
    resourceHome.findByPrimaryKey(
      task.assignedResourceId);

  ResourceVO resVO = resource.getResourceData();

  // construct a new TaskResourceVO using Task
  // and Resource data
  TaskResourceVO trVO = new TaskResourceVO(
          task.projectId, task.taskId,
          task.name, task.description,
          task.startDate, task.endDate,
          resVO);

  // add TaskResourceVO to the list
  listOfTasks.add(trVO);
}
```

Example 8.28 Implementing the Value Object Assembler

```
// add list of tasks to ProjectDetailsData
pData.listOfTasks = listOfTasks;

// add any other data to the value object
...

// return the composite value object
return pData;

}

...
}
```

Related Patterns

- **Value Object**

  The Value Object Assembler uses the Value Object pattern in order to create and transport value objects to the client. The value objects created carry the data representing the application model from the business tier to the clients requesting the data.

- **Composite Entity**

  The Composite Entity pattern promotes a coarse-grained entity bean design, where entities can produce composite value objects similar to the one produced by the Value Object Assembler. However, the Value Object Assembler is more applicable when the composite value object constructed is derived from a number of components (session beans, entity beans, DAOs, and so forth), whereas the Composite Entity pattern constructs the value object from its own data (that is, a single entity bean).

- **Session Facade**

  The Value Object Assembler is typically implemented as a stateless session bean. As such, it could be viewed as a limited special application of the Session Facade pattern. More importantly, Value Object Assembler constructs composite value objects that are immutable. Therefore, the client receiving this composite value object can only use the data for its presentation and processing purposes. The client cannot update the value object. If the client needs to update the business objects that derive the composite value object, it may have to access the Session Facade (session bean) that provides that business service.

- **Data Access Object**

  A possible strategy for the Value Object Assembler involves obtaining data for the composite value object from the persistent store without enterprise bean involvement. The Data Access Object pattern can be applied, thus leveraging its benefits to provide persistent storage access to the Value Object Assembler.

- **Service Locator**

  The Value Object Assembler needs to locate and use various business objects. The Service Locator pattern can be used in conjunction with the Value Object Assembler pattern whenever a business object or a service needs to be located.

Value List Handler

Context

The client requires a list of items from the service for presentation. The number of items in the list is unknown and can be quite large in many instances.

Problem

Most J2EE applications have a search and query requirement to search and list certain data. In some cases, such a search and query operation could yield results that can be quite large. It is impractical to return the full result set when the client's requirements are to traverse the results, rather than process the complete set. Typically, a client uses the results of a query for read-only purposes, such as displaying the result list. Often, the client views only the first few matching records, and then may discard the remaining records and attempt a new query. The search activity often does not involve an immediate transaction on the matching objects. The practice of getting a list of values represented in entity beans by calling an `ejbFind()` method, which returns a collection of remote objects, and then calling each entity bean to get the value, is very network expensive and is considered a bad practice.

There are consequences associated with using EJB finder methods that result in large results sets. Every container implementation has a certain amount of finder method overhead for creating a collection of EJBObject references. Finder method behavior performance varies, depending on a vendor's container implementation. According to the EJB specification, a container may invoke `ejbActivate()` methods on entities found by a finder method. At a minimum, a finder method returns the primary keys of the matching entities, which the container returns to the client as a collection of EJBObject references. This behavior applies for all container implementations. Some container implementations may introduce additional finder method overhead by associating the entity bean instances to these EJBObject instances to give the client access to those entity beans. However, this is a poor use of resources if the client is not interested in accessing the bean or invoking its methods. This overhead can significantly impede application performance if the application includes queries that produce many matching results.

Forces

- The application client needs an efficient query facility to avoid having to call the entity bean's `ejbFind()` method and invoking each remote object returned.

- A server-tier caching mechanism is needed to serve clients that cannot receive and process the entire results set.

- A query that is repeatedly executed on reasonably static data can be optimized to provide faster results. This depends on the application and on the implementation of this pattern.

- EJB finder methods are not suitable for browsing entire tables in the database or for searching large result sets from a table.

- Finder methods may have considerable overhead when used to find large numbers of result objects. The container may create a large number of infrastructure objects to facilitate the finders.

- EJB finder methods are not suitable for caching results. The client may not be able to handle the entire result set in a single call. If so, the client may need server-side caching and navigation functions to traverse the result set.

- EJB finder methods have predetermined query constructs and offer minimum flexibility. The EJB specification 2.0 allows a query language, EJB QL, for container-managed entity beans. EJB QL makes it easier to write portable finders and offers greater flexibility for querying.

- Client wants to scroll forward and backward within a result set.

Solution

Use a Value List Handler to control the search, cache the results, and provide the results to the client in a result set whose size and traversal meets the client's requirements.

This pattern creates a ValueListHandler to control query execution functionality and results caching. The ValueListHandler directly accesses a DAO that can execute the required query. The ValueListHandler stores the results obtained from the DAO as a collection of value objects. The client requests the ValueListHandler to provide the query results as needed. The ValueListHandler implements an Iterator pattern [GoF] to provide the solution.

Structure

The class diagram in Figure 8.29 illustrates the Value List Handler pattern.

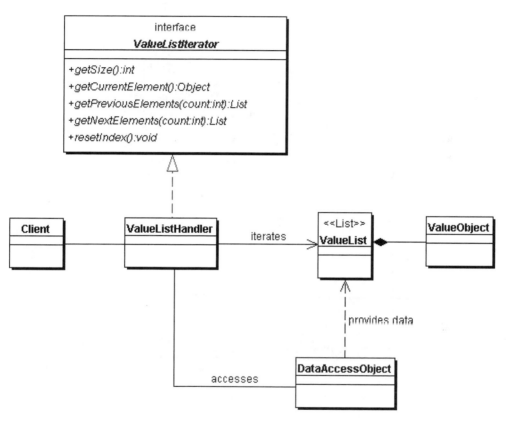

Figure 8.29 Value List Handler Class Diagram

Participants and Collaborations

The sequence diagram in Figure 8.30 shows the interactions for the Value List Handler.

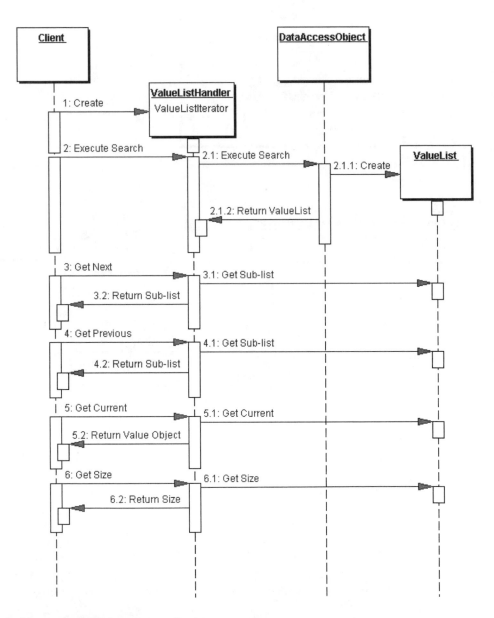

Figure 8.30 Value List Handler Sequence Diagram

ValueListIterator

This interface may provide iteration facility with the following example methods:

- `getSize()` obtains the size of the result set.
- `getCurrentElement()` obtains the current value object from the list.
- `getPreviousElements(int howMany)` obtains a collection of value objects that are in the list prior to the current element.
- `getNextElements(int howMany)` obtains a collection of value objects that are in the list after the current element.
- `resetIndex()` resets the index to the start of the list.

Depending on the need, other convenience methods can be included to be part of the ValueListIterator interface.

ValueListHandler

This is a list handler object that implements the ValueListIterator interface. The ValueListHandler executes the required query when requested by the client. The ValueListHandler obtains the query results, which it manages in a privately held collection represented by the ValueList object. The ValueListHandler creates and manipulates the ValueList collection. When the client requests the results, the ValueListHandler obtains the value objects from the cached ValueList, creates a new collection of value objects, serializes the collection, and sends it back to the client. The ValueListHandler also tracks the current index and size of the list.

DataAccessObject

The ValueListHandler can make use of a DataAccessObject to keep separate the implementation of the database access. The DataAccessObject provides a simple API to access the database (or any other persistent store), execute the query, and retrieve the results.

ValueList

The ValueList is a collection (a list) that holds the results of the query. The results are stored as value objects. If the query fails to return any matching results, then this list is empty. The ValueListHandler session bean caches ValueList to avoid repeated, unnecessary execution of the query.

ValueObject

The ValueObject represents an object view of the individual record from the query's results. It is an immutable serializable object that provides a placeholder for the data attributes of each record.

Strategies

Java Object Strategy

The ValueListHandler can be implemented as an arbitrary Java object. In this case, the ValueListHandler can be used by any client that needs the listing functionality. For applications that do not use enterprise beans, this strategy is useful. For example, simpler applications may be built using servlets, JSPs, Business Delegates, and DAOs. In this scenario, the Business Delegates can use a ValueListHandler implemented as a Java object to obtain list of values.

Stateful Session Bean Strategy

When an application uses enterprise beans in the business tier, it may be preferable to implement a session bean that uses the ValueListHandler. In this case, the session bean simply fronts an instance of a ValueListHandler. Thus, the session bean may be implemented as a stateful session bean to hold on to the list handler as its state, and thus may simply act as a facade (see "Session Facade" on page 291) or as a proxy.

Consequences

- ***Provides Alternative to EJB Finders for Large Queries***
  Typically, an EJB finder method is a resource-intensive and an expensive way of obtaining a list of items, since it involves a number of EJBObject references. The Value List Handler implements a session bean that uses a DAO to perform the query and to create a collection of value objects that match the query criteria. Because value objects have relatively low overhead compared to EJBObject references and their associated infrastructure, this pattern provides benefits when application clients require queries resulting in large result sets.

- ***Caches Query Results on Server Side***
  The result set obtained from a query execution needs to be cached when a client must display the results in small subsets rather than in one large list. However, not all browser-based

clients can perform such caching. When they cannot, the server must provide this functionality. The Value List Handler pattern provides a caching facility in the Value List Handler session bean to hold the result set obtained from a query execution. The result set is a collection of value objects that can be serialized if required.

When the client requests a collection, or a subset of a collection, the handler bean returns the requested results as a serialized collection of value objects. The client receives the collection and now has a local copy of the requested information, which the client can display or process. When the client needs an additional subset of the results, it requests the handler to return another serialized collection containing the required results. The client can process the query results in smaller, manageable chunks. The handler bean also provides the client with navigation facilities (previous and next) so that the results may be traversed forward and backward as necessary.

- *Provides Better Querying Flexibility*

  Adding a new query may require creating a new finder method or modifying an existing method, especially when using bean-managed entity beans. (With bean-managed entity beans, the developer implements the finder methods in the bean implementation.) With a container-managed entity bean, the deployer specifies the entity bean finder methods in the bean's deployment descriptor. Changes to a query for a container-managed bean require changes to the finder method specification in the deployment descriptor. Therefore, finder methods are ill-suited to handle query requirements that change dynamically. You can implement a Value List Handler to be more flexible than EJB finder methods by providing ad hoc query facilities, constructing runtime query arguments using template methods, and so forth. In other words, a Value List Handler developer can implement intelligent searching and caching algorithms without being limited by the finder methods.

- *Improves Network Performance*

  Network performance may improve because only requested data, rather than all data, is shipped (serialized) to the client on an as-needed basis. If the client displays the first few results and then abandons the query, the network bandwidth is not wasted, since the data is cached on the server side and never sent to the client. However, if the client processes the entire result set, it makes multiple remote calls to the server for the result set. When the client knows in advance that it needs the entire result set, the handler bean can provide a method that sends the client the entire result set in one method call, and the pattern's caching feature is not used.

- ***Allows Deferring Entity Bean Transactions***

  Caching results on the server side and minimizing finder overhead may improve transaction management. When the client is ready to further process an entity bean, it accesses the bean within a transaction context defined by the use case. For example, a query to display a list of books uses a Value List Handler to obtain the list. When the user wants to view a book in detail, it involves the book's entity bean in a transaction.

Sample Code

Implementing the Value List Handler as a Java Object

Consider an example where a list of Project business objects are to be retrieved and displayed. The Value List Handler pattern can be applied in this case. The sample code for this implementation is listed in Example 8.29 as ProjectListHandler, which is responsible to provide the list of Projects. This class extends the ValueListHandler base class, which provides the generic iteration functionality for all Value List Handler implementations in this application. The ValueListHandler sample code is listed in Example 8.30. The ValueListHandler implements the generic iterator interface ValueListIterator, which is shown in Example 8.32. The relevant code sample from the data access object ProjectDAO, used by ValueListHandler to execute the query and obtain matching results, is shown in Example 8.31.

Example 8.29 Implementing Value List Handler Pattern

```
package corepatterns.apps.psa.handlers;

import java.util.*;
import corepatterns.apps.psa.dao.*;
import corepatterns.apps.psa.util.*;
import corepatterns.apps.psa.core.*;

public class ProjectListHandler
extends ValueListHandler {

  private ProjectDAO dao = null;
```

Example 8.29 Implementing Value List Handler Pattern

```
// use ProjectVO as a template to determine
// search criteria
private ProjectVO projectCriteria = null;

// Client creates a ProjectVO instance, sets the
// values to use for search criteria and passes
// the ProjectVO instance as projectCriteria
// to the constructor and to setCriteria() method
public ProjectListHandler(ProjectVO projectCriteria)
throws ProjectException, ListHandlerException {
  try {
    this.projectCriteria = projectCriteria;
    this.dao = PSADAOFactory.getProjectDAO();
    executeSearch();
  } catch (Exception e) {
    // Handle exception, throw ListHandlerException
  }
}

public void setCriteria(ProjectVO projectCriteria) {
  this.projectCriteria = projectCriteria;
}

// executes search. Client can invoke this
// provided that the search criteria has been
// properly set. Used to perform search to refresh
// the list with the latest data.
public void executeSearch()
throws ListHandlerException {
  try {
    if (projectCriteria == null) {
      throw new ListHandlerException(
        "Project Criteria required...");
    }
    List resultsList =
      dao.executeSelect(projectCriteria);
    setList(resultsList);
  } catch (Exception e) {
    // Handle exception, throw ListHandlerException
  }
}
}
```

The Value List Handler is a generic iterator class that provides the iteration functionality.

Example 8.30 Implementing Generic ValueListHandler class

```java
package corepatterns.apps.psa.util;

import java.util.*;

public class ValueListHandler
implements ValueListIterator {

  protected List list;
  protected ListIterator listIterator;

  public ValueListHandler() {
  }

  protected void setList(List list)
  throws IteratorException {
    this.list = list;
    if(list != null)
      listIterator =  list.listIterator();
    else
      throw new IteratorException("List empty");
  }

  public Collection getList(){
    return list;
  }

  public int getSize() throws IteratorException{
    int size = 0;

    if (list != null)
      size = list.size();
    else
      throw new IteratorException(...); //No Data

    return size;
  }

  public Object getCurrentElement()
  throws IteratorException {

    Object obj = null;
```

Example 8.30 Implementing Generic ValueListHandler class

```
      // Will not advance iterator
      if (list != null)
      {
        int currIndex = listIterator.nextIndex();
        obj = list.get(currIndex);
      }
      else
        throw new IteratorException(...);
      return obj;

    }

    public List getPreviousElements(int count)
    throws IteratorException {
      int i = 0;
      Object object = null;
      LinkedList list = new LinkedList();
      if (listIterator != null) {
        while (listIterator.hasPrevious() && (i <
count)){
          object = listIterator.previous();
          list.add(object);
          i++;
        }
      }// end if
      else
        throw new IteratorException(...); // No data

      return list;
    }

    public List getNextElements(int count)
    throws IteratorException {
      int i = 0;
      Object object = null;
      LinkedList list = new LinkedList();
      if(listIterator != null){
        while(  listIterator.hasNext() && (i < count) ){
          object = listIterator.next();
          list.add(object);
          i++;
        }
      } // end if
      else
        throw new IteratorException(...); // No data
```

Example 8.30 Implementing Generic ValueListHandler class

```
      return list;
  }

  public void resetIndex() throws IteratorException{
    if(listIterator != null){
      listIterator = list.ListIterator();
    }
    else
      throw new IteratorException(...); // No data
  }
  ...
}
```

Example 8.31 ProjectDAO class

```
package corepatterns.apps.psa.dao;

public class ProjectDAO {
  final private String tableName = "PROJECT";

  // select statement uses fields
  final private String fields = "project_id, name," +
      "project_manager_id, start_date, end_date, " +
      " started, completed, accepted, acceptedDate," +
      " customer_id, description, status";

  // the methods relevant to the ValueListHandler
  // are shown here.
  // See Data Access Object pattern for other details.
  ...
  private List executeSelect(ProjectVO projCriteria)
  throws SQLException {

    Statement stmt= null;
    List list = null;
    Connection con = getConnection();
    StringBuffer selectStatement = new StringBuffer();
    selectStatement.append("SELECT "+ fields +
        " FROM " + tableName + "where 1=1");

    // append additional conditions to where clause
    // depending on the values specified in
    // projCriteria
```

Example 8.31 ProjectDAO class

```java
    if (projCriteria.projectId != null) {
      selectStatement.append (" AND PROJECT_ID = '" +
        projCriteria.projectId + "'");
    }
    // check and add other fields to where clause
    ...

    try {
      stmt = con.prepareStatement(selectStatement);
      stmt.setString(1, resourceID);
      ResultSet rs = stmt.executeQuery();
      list = prepareResult(rs);
      stmt.close();
    }
    finally {
      con.close();
    }
    return list;
  }

  private List prepareResult(ResultSet rs)
  throws SQLException {
    ArrayList list = new ArrayList();
    while(rs.next()) {
      int i = 1;
      ProjectVO proj = new
        ProjectVO(rs.getString(i++));
      proj.projectName = rs.getString(i++);
      proj.managerId = rs.getString(i++);
      proj.startDate = rs.getDate(i++);
      proj.endDate = rs.getDate(i++);
      proj.started = rs.getBoolean(i++);
      proj.completed = rs.getBoolean(i++);
      proj.accepted = rs.getBoolean(i++);
      proj.acceptedDate = rs.getDate(i++);
      proj.customerId = rs.getString(i++);
      proj.projectDescription = rs.getString(i++);
      proj.projectStatus = rs.getString(i++);
      list.add(proj);

    }
    return list;
  }
  ...
}
```

Example 8.32 ValueListIterator class

```
package corepatterns.apps.psa.util;

import java.util.List;

public interface ValueListIterator {

  public int getSize()
    throws IteratorException;

  public Object getCurrentElement()
    throws IteratorException;

  public List getPreviousElements(int count)
    throws IteratorException;

  public List getNextElements(int count)
    throws IteratorException;

  public void resetIndex()
    throws IteratorException;

  // other common methods as required
  ...
}
```

Related Patterns

- **Iterator [GoF]**
  This Value List Handler pattern is based on Iterator pattern, described in the GoF book, *Design Patterns: Elements of Reusable Object-Oriented Software*.

- **Session Facade**
  Since the Value List Handler is a session bean, it may appear as a specialized Session Facade. However, in isolation, it is a specialized session bean rather than a specialized Session Facade. A Session Facade has other motivations and characteristics (explained in the Session Facade pattern), and it is much coarser grained.

Service Locator

Context

Service lookup and creation involves complex interfaces and network operations.

Problem

J2EE clients interact with service components, such as EJB and JMS components, which provide business services and persistence capabilities. To interact with these components, clients must either locate the service component (referred to as a lookup operation) or create a new component. For instance, an EJB client must locate the enterprise bean's home object, which the client then uses either to find an object or to create or remove one or more enterprise beans. Similarly, a JMS client must first locate the JMS Connection Factory to obtain a JMS Connection or a JMS Session.

All J2EE application clients use the JNDI common facility to look up and create EJB and JMS components. The JNDI API enables clients to obtain an initial context object that holds the component name to object bindings. The client begins by obtaining the initial context for a bean's home object. The initial context remains valid while the client session is valid. The client provides the JNDI registered name for the required object to obtain a reference to an administered object. In the context of an EJB application, a typical administered object is an enterprise bean's home object. For JMS applications, the administered object can be a JMS Connection Factory (for a Topic or a Queue) or a JMS Destination (a Topic or a Queue).

So, locating a JNDI-administered service object is common to all clients that need to access that service object. That being the case, it is easy to see that many types of clients repeatedly use the JNDI service, and the JNDI code appears multiple times across these clients. This results in an unnecessary duplication of code in the clients that need to look up services.

Also, creating a JNDI initial context object and performing a lookup on an EJB home object utilizes significant resources. If multiple clients repeatedly require the same bean home object, such duplicate effort can negatively impact application performance.

Let us examine the lookup and creation process for various J2EE components.

1. The lookup and creation of enterprise beans relies upon the
   following:
   - A correct setup of the JNDI environment so that it con-
     nects to the naming and directory service used by the
     application. Setup entails providing the location of the
     naming service and the necessary authentication creden-
     tials to access that service.

   - The JNDI service can then provide the client with an ini-
     tial context that acts as a placeholder for the component
     name-to-object bindings. The client requests this initial
     context to look up the EJBHome object for the required
     enterprise bean by providing the JNDI name for that
     EJBHome object.

   - Find the EJBHome object using the initial context's
     lookup mechanism.

   - After obtaining the EJBHome object, create, remove, or
     find the enterprise bean, using the EJBHome object's cre-
     ate, move, and find (for entity beans only).

2. The lookup and creation of JMS components (Topic, Queue,
   QueueConnection, QueueSession, TopicConnection, TopicSession, and so forth) involves the following steps. Note that in
   these steps, Topic refers to the publish/subscribe messaging
   model and Queue refers to the point-to-point messaging model.

   - Set up the JNDI environment to the naming service used
     by the application. Setup entails providing the location of
     the naming service and the necessary authentication cre-
     dentials to access that service.

   - Obtain the initial context for the JMS service provider
     from the JNDI naming service.

   - Use the initial context to obtain a Topic or a Queue by
     supplying the JNDI name for the topic or the queue. Topic
     and Queue are JMSDestination objects.

   - Use the initial context to obtain a TopicConnectionFactory
     or a QueueConnectionFactory by supplying the JNDI
     name for the topic or queue connection factory.

   - Use the TopicConnectionFactory to obtain a TopicConnec-
     tion or QueueConnectionFactory to obtain a QueueCon-
     nection.

   - Use the TopicConnection to obtain a TopicSession or a
     QueueConnection to obtain a QueueSession.

- Use the TopicSession to obtain a TopicSubscriber or a TopicPublisher for the required Topic. Use the QueueSession to obtain a QueueReceiver or a QueueSender for the required Queue.

The process to look up and create components involves a vendor-supplied context factory implementation. This introduces vendor dependency in the application clients that need to use the JNDI lookup facility to locate the enterprise beans and JMS components, such as topics, queues, and connection factory objects.

Forces

- EJB clients need to use the JNDI API to look up EJBHome objects by using the enterprise bean's registered JNDI name.

- JMS clients need to use JNDI API to look up JMS components by using the JNDI names registered for JMS components, such as connection factories, queues, and topics.

- The context factory to use for the initial JNDI context creation is provided by the service provider vendor and is therefore vendor- dependent. The context factory is also dependent on the type of object being looked up. The context for JMS is different from the context for EJB, with different providers.

- Lookup and creation of service components could be complex and may be used repeatedly in multiple clients in the application.

- Initial context creation and service object lookups, if frequently required, can be resource-intensive and may impact application performance. This is especially true if the clients and the services are located in different tiers.

- EJB clients may need to reestablish connection to a previously accessed enterprise bean instance, having only its Handle object.

Solution

Use a Service Locator object to abstract all JNDI usage and to hide the complexities of initial context creation, EJB home object lookup, and EJB object re-creation. Multiple clients can reuse the Service Locator object to reduce code complexity, provide a single point of control, and improve performance by providing a caching facility.

This pattern reduces the client complexity that results from the client's dependency on and need to perform lookup and creation processes, which are resource-intensive. To eliminate these problems, this pattern provides a mechanism to abstract all dependencies and network details into the Service Locator.

Structure

Figure 8.31 shows the class diagram representing the relationships for the Service Locator pattern.

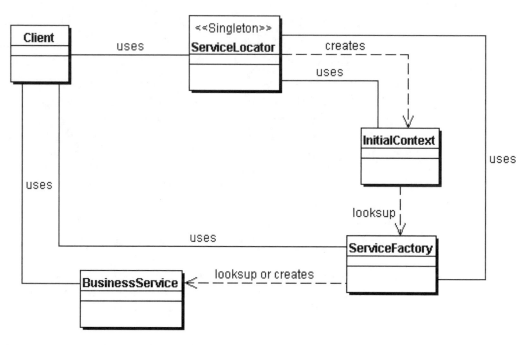

Figure 8.31 Service Locator class diagram

Participants and Responsibilities

Figure 8.32 contains the sequence diagram that shows the interaction between the various participants of the Service Locator pattern.

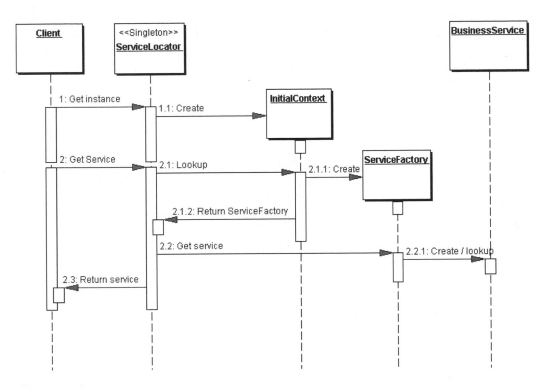

Figure 8.32 Service Locator Sequence diagram

Client

This is the client of the Service Locator. The client is an object that typically requires access to business objects such as a Business Delegate (see "Business Delegate" on page 248).

Service Locator

The Service Locator abstracts the API lookup (naming) services, vendor dependencies, lookup complexities, and business object creation, and provides a simple interface to clients. This reduces the client's complexity. In addition, the same client or other clients can reuse the Service Locator.

InitialContext

The InitialContext object is the start point in the lookup and creation process. Service providers provide the context object, which varies depending on the type of business object provided by the Service Locator's lookup and creation service. A Service Locator that provides services for multiple types of business objects (such as enterprise beans, JMS components, and so forth) utilizes multiple types of context objects, each obtained from a different provider (e.g., context provider for an EJB application server may be different from the context provider for JMS service).

ServiceFactory

The ServiceFactory object represents an object that provides life cycle management for the BusinessService objects. The ServiceFactory object for enterprise beans is an EJBHome object. The Service-Factory for JMS components can be a JMS ConnectionFactory object, such as a TopicConnectionFactory (for publish/subscribe messaging model) or a QueueConnectionFactory (for point-to-point messaging model).

BusinessService

The BusinessService is a role that is fulfilled by the service the client is seeking to access. The BusinessService object is created or looked up or removed by the ServiceFactory. The BusinessService object in the context of an EJB application is an enterprise bean. The BusinessService object in the context of a JMS application can be a Topic-Connection or a QueueConnection. The TopicConnection and QueueConnection can then be used to produce a JMSSession object, such as TopicSession or a QueueSession respectively.

Strategies

EJB Service Locator Strategy

The Service Locator for enterprise bean components uses EJBHome object, shown as BusinessHome in the role of the ServiceFactory. Once the EJBHome object is obtained, it can be cached in the ServiceLocator for future use to avoid another JNDI lookup when the client needs the home object again. Depending on the implementation, the home object can be returned to the client, which can then use it to look up, create, and remove enterprise beans. Otherwise, the ServiceLocator can retain (cache) the home object and gain the additional responsibility of proxying all client calls to the home object. The class diagram for the EJB Service Locator strategy is shown in Figure 8.33.

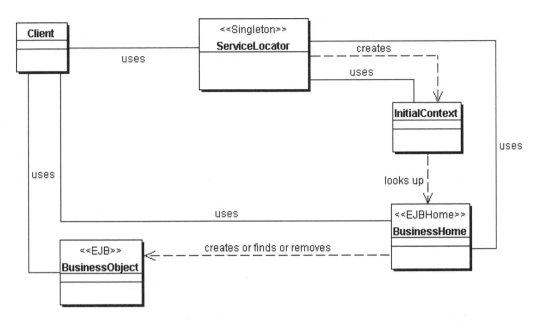

Figure 8.33 EJB Service Locator Strategy class diagram

The interaction between the participants in a Service Locator for an enterprise bean is shown in Figure 8.34.

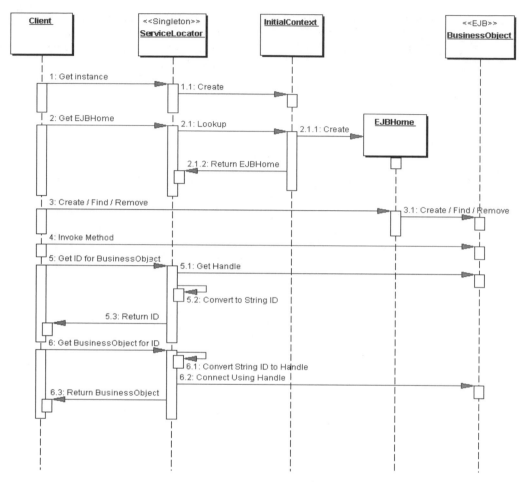

Figure 8.34 EJB Service Locator Strategy sequence diagram

JMS Queue Service Locator Strategy

This strategy is applicable to point-to-point messaging requirements. The Service Locator for JMS components uses QueueConnectionFactory objects in the role of the ServiceFactory. The QueueConnectionFactory is looked up using its JNDI name. The QueueConnectionFactory can be cached by the ServiceLocator for future use. This avoids repeated JNDI calls to look it up when the client needs it again. The ServiceLocator may otherwise hand over the QueueConnectionFactory to the client. The Client can then use it to create a QueueConnection. A QueueConnection is necessary in order to obtain a QueueSession or to create a Message, a Queue-Sender (to send messages to the queue), or a QueueReceiver (to receive messages from a queue). The class diagram for the JMS Queue Service Locator strategy is shown in Figure 8.35. In this diagram, the Queue is a JMS Destination object registered as a JNDI-administered object representing the queue. The Queue object can be directly obtained from the context by looking it up using its JNDI name.

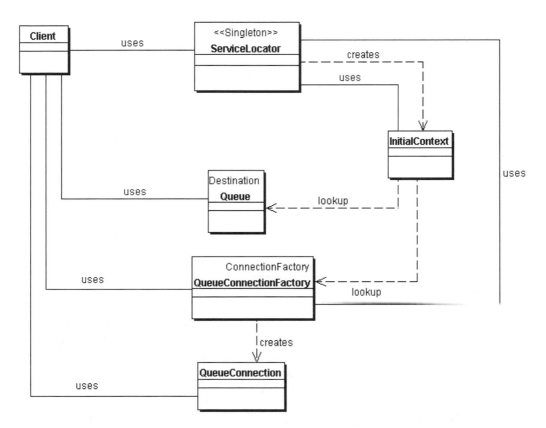

Figure 8.35 JMS Queue Service Locator strategy class diagram

The interaction between the participants in a Service Locator for point-to-point messaging using JMS Queues is shown in Figure 8.36.

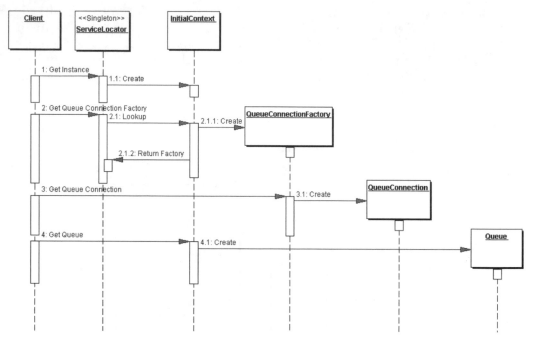

Figure 8.36 JMS Queue Service Locator Strategy sequence diagram

JMS Topic Service Locator Strategy

This strategy is applicable to publish/subscribe messaging requirements. The Service Locator for JMS components uses TopicConnectionFactory objects in the role of the ServiceFactory. The TopicConnectionFactory is looked up using its JNDI name. The TopicConnectionFactory can be cached by the ServiceLocator for future use. This avoids repeated JNDI calls to look it up when the client needs it again. The ServiceLocator may otherwise hand over the TopicConnectionFactory to the client. The Client can then use it to create a TopicConnection. A TopicConnection is necessary in order to obtain a TopicSession or to create a Message, a TopicPublisher (to publish messages to a topic), or a TopicSubscriber (to subscribe to a topic). The class diagram for the JMS Topic Service Locator strategy is shown in Figure 8.37. In this diagram, the Topic is a JMS Destination object registered as a JNDI-administered object representing the topic. The Topic object can be directly obtained from the context by looking it up using its JNDI name.

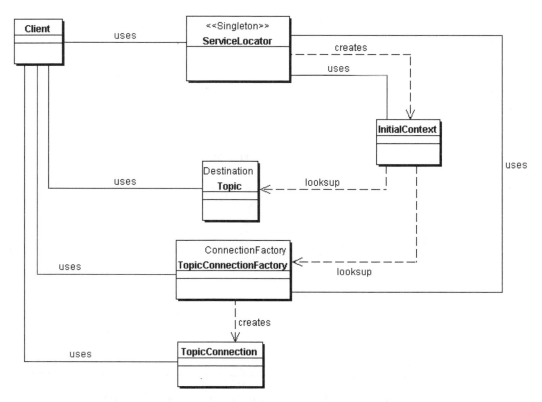

Figure 8.37 JMS Topic Service Locator strategy

The interaction between the participants in a Service Locator for publish/subscribe messaging using JMS Topics is shown in Figure 8.38.

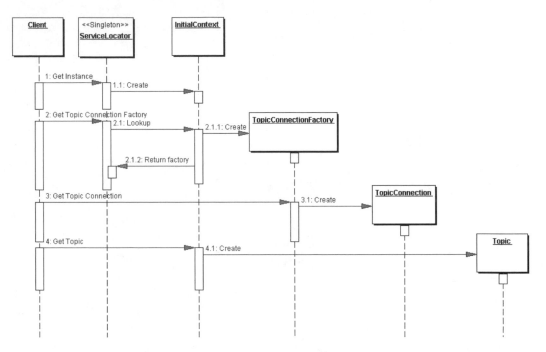

Figure 8.38 JMS Topic Service Locator Strategy sequence diagram

Combined EJB and JMS Service Locator Strategy

These strategies for EJB and JMS can be used to provide separate Service Locator implementations, since the clients for EJB and JMS may more likely be mutually exclusive. However, if there is a need to combine these strategies, it is possible to do so to provide the Service Locator for all objects—enterprise beans and JMS components.

Type Checked Service Locator Strategy

The diagrams in Figures 8.37 and 8.38 provide lookup facilities by passing in the service lookup name. For an enterprise bean lookup, the Service Locator needs a class as a parameter to the `PortableRemoteObject.narrow()` method. The Service Locator can provide a `getHome()` method, which accepts as arguments the JNDI service name and the EJBHome class object for the enterprise bean. Using this method of passing in JNDI service names and EJBHome class objects can lead to client errors. Another approach is to statically define the services in the ServiceLocator, and instead of passing in string names, the client passes in a constant. Example 8.34 illustrates such a strategy.

This strategy has trade-offs. It reduces the flexibility of lookup, which is in the Services Property Locator strategy, but add the type checking of passing in a constant to the `ServiceLocator.getHome()` method.

Service Locator Properties Strategy

This strategy helps to address the trade-offs of the type checking strategy. This strategy suggests the use of property files and/or deployment descriptors to specify the JNDI names and the EJB-Home class name. For presentation-tier clients, such properties can be specified in the presentation-tier deployment descriptors or property files. When the presentation tier accesses the business tier, it typically uses the Business Delegate pattern.

The Business Delegate interacts with the Service Locator to locate business components. If the presentation tier loads the properties on initialization and can provide a service to hand out the JNDI names and the EJB class names for the required enterprise bean, then the Business Delegate could request this service to obtain them. Once the Business Delegate has the JNDI name and the EJBHome Class name, it can request the Service Locator for the EJBHome by passing these properties as arguments.

The Service Locator can in turn use `Class.forName(EJBHome ClassName)` to obtain the EJBHome Class object and go about its business of looking up the EJBHome and using the `Portable RemoteObject.narrow()` method to cast the object, as shown by the `getHome()` method in the ServiceLocator sample code in Example 8.33. The only thing that changes is where the JNDI name and the Class objects are coming from. Thus, this strategy avoids hardcoded JNDI names in the code and provides for flexibility of deployment. However, due to the lack of type checking, there is scope for avoiding errors and mismatches in specifying the JNDI names in different deployment descriptors.

Consequences

- ### Abstracts Complexity
  The Service Locator pattern encapsulates the complexity of this lookup and creation process (described in the problem) and keeps it hidden from the client. The client does not need to deal with the lookup of component factory objects (EJBHome, QueueConnectionFactory, and TopicConnectionFactory, among others) because the ServiceLocator is delegated that responsibility.

- ***Provides Uniform Service Access to Clients***
  The Service Locator pattern abstracts all the complexities, as explained previously. In doing so, it provides a very useful and precise interface that all clients can use. The pattern interface ensures that all types of clients in the application uniformly access business objects, in terms of lookup and creation. This uniformity reduces development and maintenance overhead.

- ***Facilitates Adding New Business Components***
  Because clients of enterprise beans are not aware of the EJB-Home objects, it's possible to add new EJBHome objects for enterprise beans developed and deployed at a later time without impacting the clients. JMS clients are not directly aware of the JMS connection factories, so new connection factories can be added without impacting the clients.

- ***Improves Network Performance***
  The clients are not involved in JNDI lookup and factory/home object creation. Because the Service Locator performs this work, it can aggregate the network calls required to look up and create business objects.

- ***Improves Client Performance by Caching***
  The Service Locator can cache the initial context objects and references to the factory objects (EJBHome, JMS connection factories) to eliminate unnecessary JNDI activity that occurs when obtaining the initial context and the other objects. This improves the application performance.

Sample Code

Implementing Service Locator Pattern

A sample implementation of the Service Locator pattern is shown in Example 8.33. An example for implementing the Type Checked Service Locator strategy is listed in Example 8.34.

Example 8.33 Implementing Service Locator

```
package corepatterns.apps.psa.util;
import java.util.*;
import javax.naming.*;
import java.rmi.RemoteException;
import javax.ejb.*;
import javax.rmi.PortableRemoteObject;
import java.io.*;

public class ServiceLocator {
  private static ServiceLocator me;
  InitialContext context = null;

  private ServiceLocator()
  throws ServiceLocatorException {
    try {
      context = new InitialContext();
    } catch(NamingException ne) {
      throw new ServiceLocatorException(...);
    }
  }

  // Returns the instance of ServiceLocator class
  public static ServiceLocator getInstance()
  throws ServiceLocatorException {
    if (me == null) {
      me = new ServiceLocator();
    }
    return me;
  }

  // Converts the serialized string into EJBHandle
  // then to EJBObject.
  public EJBObject getService(String id)
  throws ServiceLocatorException {
    if (id == null) {
      throw new ServiceLocatorException(...);
    }
    try {
      byte[] bytes = new String(id).getBytes();
      InputStream io = new
        ByteArrayInputStream(bytes);
      ObjectInputStream os = new
        ObjectInputStream(io);
      javax.ejb.Handle handle =
        (javax.ejb.Handle)os.readObject();
```

Example 8.33 Implementing Service Locator

```java
      return handle.getEJBObject();
    } catch(Exception ex) {
      throw new ServiceLocatorException(...);
    }
  }

  // Returns the String that represents the given
  // EJBObject's handle in serialized format.
  protected String getId(EJBObject session)
  throws ServiceLocatorException {
    try {
      javax.ejb.Handle handle = session.getHandle();
      ByteArrayOutputStream fo = new
        ByteArrayOutputStream();
      ObjectOutputStream so = new
        ObjectOutputStream(fo);
      so.writeObject(handle);
      so.flush();
      so.close();
      return new String(fo.toByteArray());
    } catch(RemoteException ex) {
      throw new ServiceLocatorException(...);
    } catch(IOException ex) {
      throw new ServiceLocatorException(...);
    }
    return null;
  }

  // Returns the EJBHome object for requested service
  // name. Throws ServiceLocatorException If Any Error
  // occurs in lookup
  public EJBHome getHome(String name, Class clazz)
  throws ServiceLocatorException {
    try {
      Object objref = context.lookup(name);
      EJBHome home = (EJBHome)
        PortableRemoteObject.narrow(objref, clazz);
      return home;
    } catch(NamingException ex) {
      throw new ServiceLocatorException(...);
    }
  }
}
```

Implementing Type Checked Service Locator Strategy

Example 8.34 Implementing Type Checked Service Locator Strategy

```java
package corepatterns.apps.psa.util;
// imports
...

public class ServiceLocator {
  // singleton's private instance
  private static ServiceLocator me;

  static {
    me = new ServiceLocator();
  }

  private ServiceLocator() {}

  // returns the Service Locator instance
  static public ServiceLocator getInstance() {
    return me;
  }


  // Services Constants Inner Class - service objects
  public class Services {
    final public static int PROJECT  = 0;
    final public static int RESOURCE = 1;
  }

  // Project EJB related constants
  final static Class  PROJECT_CLASS =
  ProjectHome.class;
  final static String PROJECT_NAME  = "Project";

  // Resource EJB related constants

  final static Class  RESOURCE_CLASS =
    ResourceHome.class;
  final static String RESOURCE_NAME  = "Resource";

  // Returns the Class for the required service
  static private Class getServiceClass(int service){
    switch( service ) {
      case Services.PROJECT:
       return PROJECT_CLASS;
      case Services.RESOURCE:
```

Example 8.34 Implementing Type Checked Service Locator Strategy

```
      return RESOURCE_CLASS;
    }
    return null;
}

// returns the JNDI name for the required service
static private String getServiceName(int service){
  switch( service ) {
    case Services.PROJECT:
      return PROJECT_NAME;
    case Services.RESOURCE:
      return RESOURCE_NAME;
  }
  return null;
}

/* gets the EJBHome for the given service using the
** JNDI name and the Class for the EJBHome
*/
public EJBHome getHome( int s )
  throws ServiceLocatorException {
  EJBHome home = null;
  try {
      Context initial  = new InitialContext();

    // Look up using the service name from
    // defined constant
    Object objref =
      initial.lookup(getServiceName(s));

    // Narrow using the EJBHome Class from
    // defined constant
    Object obj = PortableRemoteObject.narrow(
            objref, getServiceClass(s));
    home = (EJBHome)obj;
  }
  catch( NamingException ex ) {
      throw new ServiceLocatorException(...);
  }
  catch( Exception ex ) {
      throw new ServiceLocatorException(...);
  }
  return home;
  }
}
```

The client code to use the Service Locator for this strategy may look like the code in Example 8.35.

Example 8.35 Client Code for Using the Service Locator

```java
public class ServiceLocatorTester {
  public static void main( String[] args ) {
    ServiceLocator serviceLocator =
      ServiceLocator.getInstance();
    try {
      ProjectHome projectHome = (ProjectHome)
        serviceLocator.getHome(
          ServiceLocator.Services.PROJECT );
    }
    catch( ServiceException ex ) {
      // client handles exception
      System.out.println( ex.getMessage( ));
    }
  }
}
```

This strategy is about applying type checking to client lookup. It encapsulates the static service values inside the ServiceLocator and creates an inner class Services, which declares the service constants (PROJECT and RESOURCE). The Tester client gets an instance to the ServiceLocator singleton and calls getHome(), passing in the PROJECT. ServiceLocator in turn gets the JNDI entry name and the Home class and returns the EJBHome.

Related Patterns

- **Business Delegate**
  The Business Delegate pattern uses Service Locator to gain access to the business service objects such as EJB objects, JMS topics, and JMS queues. This separates the complexity of service location from the Business Delegate, leading to loose coupling and increased manageability.

- **Session Facade**
  The Session Facade pattern uses Service Locator to gain access to the enterprise beans that are involved in a workflow. The Session Facade could directly use the Service Locator or delegate the work to a Business Delegate (See "Business Delegate" on page 248.).

- **Value Object Assembler**
  The Value Object Assembler pattern uses Service Locator to gain access to the various enterprise beans it needs to access to build its composite value object. The Value Object Assembler could directly use the Service Locator or delegate the work to a Business Delegate (See "Business Delegate" on page 248.).

INTEGRATION TIER PATTERNS

Topics in This Chapter

- Data Access Object
- Service Activator

Chapter 9

Data Access Object

Context

Access to data varies depending on the source of the data. Access to persistent storage, such as to a database, varies greatly depending on the type of storage (relational databases, object-oriented databases, flat files, and so forth) and the vendor implementation.

Problem

Many real-world J2EE applications need to use persistent data at some point. For many applications, persistent storage is implemented with different mechanisms, and there are marked differences in the APIs used to access these different persistent storage mechanisms. Other applications may need to access data that resides on separate systems. For example, the data may reside in mainframe systems, Lightweight Directory Access Protocol (LDAP) repositories, and so forth. Another example is where data is provided by services through external systems such as business-to-business (B2B) integration systems, credit card bureau service, and so forth.

Typically, applications use shared distributed components such as entity beans to represent persistent data. An application is considered to employ bean-managed persistence (BMP) for its entity beans when these entity beans explicitly access the persistent storage—the entity bean includes code to directly access the persistent storage. An application with simpler requirements may forego using entity beans and instead use session beans or servlets to directly access the persistent storage to retrieve and modify the data. Or, the application could use entity beans with container-managed persistence, and thus let the container handle the transaction and persistent details.

Applications can use the JDBC API to access data residing in a relational database management system (RDBMS). The JDBC API enables standard access and manipulation of data in persistent storage, such as a relational database. JDBC enables J2EE applications to use SQL statements, which are the standard means for accessing RDBMS tables. However, even within an RDBMS environment, the actual syntax and format of the SQL statements may vary depending on the particular database product.

There is even greater variation with different types of persistent storage. Access mechanisms, supported APIs, and features vary between different types of persistent stores such as RDBMS, object-oriented databases, flat files, and so forth. Applications that need to access data from a legacy or disparate system (such as a mainframe, or B2B service) are often required to use APIs that may be proprietary. Such disparate data sources offer challenges to the application and can potentially create a direct dependency between application code and data access code. When business components—entity beans, session beans, and even presentation components like servlets and helper objects for Java Server Pages (JSPs)—need to access a data source, they can use the appropriate API to achieve connectivity and manipulate the data source. But including the connectivity and data access code within these components introduces a tight coupling between the components and the data source implementation. Such code dependencies in components make it difficult and tedious to migrate the application from one type of data source to another. When the data source changes, the components need to be changed to handle the new type of data source.

Forces

- Components such as bean-managed entity beans, session beans, servlets, and other objects like helpers for JSPs need to retrieve and store information from persistent stores and other data sources like legacy systems, B2B, LDAP, and so forth.

- Persistent storage APIs vary depending on the product vendor. Other data sources may have APIs that are nonstandard and/or proprietary. These APIs and their capabilities also vary depending on the type of storage—RDBMS, object-oriented database management system (OODBMS), XML documents, flat files, and so forth. There is a lack of uniform APIs to address the requirements to access such disparate systems.

- Components typically use proprietary APIs to access external and/or legacy systems to retrieve and store data.

- Portability of the components is directly affected when specific access mechanisms and APIs are included in the components.

- Components need to be transparent to the actual persistent store or data source implementation to provide easy migration to different vendor products, different storage types, and different data source types.

Solution

Use a Data Access Object (DAO) to abstract and encapsulate all access to the data source. The DAO manages the connection with the data source to obtain and store data.

The DAO implements the access mechanism required to work with the data source. The data source could be a persistent store like an RDBMS, an external service like a B2B exchange, a repository like an LDAP database, or a business service accessed via CORBA Internet Inter-ORB Protocol (IIOP) or low-level sockets. The business component that relies on the DAO uses the simpler interface exposed by the DAO for its clients. The DAO completely hides the data source implementation details from its clients. Because the interface exposed by the DAO to clients does not change when the underlying data source implementation changes, this pattern allows the DAO to adapt to different storage schemes without affecting its clients or business components. Essentially, the DAO acts as an adapter between the component and the data source.

Structure

Figure 9.1 shows the class diagram representing the relationships for the DAO pattern.

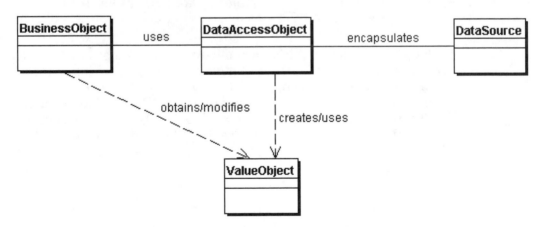

Figure 9.1 Data Access Object

Participants and Responsibilities

Figure 9.2 contains the sequence diagram that shows the interaction between the various participants in this pattern.

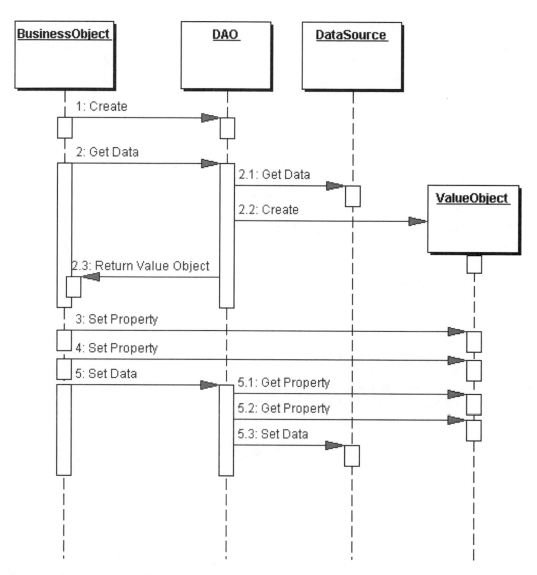

Figure 9.2 Data Access Object sequence diagram

BusinessObject

The BusinessObject represents the data client. It is the object that requires access to the data source to obtain and store data. A BusinessObject may be implemented as a session bean, entity bean, or some other Java object, in addition to a servlet or helper bean that accesses the data source.

DataAccessObject

The DataAccessObject is the primary object of this pattern. The DataAccessObject abstracts the underlying data access implementation for the BusinessObject to enable transparent access to the data source. The BusinessObject also delegates data load and store operations to the DataAccessObject.

DataSource

This represents a data source implementation. A data source could be a database such as an RDBMS, OODBMS, XML repository, flat file system, and so forth. A data source can also be another system (legacy/mainframe), service (B2B service or credit card bureau), or some kind of repository (LDAP).

ValueObject

This represents a value object used as a data carrier. The DataAccessObject may use a value object to return data to the client. The DataAccessObject may also receive the data from the client in a value object to update the data in the data source.

Strategies

Automatic DAO Code Generation Strategy

Since each BusinessObject corresponds to a specific DAO, it is possible to establish relationships between the BusinessObject, DAO, and underlying implementations (such as the tables in an RDBMS). Once the relationships are established, it is possible to write a simple application-specific code-generation utility that generates the code for all DAOs required by the application. The metadata to generate the DAO can come from a developer-defined descriptor file. Alternatively, the code generator can automatically introspect the database and provide the necessary DAOs to access the database. If the requirements for DAOs are sufficiently complex, consider using third-party tools that provide object-to-relational mapping for RDBMS databases. These tools typically include GUI tools to map the business objects to the persistent storage objects and thereby define the intermediary DAOs. The tools automatically generate the code once the mapping is complete, and may provide other value-added features such as results caching, query caching, integration with application servers, integration with other third-party products (e.g., distributed caching), and so forth.

Factory for Data Access Objects Strategy

The DAO pattern can be made highly flexible by adopting the Abstract Factory [GoF] and the Factory Method [GoF] patterns (see "Related Patterns" in this chapter).

When the underlying storage is not subject to change from one implementation to another, this strategy can be implemented using the Factory Method pattern to produce a number of DAOs needed by the application. The class diagram for this case is shown in Figure 9.3.

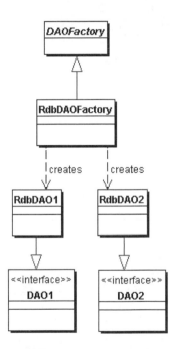

Figure 9.3 Factory for Data Access Object strategy using Factory Method

When the underlying storage is subject to change from one implementation to another, this strategy may be implemented using the Abstract Factory pattern. The Abstract Factory can in turn build on and use the Factory Method implementation, as suggested in *Design Patterns: Elements of Reusable Object-Oriented Software* [GoF]. In this case, this strategy provides an abstract DAO factory object (Abstract Factory) that can construct various types of concrete DAO factories, each factory supporting a different type of persistent storage implementation. Once you obtain the concrete DAO factory for a specific implementation, you use it to produce DAOs supported and implemented in that implementation.

The class diagram for this strategy is shown in Figure 9.4. This class diagram shows a base DAO factory, which is an abstract class that is inherited and implemented by different concrete DAO factories to support storage implementation-specific access. The client can obtain a concrete DAO factory implementation such as RdbDAO-Factory and use it to obtain concrete DAOs that work with that specific storage implementation. For example, the data client can obtain an RdbDAOFactory and use it to get specific DAOs such as RdbCustomerDAO, RdbAccountDAO, and so forth. The DAOs can extend and implement a generic base class (shown as DAO1 and DAO2) that specifically describe the DAO requirements for the business object it supports. Each concrete DAO is responsible for connecting to the data source and obtaining and manipulating data for the business object it supports.

The sample implementation for the DAO pattern and its strategies is shown in the "Sample Code" section of this chapter.

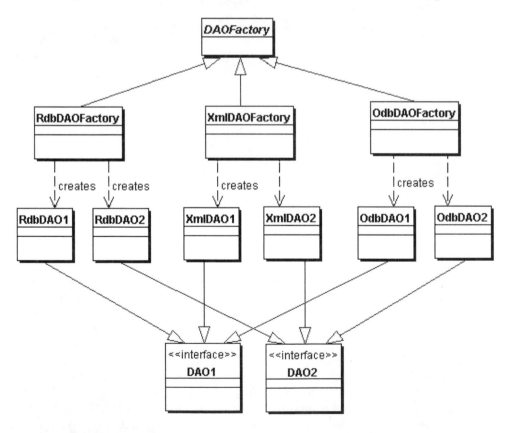

Figure 9.4 Factory for Data Access Object strategy using Abstract Factory

The sequence diagram describing the interactions for this strategy is shown in Figure 9.5.

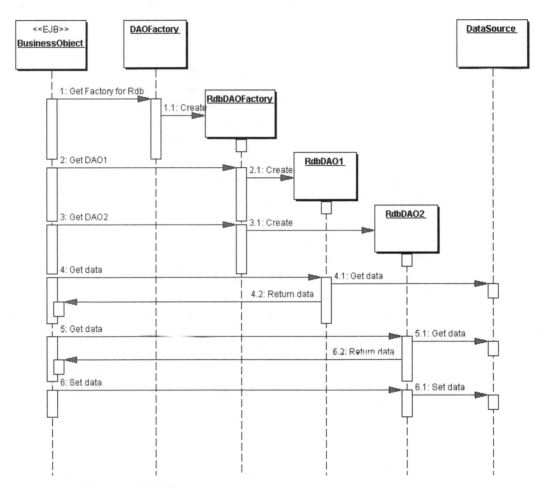

Figure 9.5 Factory for Data Access Objects using Abstract Factory sequence diagram

Consequences

- ***Enables Transparency***

  Business objects can use the data source without knowing the specific details of the data source's implementation. Access is transparent because the implementation details are hidden inside the DAO.

- *Enables Easier Migration*

  A layer of DAOs makes it easier for an application to migrate to a different database implementation. The business objects have no knowledge of the underlying data implementation. Thus, the migration involves changes only to the DAO layer. Further, if employing a factory strategy, it is possible to provide a concrete factory implementation for each underlying storage implementation. In this case, migrating to a different storage implementation means providing a new factory implementation to the application.

- *Reduces Code Complexity in Business Objects*

  Because the DAOs manage all the data access complexities, it simplifies the code in the business objects and other data clients that use the DAOs. All implementation-related code (such as SQL statements) is contained in the DAO and not in the business object. This improves code readability and development productivity.

- *Centralizes All Data Access into a Separate Layer*

  Because all data access operations are now delegated to the DAOs, the separate data access layer can be viewed as the layer that can isolate the rest of the application from the data access implementation. This centralization makes the application easier to maintain and manage.

- *Not Useful for Container-Managed Persistence*

  Because the EJB container manages entity beans with container-managed persistence (CMP), the container automatically services all persistent storage access. Applications using container-managed entity beans do not need a DAO layer, since the application server transparently provides this functionality. However, DAOs are still useful when a combination of CMP (for entity beans) and BMP (for session beans, servlets) is required.

- *Adds Extra Layer*

  The DAOs create an additional layer of objects between the data client and the data source that need to be designed and implemented to leverage the benefits of this pattern. But the benefit realized by choosing this approach pays off for the additional effort.

- *Needs Class Hierarchy Design*

  When using a factory strategy, the hierarchy of concrete factories and the hierarchy of concrete products produced by the factories need to be designed and implemented. This additional effort needs to be considered if there is sufficient justification warranting such flexibility. This increases the complexity of the design. However, you can choose to implement the factory strategy starting with the Factory Method pattern first, and then move towards the Abstract Factory if necessary.

Sample Code

Implementing Data Access Object pattern

An example DAO code for a persistent object that represents Customer information is shown in Example 9.4. The CloudscapeCustomerDAO creates a Customer value object when the `findCustomer()` method is invoked.

The sample code to use the DAO is shown in Example 9.6. The class diagram for this example is shown in Figure 9.6.

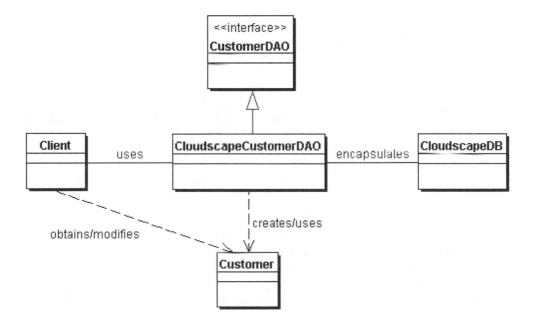

Figure 9.6 Implementing the DAO pattern

Implementing Factory for Data Access Objects Strategy

Using Factory Method Pattern

Consider an example where we are implementing this strategy in which a DAO factory produces many DAOs for a single database implementation (e.g., Oracle). The factory produces DAOs such as CustomerDAO, AccountDAO, OrderDAO, and so forth. The class diagram for this example is shown in Figure 9.7.

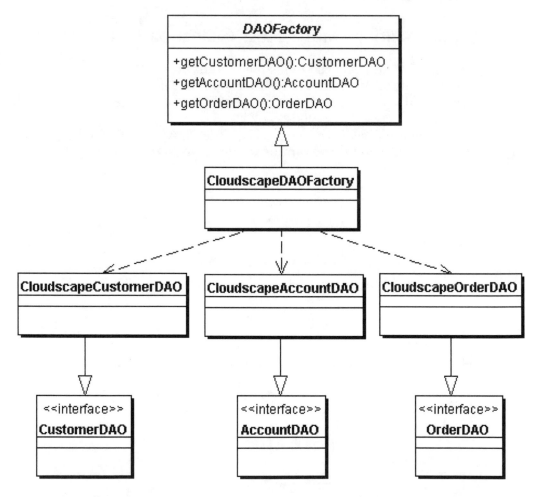

Figure 9.7 Implementing the Factory for DAO strategy using Factory Method

The example code for the DAO factory (CloudscapeDAOFactory) is listed in Example 9.2.

Using Abstract Factory Pattern

Consider an example where we are considering implementing this strategy for three different databases. In this case, the Abstract Factory pattern can be employed. The class diagram for this example is shown in Figure 9.8. The sample code in Example 9.1 shows code excerpt for the abstract DAOFactory class. This factory produces DAOs such as CustomerDAO, AccountDAO, OrderDAO, and so forth. This strategy uses the Factory Method implementation in the factories produced by the Abstract Factory.

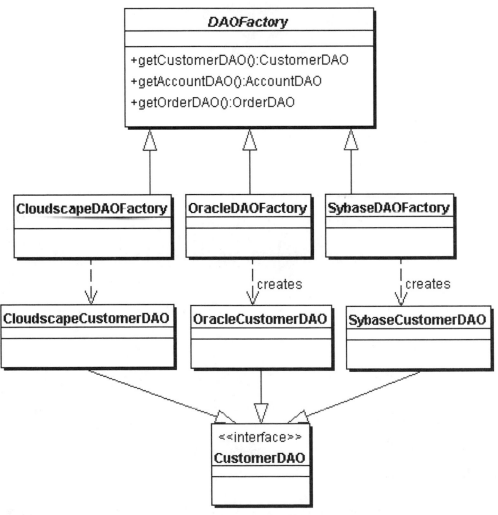

Figure 9.8 Implementing the Factory for DAO strategy using Abstract Factory

Example 9.1 Abstract DAOFactory Class

```
// Abstract class DAO Factory
public abstract class DAOFactory {

    // List of DAO types supported by the factory
    public static final int CLOUDSCAPE = 1;
    public static final int ORACLE = 2;
    public static final int SYBASE = 3;
    ...


    // There will be a method for each DAO that can be
    // created. The concrete factories will have to
    // implement these methods.
    public abstract CustomerDAO getCustomerDAO();
    public abstract AccountDAO getAccountDAO();
    public abstract OrderDAO getOrderDAO();
    ...

    public static DAOFactory getDAOFactory(
        int whichFactory) {

      switch (whichFactory) {
        case CLOUDSCAPE:
            return new CloudscapeDAOFactory();
        case ORACLE   :
            return new OracleDAOFactory();
        case SYBASE   :
            return new SybaseDAOFactory();
        ...
        default           :
            return null;
      }
    }
}
```

The sample code for CloudscapeDAOFactory is shown in Example 9.2. The implementation for OracleDAOFactory and SybaseDAOFactory are similar except for specifics of each implementation, such as JDBC driver, database URL, and differences in SQL syntax, if any.

Example 9.2 Concrete DAOFactory Implementation for Cloudscape

```java
// Cloudscape concrete DAO Factory implementation
import java.sql.*;

public class CloudscapeDAOFactory extends DAOFactory {
  public static final String DRIVER=
    "COM.cloudscape.core.RmiJdbcDriver";
  public static final String DBURL=
    "jdbc:cloudscape:rmi://localhost:1099/CoreJ2EEDB";

  // method to create Cloudscape connections
  public static Connection createConnection() {
    // Use DRIVER and DBURL to create a connection
    // Recommend connection pool implementation/usage
  }
  public CustomerDAO getCustomerDAO() {
    // CloudscapeCustomerDAO implements CustomerDAO
    return new CloudscapeCustomerDAO();
  }
  public AccountDAO getAccountDAO() {
    // CloudscapeAccountDAO implements AccountDAO
    return new CloudscapeAccountDAO();
  }
  public OrderDAO getOrderDAO() {
    // CloudscapeOrderDAO implements OrderDAO
    return new CloudscapeOrderDAO();
  }
  ...
}
```

The CustomerDAO interface shown in Example 9.3 defines the DAO methods for Customer persistent object that are implemented by all concrete DAO implementations, such as CloudscapeCustomer-DAO, OracleCustomerDAO, and SybaseCustomerDAO. Similar, but not listed here, are AccountDAO and OrderDAO interfaces that define the DAO methods for Account and Order business objects respectively.

Example 9.3 Base DAO Interface for Customer

```
// Interface that all CustomerDAOs must support
public interface CustomerDAO {
  public int insertCustomer(...);
  public boolean deleteCustomer(...);
  public Customer findCustomer(...);
  public boolean updateCustomer(...);
  public RowSet selectCustomersRS(...);
  public Collection selectCustomersVO(...);
  ...
}
```

The CloudscapeCustomerDAO implements the CustomerDAO as shown in Example 9.4. The implementation of other DAOs, such as CloudscapeAccountDAO, CloudscapeOrderDAO, OracleCustomer-DAO, OracleAccountDAO, and so forth, are similar.

Example 9.4 Cloudscape DAO Implementation for Customer

```
// CloudscapeCustomerDAO implementation of the
// CustomerDAO interface. This class can contain all
// Cloudscape specific code and SQL statements.
// The client is thus shielded from knowing
// these implementation details.

import java.sql.*;

public class CloudscapeCustomerDAO implements
    CustomerDAO {

  public CloudscapeCustomerDAO() {
    // initialization
  }

  // The following methods can use
  // CloudscapeDAOFactory.createConnection()
  // to get a connection as required

  public int insertCustomer(...) {
    // Implement insert customer here.
    // Return newly created customer number
    // or a -1 on error
  }
```

Example 9.4 Cloudscape DAO Implementation for Customer

```
public boolean deleteCustomer(...) {
  // Implement delete customer here
  // Return true on success, false on failure
}

public Customer findCustomer(...) {
  // Implement find a customer here using supplied
  // argument values as search criteria
  // Return a value object if found,
  // return null on error or if not found
}

public boolean updateCustomer(...) {
  // implement update record here using data
  // from the customerData value object
  // Return true on success, false on failure or
  // error
}

public RowSet selectCustomersRS(...) {
  // implement search customers here using the
  // supplied criteria.
  // Return a RowSet.
}

public Collection selectCustomersVO(...) {
  // implement search customers here using the
  // supplied criteria.
  // Alternatively, implement to return a Collection
  // of value objects.
}
...
}
```

The Customer value object class is shown in Example 9.5. This is used by the DAOs to send and receive data from the clients. The usage of value objects is discussed in detail in the Value Object pattern.

Example 9.5 Customer Value Object

```
public class Customer implements java.io.Serializable
  {
  // member variables
  int CustomerNumber;
  String name;
  String streetAddress;
  String city;
  ...

  // getter and setter methods...
  ...
  }
```

Example 9.6 shows the usage of the DAO factory and the DAO. If the implementation changes from Cloudscape to another product, the only required change is the `getDAOFactory()` method call to the DAO factory to obtain a different factory.

Example 9.6 Using a DAO and DAO Factory – Client Code

```
...
// create the required DAO Factory
DAOFactory cloudscapeFactory =
  DAOFactory.getDAOFactory(DAOFactory.DAOCLOUDSCAPE);

// Create a DAO
CustomerDAO custDAO =
  cloudscapeFactory.getCustomerDAO();

// create a new customer
int newCustNo = custDAO.insertCustomer(...);

// Find a customer object. Get the value object.
Customer cust = custDAO.findCustomer(...);

// modify the values in the value object.
cust.setAddress(...);
cust.setEmail(...);
// update the customer object using the DAO
custDAO.updateCustomer(cust);

// delete a customer object
custDAO.deleteCustomer(...);
```

Example 9.6 Using a DAO and DAO Factory – Client Code

```
// select all customers in the same city
Customer criteria=new Customer();
criteria.setCity("New York");
Collection customersList =
  custDAO.selectCustomersVO(criteria);
// returns customersList - collection of Customer
// value objects. iterate through this collection to
// get values.

...
```

Related Patterns

- **Value Object**

  A DAO uses value objects to transport data to and from its clients.

- **Factory Method [GoF] and Abstract Factory [GoF]**

  The *Factory for Data Access Objects Strategy* uses the Factory Method pattern to implement the concrete factories and its products (DAOs). For added flexibility, the Abstract Factory pattern may be employed as discussed in the strategies.

- **Broker [POSA1]**

  The DAO pattern is related to the Broker pattern, which describes approaches for decoupling clients and servers in distributed systems. The DAO pattern more specifically applies this pattern to decouple the resource tier from clients in another tier, such as the business or presentation tier.

Service Activator

Context

Enterprise beans and other business services need a way to be activated asynchronously.

Problem

When a client needs to access an enterprise bean, it first looks up the bean's home object. The client requests the EJB home to provide a remote reference to the required enterprise bean. The client then invokes business method calls on the remote reference to access the enterprise bean services. All these method calls, such as lookup and remote method calls, are synchronous. The client has to wait until these methods return.

Another factor to consider is the life cycle of an enterprise bean. The EJB specification permits the container to passivate an enterprise bean to secondary storage. As a result, the EJB container has no mechanism by which it can provide a process-like service to keep an enterprise bean constantly in an activated and ready state. Because the client must interact with the enterprise bean using the bean's remote interface, even if the bean is in an activated state in the container, the client still needs to obtain its remote interface via the lookup process and still interacts with the bean in a synchronous manner.

If an application needs synchronous processing for its server-side business components, then enterprise beans are an appropriate choice. Some application clients may require asynchronous processing for the server-side business objects because the clients do not need to wait or do not have the time to wait for the processing to complete. In cases where the application needs a form of asynchronous processing, enterprise beans do not offer this capability in implementations prior to EJB 2.0.

EJB 2.0 provides integration by introducing message-driven bean, which is a special type of stateless session bean that offers asynchronous invocation capabilities. However, the new specification does not offer asynchronous invocation for other types of enterprise beans, such as stateful or entity beans.

In general, a business service such as a session or entity bean provides only synchronous processing and thus presents a challenge to implementing asynchronous processing.

Forces

- Enterprise beans are exposed to their clients via their remote interfaces, which allow only synchronous access.
- The container manages enterprise beans, allowing interactions only via the remote references. The EJB container does not allow direct access to the bean implementation and its methods. Thus, implementing the JMS message listener in an enterprise bean is not feasible, since this violates the EJB specification by permitting direct access to the bean implementation.
- An application needs to provide a publish/subscribe or point-to-point messaging framework where clients can publish requests to enterprise beans for asynchronous processing.
- Clients need asynchronous processing capabilities from the enterprise beans and other business components that can only provide synchronous access, so that the client can send a request for processing without waiting for the results.
- Clients want to use the message-oriented middleware (MOM) interfaces offered by the Java Messaging Service (JMS). These interfaces are not integrated into EJB server products that are based on the pre-EJB 2.0 specification.
- An application needs to provide daemon-like service so that an enterprise bean can be in a quiet mode until an event (or a message) triggers its activity.
- Enterprise beans are subject to the container life cycle management, which includes passivation due to time-outs, inactivity and resource management. The client will have to invoke on an enterprise bean to activate it again.
- EJB 2.0 introduces a message-driven bean as a stateless session bean, but it is not possible to invoke other types of enterprise beans asynchronously.

Solution

Use a Service Activator to receive asynchronous client requests and messages. On receiving a message, the Service Activator locates and invokes the necessary business methods on the business service components to fulfill the request asynchronously.

The ServiceActivator is a JMS Listener and delegation service that requires implementing the JMS message listener—making it a JMS listener object that can listen to JMS messages. The ServiceActivator can be implemented as a standalone service. Clients act as the message generator, generating events based on their activity.

Any client that needs to asynchronously invoke a business service, such as an enterprise bean, may create and send a message to the Service Activator. The Service Activator receives the message and parses it to interpret the client request. Once the client's request is parsed or unmarshalled, the Service Activator identifies and locates the necessary business service component and invokes business methods to complete processing of the client's request asynchronously.

The Service Activator may optionally send an acknowledgement to the client after successfully completing the request processing. The Service Activator may also notify the client or other services on failure events if it fails to complete the asynchronous request processing.

The Service Activator may use the services of a Service Locator to locate a business component. See "Service Locator" on page 367.

Structure

Figure 9.9 represents the class relationships for the Service Activator pattern.

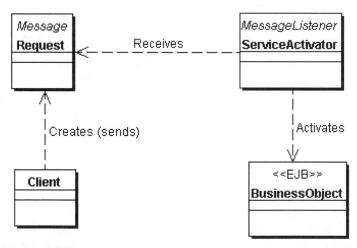

Figure 9.9 Service Activator class diagram

Participants and Responsibilities

Figure 9.10 shows the interactions between the various participants in the Service Activator pattern.

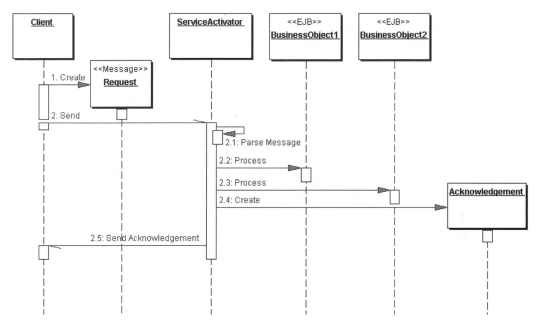

Figure 9.10 Service Activator sequence diagram

Client

The client requires an asynchronous processing facility from the business objects participating in a workflow. The client can be any type of application that has the capability to create and send JMS messages. The client can also be an EJB component that needs to invoke another EJB component's business methods in an asynchronous manner. The client can use the services offered by the Service Locator pattern to look up or create EJB components, JMS services, and JMS objects, as necessary.

Request

The Request is the message object created by the client and sent to the ServiceActivator via the MOM. According to the JMS specification, the Request is an object that implements the javax.jms.Message interface. The JMS API provides several message types, such as TextMessage, ObjectMessage, and so forth, that can be used as request objects.

ServiceActivator

The ServiceActivator is the main class of the pattern. It implements the javax.jms.MessageListener interface, which is defined by the JMS specification. The ServiceActivator implements an `onMessage()` method that is invoked when a new message arrives. The ServiceActivator parses (unmarshals) the message (request) to determine what needs to be done. The ServiceActivator may use the services offered by a Service Locator (see Service Locator) pattern to look up or create Business Service components such as enterprise beans.

BusinessObject

BusinessObject is the target object to which the client needs access in an asynchronous mode. The business object is a role fulfilled by either a session or entity bean. It is also possible that the BusinessObject is an external service instead of an entity bean.

Strategies

Entity Bean Strategy

Both session and entity beans can fulfill the role of a BusinessObject. When J2EE applications implement a Session Façade pattern to provide coarse-grained access to entity beans and to encapsulate the workflow, then the session bean from the Session Façade fulfills the BusinessObject role.

In simple applications with minimal workflow, an entity bean may fulfill the BusinessObject role. However, for complex workflow involving multiple entity beans and other business objects, the ServiceActivator typically interacts with a Session Facade which encapsulates such workflow.

Session Bean Strategy

When a session bean fulfills the role of the BusinessObject, the business requirements determine whether the bean should be stateful or stateless. Since the client for the BusinessObject is a ServiceActivator that activates the BusinessObject on receiving a new message, the workflow to process the message can define whether the bean should be stateful or not. In most cases, a message delivery simply activates a single method in the BusinessObject that delegates the processing of the message within. A stateless session bean can be used in these cases. If the ServiceActivator needs to invoke multiple methods in the BusinessObject or to work with more than one BusinessObject to fulfill the processing requirements for a message, it may be useful to consider a stateful session bean to retain state between multiple invocations. See "Stateless Session Facade Strategy" on page 296 and "Stateful Session Facade Strategy" on page 297.

ServiceActivator Server Strategy

The most straightforward strategy for implementing the listener or ServiceActivator is as a standalone JMS application that listens and processes JMS messages.

An alternative is to implement the ServiceActivator as a service of the application server. This may make it easier to manage the ServiceActivator, because it uses the application server features to monitor the ServiceActivator state and to start, restart, and stop the ServiceActivator as needed, either manually or automatically.

Enterprise Bean as Client Strategy

The Client can be any client, including another enterprise bean that requires asynchronous processing from the enterprise bean. When integrating legacy applications to the J2EE platform, it is logical to choose Java application clients to act as the message generators based on the activity in the legacy system. The ServiceActivator can receive messages and perform the necessary enterprise bean invocations to process the request from the legacy system.

Consequences

- ### Integrates JMS into Pre-EJB 2.0 Implementations

  Prior to the EJB 2.0 specification, there was no integration between enterprise bean and JMS components. This pattern provides a means to integrate JMS into an EJB application and enable asynchronous processing. The EJB 2.0 specification defines a new type of session bean, called a message-driven bean, to integrate JMS and EJB components. This special bean implements the JMS Message Listener interface and it receives asynchronous messages. In this case, the application server plays the role of the Service Activator. This pattern makes it possible to run applications in EJB 2.0 implementations as well as pre-EJB 2.0 implementations.

- ### Provides Asynchronous Processing for any Enterprise Beans

  In EJB 2.0, the message-driven bean is a stateless session bean. Using the Service Activator pattern, it is possible to provide asynchronous invocation on all types of enterprise beans, including stateless session beans, stateful session beans, and entity beans. As previously explained, since the Service Activator is implemented in its own right, without any limitations of the message-driven bean, the Service Activator can perform asynchronous invocations on any type of business service. Thus, this pattern provides a way to enable asynchronous processing for clients that either have no need to wait for the results or do not want to wait for processing to complete. The processing can be deferred and performed at a later time, enabling the client to complete the service in less time.

- ***Standalone Process***

  The Service Activator can be run as a standalone process. However, in a critical application, Service Activator needs to be monitored to ensure availability. The additional management and maintenance of this process can add to application support overhead.

Sample Code

Consider an order processing application where the customers shop online and the order fulfillment process happens in the background. In some cases, order fulfillment may be outsourced to a third-party warehouse. In such cases, the online store needs to invoke these fulfillment services asynchronously. This is an example that demonstrates usage of point-to-point (PTP) messaging to accomplish asynchronous processing. However, using publish/subscribe messaging would be similar, except that Topic is used instead of a Queue. Choosing which method to use, PTP or publish/subscribe, depends on the business and application requirements, and hence is outside the scope of this pattern.

The class diagram with only the relevant methods for this example is shown in Figure 9.11.

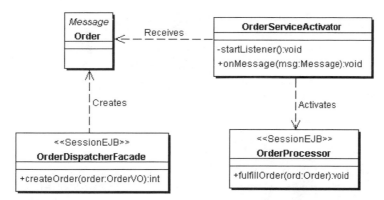

Figure 9.11 Service Activator for Order Processing example – class diagram

The code excerpt shown in Example 9.7 demonstrates a sample Service Activator implementation. This is the class that can be instantiated in an application server or run in a stand-alone server, as explained in the Service Activator Server strategy.

Example 9.7 Order Service Activator

```
public class OrderServiceActivator implements
  javax.jms.MessageListener{

  // Queue session and receiver. see JMS API for
  // details
  private QueueSession orderQueueSession;
  private QueueReceiver orderQueueReceiver;

  // Note: values should come from property files or
  // environment instead of hard coding.
  private String connFactoryName =
    "PendingOrdersQueueFactory";
  private String queueName = "PendingOrders";

  // use a service locator to locate administered
  // JMS components such as a Queue or a Queue
  // Connection factory
  private JMSServiceLocator serviceLocator;

  public OrderServiceActivator(String connFactoryName,
      String queueName) {
    super();
    this.connFactoryName = connFactoryName;
    this.queueName = queueName;
```

Example 9.7 Order Service Activator

```
    startListener();
}

private void startListener() {
  try {
    serviceLocator = new JMSServiceLocator
         (connFactoryName);
    qConnFactory =
       serviceLocator.getQueueConnectionFactory();
    qConn = qConnFactory.createQueueConnection();

    // See JMS API for method usage and arguments
    orderQueueSession = qConn.createQueueSession
(...);
    Queue ordersQueue =
           serviceLocator.getQueue(queueName);
    orderQueueReceiver =
      orderQueueSession.createReceiver(ordersQueue);
    orderQueueReceiver.setMessageListener(this);
  }
  catch (JMSException excp) {
    // handle error
  }
}

// The JMS API specifies the onMessage method in the
// javax.jms.MessageListener interface.
// This method is asynchronously invoked
// when a message arrives on the Queue being
// listened to by the ServiceActivator.
// See JMS Specification and API for more details.
public void onMessage(Message msg) {
  try {
      // parse Message msg. See JMS API for Message.
      ...

      // Invoke business method on an enterprise
      // bean using the bean's business delegate.
```

This example demonstrates using the Business Delegate pattern between business and integration tiers. OrderProcessorDelegate logically resides in the integration tier and accesses the Order Processor session bean, which resides in the business tier.

Example 9.7 Order Service Activator

```
                // OrderProcessorDelegate is the business
                // delegate for OrderProcessor Session bean.
                // See Business Delegate pattern for details.
                  OrderProcessorDelegate orderProcDeleg =
                     new OrderProcessorDelegate();

                // Use data values from the parsed message to
                // invoke business method on bean via delegate
                orderProcDeleg.fulfillOrder(...);

                // send any acknowledgement here...
            }
            catch (JMSException jmsexcp) {
               // Handle JMSExceptions, if any
            }
            catch (Exception excp) {
               // Handle any other exceptions
            }
        }

    public void close() {
        try {
           // cleanup before closing
           orderQueueReceiver.setMessageListener (null);
           orderQueueSession.close();
        }
        catch(Exception excp) {
           // Handle exception - Failure to close
        }
      }
    }
```

The sample session facade code responsible to dispatch orders to this asynchronous service is shown in the code excerpt in Example 9.8. The Service Activator client can be a session bean that implements the Session Façade pattern to provide order processing services to the online store application. When the session bean's `createOrder()` method is called, after successfully validating and creating a new order, it invokes `sendOrder()` to dispatch the new order to the backend order fulfillment service.

Example 9.8 Session Facade as Client for Service Activator

```
// imports...
public class OrderDispatcherFacade
  implements javax.ejb.SessionBean {
  ...
  // business method to create new Order
  public int createOrder(...) throws OrderException {

    // create new business order entity bean
    ...

    // successfully created Order. send Order to
    // asynchronous backend processing
    OrderSender orderSender = new OrderSender();
    orderSender.sendOrder(order);

    // close the sender, if done...
    orderSender.close();

    // other processing
    ...
  }
}
```

The JMS code can be separated into a different class so that it can be reused by different clients. This JMS delegate class is shown as OrderSender in the Example 9.9 code listing.

Example 9.9 OrderSender: Used to Dispatch Orders to Queue

```
// imports...
public class OrderSender {
  // Queue session and sender: see JMS API for details
  private QueueSession orderQueueSession;
  private QueueSender orderQueueSender;

  // These values could come from some property files
  private String connFactoryName =
    "PendingOrdersQueueFactory";
  private String queueName = "PendingOrders";

  // use a service locator to locate administered
  // JMS components such as a Queue or a Queue.
  // Connection factory
  private JMSServiceLocator serviceLocator;
  ...
```

Example 9.9 OrderSender: Used to Dispatch Orders to Queue

```
// method to initialize and create queue sender
private void createSender() {
  try {
    // using ServiceLocator and getting Queue
    // Connection Factory is similar to the
    // Service Activator code.
    serviceLocator = new JMSServiceLocator
        (connFactoryName);
    qConnFactory =
        serviceLocator.getQueueConnectionFactory();
    qConn = qConnFactory.createQueueConnection();

    // See JMS API for method usage and arguments
    orderQueueSession = qConn.createQueueSession
        (...);
    Queue ordersQueue =
            serviceLocator.getQueue(queueName);
    orderQueueSender =
        orderQueueSession.createSender(ordersQueue);
  catch(Exception excp) {
    // Handle exception - Failure to create sender
  }
}

// method to dispatch order to fulfillment service
// for asynchronous processing
public void sendOrder(Order newOrder) {

    // create a new Message to send Order object
    ObjectMessage objMessage =
      queueSession.createObjectMessage(order);

    // set object message properties and delivery
    // mode as required.
    // See JMS API for ObjectMessage

    // Set the Order into the object message
     objMessage.setObject(order);

    // send the message to the Queue
    orderQueueSender.send(objMessage);

    ...
  } catch (Exception e) {
    // Handle exceptions
```

Example 9.9 OrderSender: Used to Dispatch Orders to Queue

```
        }
        ...
    }
    ...
    public void close() {
        try {
            // cleanup before closing
            orderQueueReceiver.setMessageListener (null);
            orderQueueSession.close();
        }
        catch(Exception excp) {
            // Handle exception - Failure to close
        }
    }
}
```

Related Patterns

- **Session Facade**

  The Session Facade pattern encapsulates the complexity of the system and provides coarse-grained access to business objects. This Service Activator pattern may access a Session Façade as the primary business object to invoke business service methods in the Session Façade asynchronously on behalf of the client.

- **Business Delegate**

  The Service Activator pattern may use a Business Delegate to access the Session Façade or other enterprise bean implementations. This results in simpler code for the Service Activator and results in Business Delegate reuse across different tiers, as intended by the Business Delegate pattern.

- **Service Locator**

  The client can use the Service Locator pattern to look up and create JMS-related service objects. The Service Activator can use the Service Locator pattern to look up and create enterprise bean components.

- **Half-Sync/Half-Async [POSA2]**

  The Service Activator pattern is related to the Half-Sync/Half-Async pattern, which describes architectural decoupling of synchronous and asynchronous processing by suggesting different layers for synchronous, asynchronous and an intermediate queueing layer inbetween.

J2EE PATTERNS
APPLIED

Epilogue

In this chapter we present an example of using the J2EE patterns in an application. Our experiences have shown us that using the pattern catalog can improve the efficiency and quality of your software development process. It is important to understand how to leverage the pattern catalog, and that's what we illustrate in this chapter. Leveraging the pattern catalog does not in itself require a new development process or a new methodology. Rather, it shows how to integrate the patterns in the catalog into your present design process or approach, so that your approach improves and produces a better, more robust solution.

This chapter shows you a sampling of ways to apply the patterns to real-world examples. We go directly to the patterns and pattern realizations to describe how the patterns are applied to an example. We want to emphasize that these ideas are a sampling of many possibilities. They are meant to get you thinking creatively with the patterns. You will benefit by applying approaches similar to ours, and you will gain confidence in applying the patterns to your own design problems in new and unique ways.

PSA Overview

This example deals with the domain of professional services automation, also known as PSA. PSA is a set of software and services used by professional services organizations to help operate more effectively. PSA may cover a wide range of processes, including project bidding and team, skill, project, and customer management.

Our intention with this example is to address a small set of basic requirements of a professional services organization. The PSA system must be flexible, providing different services based on the particular role of the user.

- Project managers will search the PSA system for matching resources, check on the availability of a particular resource, and schedule an available resource for a specific project.
- Consultants (hereafter known as "resources") accept and manage their assignments, their availability, and the listing of their current skill set.
- Project administrators are "super" project managers, as they can act on behalf of a project manager. In addition, they perform administrative tasks, such as creating new projects and managing the care and feeding of project information over its lifetime.

Each of the three roles share common functional requirements:

- Searching based on projects, resources, skills.
- Managing resource information (address, email, phone, etc.).
- Other packaged and ad hoc reports and queries.

Use Case Model

The following use case model is derived from the functional requirements for the PSA application. In the model, we've identified the following actors for the PSA application, as shown in Table E-1 .

Table E-1 PSA Actors

Actor	*Description*
Resource	An employee who can be assigned to work on a project.
Project Manager	An employee who can be assigned to manage and execute a project.
Administrator	An employee who provides administrative support to the PS organization.
Resource Manager	An employee who is responsible to manage a group of resources.

Figure E.1 shows the use case model for the PSA application.

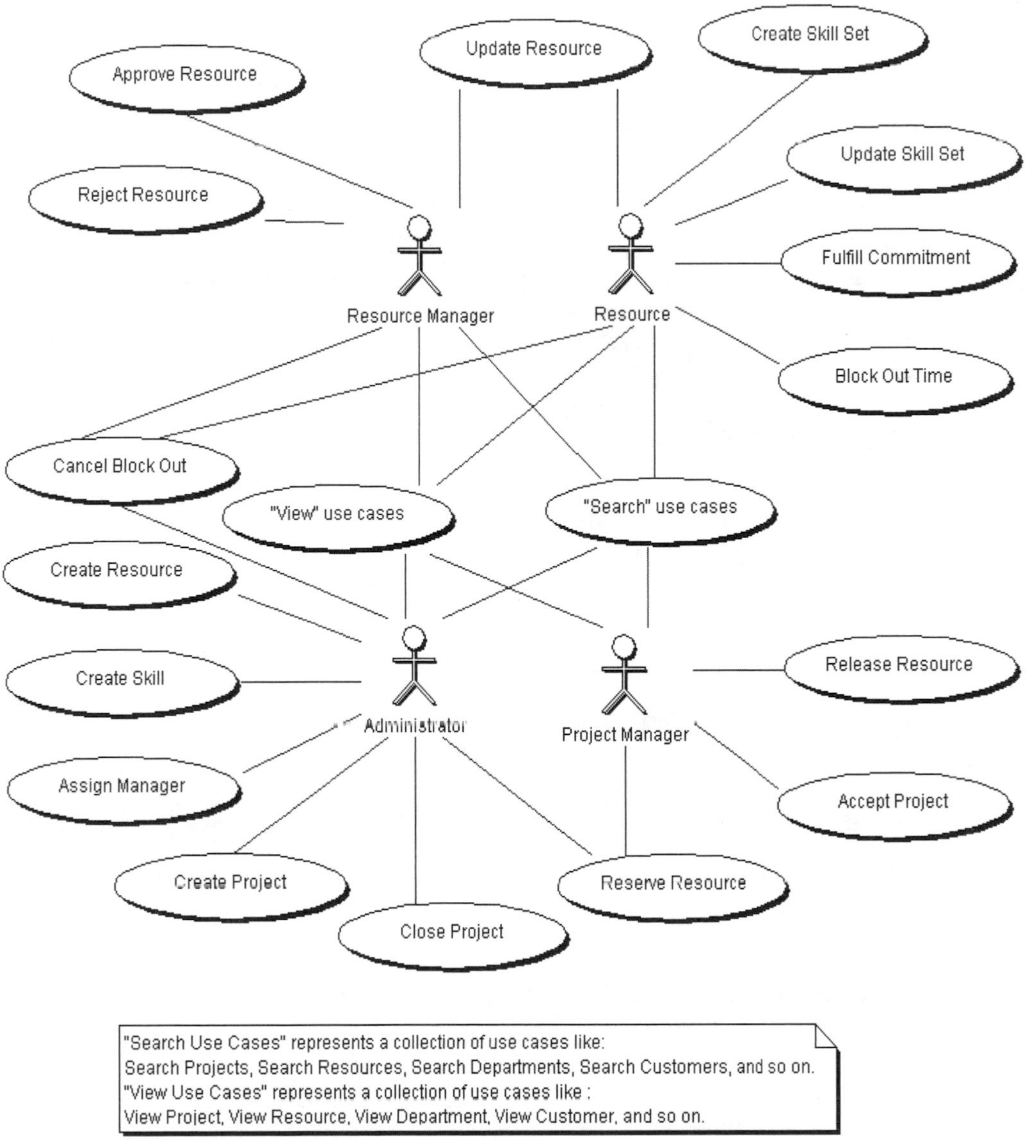

Figure E.1 Use case model

Use Cases, Patterns, and Pattern Frameworks

In this section we apply the patterns based on the use cases. The goal of this section is to focus on the realized patterns, not the process from which we arrived at the pattern selection. The approach we take is to show the pattern framework and then the realized pattern framework. We define a pattern framework as a set of patterns commonly used in combination to solve a problem.

We are confident that as you see these examples and begin applying the J2EE patterns to your solutions, you will be able to quickly identify the proper patterns.

Create Project Use Case

In this use case, the administrator creates a project. See Figure E.2. The project contains information such as the start and end dates, customer name, and skills required.

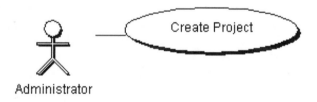

Figure E.2 Create Project use case

Pattern Identification

We use the following presentation patterns:

- Intercepting Filter—A filter checks user privileges for creating a project.

- Front Controller—A controller acts as the initial point of contact for generating the form for project creation, and subsequently handles submission of this form. The controller delegates project creation-related processing to its helpers, which in turn delegate much of this processing to the business tier.

- View Helper—The view delegates to its helpers in order to generate dynamic portions of the display.
- Composite View—The view includes a header and a footer to create the Create Project page. This is a very simple example of a composite view.

We use the following business patterns:

- Business Delegate—A business delegate interacts with the business tier for creating a project.
- Service Locator—A business delegate uses a service locator to look up the project components.
- Session Facade—The business delegate interacts with a session bean, which interacts with the project entity when creating a project.
- Value Object—A project value object encapsulates the project data, which is passed from the presentation tier to the business tier.

We use the following integration pattern:

- Data Access Object—A data access object abstracts and encapsulates access to the project tables.

Figure E.3 shows the pattern framework for the Create Project use case. It shows the patterns used in presentation, business, and integration.

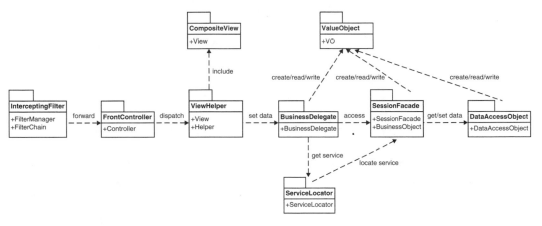

Figure E.3 Create Project pattern framework

Pattern Realization

Figure E.4 shows the realized patterns for the Create Project use case. This diagram provides a breakdown by tiers. The following list matches the name of an implementation class with the pattern from which it is realized.

- Presentation—The Create Project form is shown in Figure E.5.

Class	Pattern
LoginCheckFilter	Intercepting Filter
PSAController	Front Controller
CreateProjectForm, header, footer	Composite View
ProjectView, currentDate, listCustomers	View Helper

- Business

Class	Pattern
ProjectDelegate	Business Delegate
PSAServiceLocator	Service Locator
ProjectManagerSession	Session Facade
ProjectEntity	Session Facade
ProjectVO	Value Object

- Integration

Class	Pattern
ProjectDAO	Data Access Object

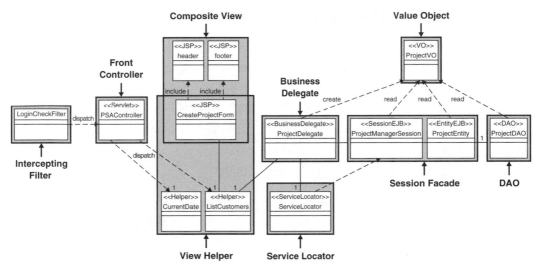

Figure E.4 Create Project realized patterns

Figure E.5 Create Project Form

Reserve Resource Use Case

In the Reserve Resource use case, the project manager must reserve a resource for use on a project. See Figure E.6. The reservation is comprised of a length of time and a number of hours per week. After the resource is reserved, the resource manager must approve him. Once the resource manager approves the resource, the resource is officially assigned to the project.

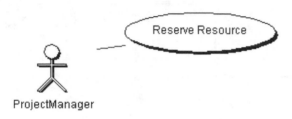

Figure E.6 Reserve Resource use case

Pattern Identification

Figure E.7 contains the pattern framework for the Reserve Resource use case. It shows the patterns used in presentation, business, and integration. We use the following presentation patterns:

- Intercepting Filter—A filter checks user privileges for reserving a resource.

- Front Controller—A controller acts as the initial point of contact for reserving a resource. The controller delegates resource reservation-related processing to its helpers, which in turn delegate much of this processing to the business tier.

- View Helper—The view delegates to its helpers in order to generate dynamic portions of the display.

- Composite View—The view includes a header and a footer to create the Reserve Resource page. This is a very simple example of a composite view.

We use the following business patterns:

- Business Delegate—A business delegate interacts with the business tier for reserving a resource.

- Service Locator—A business delegate uses a service locator to look up the resource components.

- Session Facade—The business delegate interacts with a session bean, which interacts with the project entity when reserving a resource.

- Value Object—A commitment value object encapsulates the commitment data, which is passed from the presentation tier to the business tier.

- Composite Entity—A project entity acts as a coarse-grained object to the dependent commitment objects.

We use the following integration patterns:

- Data Access Object—A data access object abstracts and encapsulates access to the resource and commitment tables.

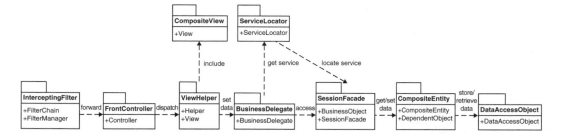

Figure E.7 Reserve Resource pattern framework

Pattern Realization

Figure E.8 shows the realized patterns for the Reserve Resource use case. The following list matches the name of an implementation class with the pattern from which it is realized:

- Presentation—The Reserve Resource form is shown in Figure E.9.

Class	*Pattern*
LoginCheckFilter	Intercepting Filter
PSAController	Front Controller
ReserveResourceForm, header, footer	Composite View
ReserveResourceForm, ResourceHelper	View Helper

- Business

Class	Pattern
ProjectDelegate	Business Delegate
PSAServiceLocator	Service Locator
ProjectManagerSession	Session Façade
ProjectEntity	Session Facade, Composite Entity
Commitment	Composite Entity
CommitmentVO	Value Object

- Integration

Class	Pattern
ProjectDAO	Data Access Object
CommitmentsDAO	Data Access Object

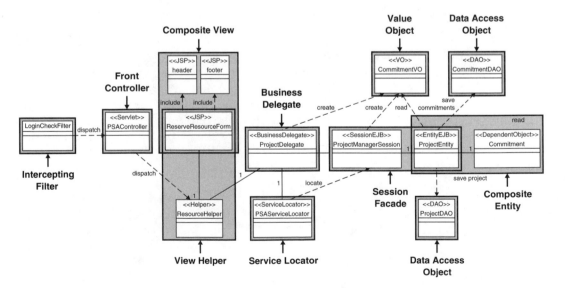

Figure E.8 Reserve Resource realized patterns

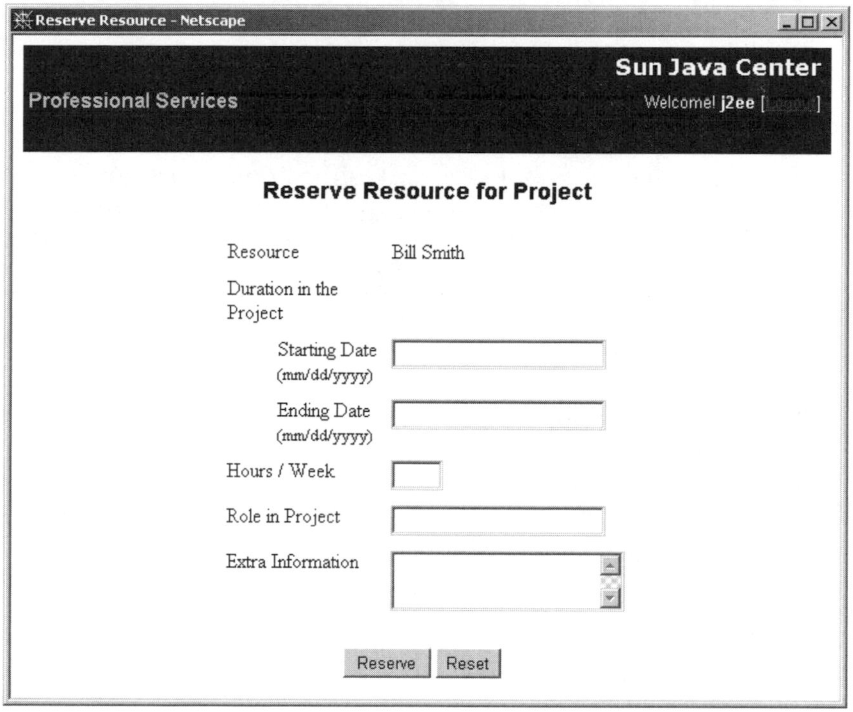

Figure E.9 Reserve Resources Form

Find Available Resources Use Case

In the Find Available Resources use case, the project manager searches for available resources for a project by start date, end date, and skills. See Figure E.10.

Figure E.10 Reserve Resource use case

Pattern Identification

For this use case, we use the following presentation patterns:

- Intercepting Filter—A filter checks user privileges for searching for available resources.
- Front Controller—A controller acts as the initial point of contact for searching for resources. The controller delegates resource availability-related processing to its helpers, which in turn delegate much of this processing to the business tier.
- View Helper—The view delegates to its helpers in order to generate dynamic portions of the display.
- Composite View—The view includes a header and a footer to create the search for available resources page. This is a very simple example of a composite view.

We use the following business patterns:

- Business Delegate—A business delegate interacts with the business tier when searching for available resources.
- Service Locator—A business delegate uses a service locator to look up the resource components.
- Session Facade—The business delegate interacts with a session bean, which interacts with the list handler when searching for available resources.
- Value Object—The commitment value object encapsulates the commitment data, which is passed from the presentation tier to the business tier.
- Composite Entity—A project entity acts as a coarse-grained object to the dependent commitment objects.
- Value List Handler—A value list handler controls the lookup, cache, and iteration of the resources.

We use the following integration patterns:

- Data Access Object—A data access object abstracts and encapsulates access to commitments and resource tables.

Figure E.11 is the pattern framework for the Find Available Resources use case. It shows the patterns used in presentation, business, and integration.

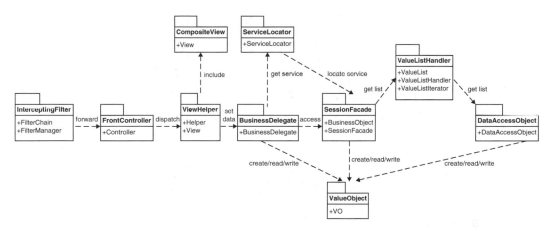

Figure E.11 Find Available Resources pattern framework

Pattern Realization

Figure E.12 shows the realized patterns for the Find Available Resources use case. The following list matches the name of an implementation class with the pattern from which it is realized:

- Presentation—The Find Available Resources form is shown in Figure E.13.

Class	Pattern
LoginCheckFilter	Intercepting Filter
PSAController	Front Controller
FindAvailableResourcesForm, Resource-Helper	View Helper
FindAvailableResourcesForm, header, footer	Composite View

- Business

Class	Pattern
ResourceDelegate	Business Delegate
PSAServiceLocator	Service Locator
ResourceAdminSession	Session Facade
ResourceListHandler, ResourcesList	Value List Handler
ResourceVO	Value Object

- Integration

Class	Pattern
ResourceDAO	Session Facade, Data Access Object

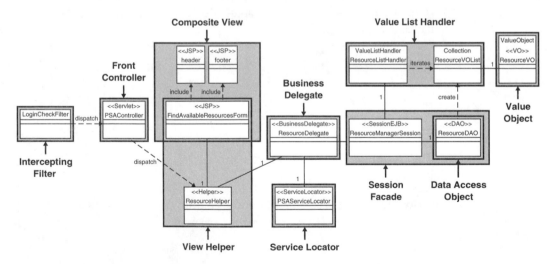

Figure E.12 Find Available Resources realized patterns

Figure E.13 Find Available Resources Form

BIBLIOGRAPHY

[Alex] Christopher Alexander, "The Timeless Way of Building", Oxford University Press, New York, 1979

[Alex2] Christopher Alexander, Sara Ishikawa, Murray Silverstein, Max Jacobson, Ingrid Fiksdahl-King, and Shlomo Angel, "A Pattern Language", Oxford University Press, New York, 1977

[Arnold] Ken Arnold, David Holmes, and James Gosling, "The Java Programming Language, Third Edition: The Java Series", Addison Wesley, 2000

[Bergsten] Hans Bergsten, "JavaServer Pages", O'Reilly & Associates, Inc., 2001.

[Booch] Grady Booch, James Rumbaugh, and Ivar Jacobson, "The Unified Modeling Language User Guide", Addison Wesley, 1998.

[Brown] William H. Brown, Raphael C. Malveau, Hays W. "Skip" McCormick III and Thomas J. Mowbray, "Anti-Patterns: Refactoring Software, Architectures and Projects in Crisis", Wiley Press, 1998

[Coplien] Jim O. Coplien, Douglas C. Schmidt (Editors), "Pattern Languages of Program Design", Addison Wesley, 1995

[Fowler] Martin Fowler, "Refactorings - Improving the Design Of Existing Code", Addison Wesley, 1999

[Fowler2] Martin Fowler, "Analysis Patterns: Reusable Object Models", Addison Wesley, 1997

[Fowler3] Martin Fowler and Kendall Scott, "UML Distilled : A Brief Guide to the Standard Object Modeling Language, Second Edition", Addison Wesley, 2000.

[Gabriel] Richard P. Gabriel, "Patterns of Software: Tales from the Software Community", Oxford University Press, 1998

[Geary] David M. Geary, "Advanced JavaServer Pages", Sun Microsystems Press/Prentice Hall PTR, 2001

[GoF] Erich Gamma, Richard Helm, Ralph Johnson, and John Vlissides, "Design Patterns: Elements of Reusable Object-Oriented Software", Addison Wesley, 1994

[Gosling] James Gosling, Bill Joy, Guy Steele, and Gilad Bracha, "The Java Language Specification, Second Edition: The Java Series", Addison Wesley, 2000

[Haefel] Richard Monson-Haefel, "Enterprise JavaBeans, Second Edition", O'Reilly & Associates, Inc., 2000

[Harrison] Niel Harrison, Brian Foote and Hans Rohnert (Editors), "Pattern Languages of Program Design 4", Addison Wesley, 1999

[Jacobsen] Ivar Jacobson, Magnus Christerson, Patrik Jonsson, and Gunnar Overgaard, "Object-Oriented Software Engineering-A Use Case Driven Approach", Addison-Wesley, ACM Press, 1992-98

[POSA1] Frank Buschmann, Regine Meunier, Hans Rohnert, Peter Sommerlad, and Michael Stal, "Pattern-Oriented Software Architecture-A System of patterns", Wiley Press, 1996-2000

[POSA2] Douglas Schmidt, Michael Stal, Hans Rohnert, and Frank Buschmann, "Pattern-Oriented Software Architecture-Volume 2: Patterns for Concurrent and Networked Objects", Wiley Press, 2000

[Shannon] Bill Shannon, Mark Hapner, Vlada Matena, James Davidson, Eduardo Pelegri-Llopart, Larry Cable and the Enterprise Team, "Java 2 Platform, Enterprise Edition: Platform and Component Specifications", Addison Wesley, 2000

[Martin] Robert Martin, Dirk Riehle, and Frank Buschmann (Editors), "Pattern Languages of Program Design 3", Addison Wesley, 1998

[Rosenberg] Doug Rosenberg, with Kendall Scott, "Use Case Driven Object Modeling with UML", Addison Wesley, 1999.

[Rumbaugh] James Rumbaugh, Ivar Jacobson, and Grady Booch, "The Unified Modeling Language Reference Manual", Addison Wesley, 1999.

[Vlissides] John M. Vlissides, Jim O. Coplien, and Norman L. Kerth (Editors), "Pattern Languages of Program Design 2", Addison Wesley, 1996

[Vlissides2] John Vlissides, "Pattern Hatching: Design Patterns Applied", Addison Wesley, 1998

Online References

[EJBHome] Enterprise Java Beans (EJB) Home Page and Specification
http://java.sun.com/products/ejb/
EJB 2.0 (Final Draft) Specification:
http://java.sun.com/products/ejb/2.0.html

[Hillside] Hillside.net - Patterns Home Page
http://hillside.net/patterns

[JakartaTaglibs] The Jakarta "Taglibs" Project
http://www.jakarta.apache.org/taglibs/index.html

[JavaHome] Java Home Page
http://java.sun.com

[J2EEHome] Java 2 Enterprise Edition (J2EE) Home Page
http://java.sun.com/j2ee/

[JDBCHome] Java Database Connectivity (JDBC) Technology Home page and Specification
http://java.sun.com/products/jdbc/

[JNDIHome] Java Naming and Directory Interface (JNDI) Home page and Specification
http://java.sun.com/products/jndi/

[JSPHome] Java Server Pages (JSP) Home page and Specification
http://java.sun.com/products/jsp/

[JMSHome] Java Message Service (JMS) Home page and Specification
http://java.sun.com/products/jms/

[Portland] The Portland Pattern Repository
http://www.c2.com/cgi/wiki?PortlandPatternRepository

[Resonate]
http://www.resonate.com

[ServletHome] Java Servlet Technology Home page and Specification
http://java.sun.com/products/servlet/

[Struts] http://jakarta.apache.org/struts/index.html

[TS1341] Daniel Malks and Deepak Alur, "Prototyping Patterns for the J2EE Platform", JavaOne 2000, San Francisco
http://jsp.java.sun.com/javaone/javaone2000/event.jsp?eventId=1341

Index

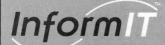

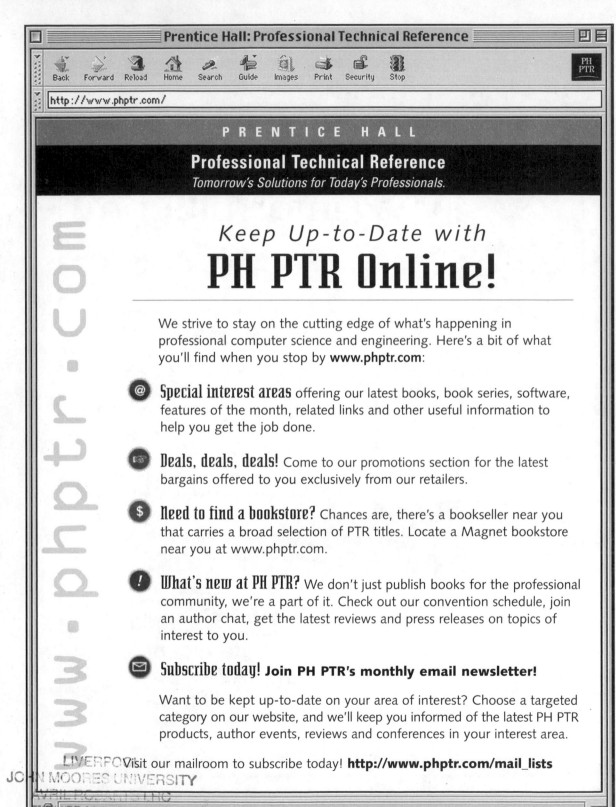